A SHORT REFERENCE GRAMMAR OF MOROCCAN ARABIC with Audio CD

Richard S. Harrell

With an appendix of texts in
Urban Moroccan Arabic by
Louis Brunot

Georgetown University Press
Washington, D.C.

Georgetown University Press, Washington, D.C.

Printed in Canada

10 9 8 7 6 5 4 3 2 1 2004

This book is printed on acid-free paper meeting
the requirements of the American National Standard
for Permanence in Paper for Printed Library Materials.

The research reported herein was performed pursuant to a contract with the
United States Office of Education, Department of Health, Education, and Welfare.

Library of Congress Cataloging-in-Publication Data

Harrell, Richard S. (Richard Slade), 1928–1964.
A short reference grammar of Moroccan Arabic : with audio CD / Richard S. Harrell ; with an appendix of texts in urban Moroccan Arabic by Louis Brunot.
p. cm. — (Georgetown classics in Arabic language and linguistics)
Originally published: Washington, D.C. : Georgetown University Press, 1962, in series: Arabic series / Georgetown University, Institute of Languages and Linguistics ; no. 1.
ISBN 1-58901-009-4 (pbk. : alk. paper)
1. Arabic language—Dialects—Morocco. 2. Arabic language—Grammar.
I. Title. II. Series.

PJ6763.H315 2004
492.7'7'0964—dc22

2003049544

Georgetown Classics in Arabic Language and Linguistics

Karin C. Ryding and Margaret Nydell, series editors

For some time, Georgetown University Press has been interested in making available seminal publications in Arabic language and linguistics that have gone out of print. Some of the most meticulous and creative scholarship of the last century was devoted to the analysis of Arabic language and to producing detailed reference works and textbooks of the highest quality. Although some of the material is dated in terms of theoretical approaches, the content and methodology of the books considered for the reprint series is still valid and, in some cases, unsurpassed.

With global awareness now refocused on the Arab world, and with renewed interest in Arab culture, society, and political life, it is essential to provide easy access to classic reference materials, such as dictionaries and reference grammars, and to language teaching materials. The components of this series have been chosen for their quality of research and scholarship, and have been updated with new bibliographies and introductions to provide readers with resources for further study.

Georgetown University Press hereby hopes to serve the growing national and international need for reference works on Arabic language and culture, as well as provide access to quality textbooks and audiovisual resources for teaching Arabic language in its written and spoken forms.

Books in the Georgetown Classics in Arabic Language and Linguistics series

Arabic Language Handbook
Mary Catherine Bateson

A Basic Course in Iraqi Arabic with Audio MP3 Files
Wallace M. Erwin

A Basic Course in Moroccan Arabic
Richard S. Harrell with Mohammed Abu-Talib and William S. Carroll

A Dictionary of Iraqi Arabic: English–Arabic, Arabic–English
B. E. Clarity, Karl Stowasser, Ronald G. Wolfe, D. R. Woodhead, and Wayne Beene, Editors

A Short Reference Grammar of Iraqi Arabic
Wallace M. Erwin

A Short Reference Grammar of Moroccan Arabic with Audio CD
Richard S. Harrell

To my French colleagues
Louis Brunot
and
G.-S. Colin

Contents

APPENDIX: Texts in Urban Moroccan Arabic
Collected and annotated by Louis Brunot
Edited by Richard S. Harrell

Contents of the CD Recording

The audio CD included with this book was remastered from the original audiocassettes, and the sound quality reflects the early technology of the originals.

Track	Page	Section	Time
1	—	Information and Copyright	(0:56)
2	3–4	I.1.a. "turkey" to "to dream"	(1:14)
3	4	I.1.a. "second" to "to visit"	(0:54)
4	4–5	I.1.a. "satchel" to "we didn't see him"	(0:48)
5	5	I.1.a. "to repent" to "to rise, to get up"	(0:29)
6	5	I.1.a. "dog" to "to split"	(0:43)
7	6	I.1.a. "to go out" to "to chew"	(0:59)
8	6–7	I.1.a. "shame" to "he built it"	(1:37)
9	7	I.1.a. "Islam" to "to instruct, to educate"	(0:18)
10	7	I.1.a. "prophet" to "darkness"	(1:08)
11	9	I.1.b. "to fly" to "day after tomorrow"	(1:06)
12	9	I.1.c. "room" to "viscera"	(1:12)
13	11	I.2. "room" to "walls"	(1:09)
14	11–12	I.2. "death" to "I saw him"	(0:54)
15	12	I.2. "tea" to "this"	(0:41)
16	12	I.2. "to say" to "to polish"	(0:42)
17	12–13	I.2. "to fly" to "God, Allah"	(0:39)
18	13	I.2. "excellent" to "I saw them"	(0:29)
19	13	I.2. "at six o'clock" to "to confess"	(0:33)
20	13	I.2. "to present" to "tomorrow"	(0:51)
21	14	I.2. "wedding" to "I sold"	(0:24)
22	14	I.2. "jail" to "some"	(0:29)
23	16	II.1. "two" to "married"	(1:00)
24	18	II.5.a. "he sent" to "my husband"	(1:11)
25	18–19	II.5.b. "he found" to "they enter"	(1:11)
26	19	II.5.c. "she saw" to "she saw him"	(0:26)
27	19	II.5.c. "she found" to "she sent him"	(1:01)
			Total: (23:17)

Arabic Research at Georgetown University

In the thirty-five years since the original publication of Wallace M. Erwin's *A Basic Course in Iraqi Arabic*, the world of research in Arabic theoretical linguistics has expanded but the production of professional quality textbooks in colloquial Arabic has remained limited. Despite the passage of years, the Richard Slade Harrell Arabic Series has consistently been in demand from Georgetown University Press because of the quality of research that went into its composition, the solid theoretical foundations for its methodology, and the comprehensive coverage of regional Arabic speech communities.

The Arabic Department at Georgetown University (now Department of Arabic Language, Literature and Linguistics) recognizes the need to sustain the tradition of research and publication in Arabic dialects and has continued dialectology field research and textbook production, most notably with Margaret (Omar) Nydell's Syrian Arabic Video Course, a three-year research project funded by the Center for the Advancement of Language Learning from 1991 to 1994.

Currently, Dr. Nydell is leading a four-year dialectology research project aimed at producing "conversion" courses to assist learners of Modern Standard Arabic in converting their knowledge and skills of written Arabic to proficiency in selected Arabic dialects. This project is part of a proposal prepared by the National Capital Language Resource Center under the directorship of Dr. James E. Alatis and Dr. Anna Chamot. The first Arabic dialect tackled under this research project was Iraqi, and the Iraqi conversion short course was field tested successfully in the summer of 2003. In developing the materials for the conversion course, the most authoritative English sources of information were the two seminal texts produced by Wallace Erwin and published by Georgetown University Press in the 1960s, and which the Press is reissuing this year, *A Basic Course in Iraqi Arabic* and *A Short Reference Grammar of Iraqi Arabic*.

We pay tribute to the tradition initiated and led by Richard Harrell, the founder of this series and of the original Arabic Research Program at Georgetown University. Harrell's scholarship and creative energy set a standard in the field and yielded an unprecedented and as yet unsurpassed series of, as he put it, "practical tools for the increasing number of Americans whose lives bring them into contact with the Arab world."

For more information about the Department of Arabic Language, Literature and Linguistics at Georgetown University, its course offerings, its degree programs, and its research agenda, see www.georgetown.edu/departments/arabic.

Karin C. Ryding
Sultan Qaboos bin Said Professor of Arabic

The History of the Arabic Research Program Institute of Languages and Linguistics Georgetown University

The Arabic Research Program was established in June of 1960 as a contract between Georgetown University and the United States Office of Education under the provisions of the Language Development Program of the National Defense Education Act.

The first two years of the research program, 1960–1962 (contract number SAE-8706), were devoted to the production of six books, a reference grammar and a conversational English-Arabic dictionary in the cultivated spoken forms of Moroccan, Syrian, and Iraqi Arabic. The second two years of the research program, 1962–64 (contract number OE-2-14-029), call for the further production of Arabic-English dictionaries in each of the three varieties of Arabic mentioned above, as well as comprehensive basic courses in the Moroccan and Iraqi varities.

The eleven books of this series, of which the present volume is one, are designed to serve as practical tools for the increasing number of Americans whose lives bring them into contact with the Arab world. The dictionaries, the reference grammars, and the basic courses are oriented toward the educated American who is a layman in linguistic matters. Although it is hoped that the scientific linguist and the specialist in Arabic dialectology will find these books both of interest and of use, matters of purely scientific and theoretical importance have not been directly treated as such, and specialized scientific terminology has been avoided as much as possible.

As is usual, the authors or editors of the individual books bear final scholarly responsibility for the contents, but there has been a large amount of informal cooperation in our work. Criticism, consultation, and discussion have gone on constantly among the senior professional members of the staff. The contribution of more junior research assistants, both Arab and American, is also not be underestimated. Their painstaking assembling and ordering of raw data, often in manners requiring considerable creative intelligence, has been the necessary prerequisite for further progress.

Staff work has been especially important in the preparation of the dictionaries. Although the contributing staff members are named on the title page of the individual dictionaries, special mention must be made of Mr. Karl Stowasser's work. His lexicographical experience, acquired in his work on the English version of Professor Wehr's *Arabisches Worterbuch für die Schriftsprache der Gegenwart* (Hans Wehr, *A Dictionary of Modern Written Arabic,* ed. J. Milton Cowen [Ithaca, N.Y.: Cornell University Press, 1961]), along with his thorough knowledge of Arabic, has been critically important for all our lexicographical work, covering the entire range from typography to substantive entries in the dictionaries.

In most cases the books prepared by the Arabic Research Program are the first of their kind in English, and in some cases the first in any language. The preparation of them has been a rewarding experience. It is hoped that the public use of them will be equally so. The undersigned, on behalf of the entire staff, would like to ask the same indulgence of the reader as Samuel Johnson requested in his first English dictionary: To remember that although much has been left out, much has been included.

Richard S. Harrell
Associated Professor of Linguistics
Georgetown University
Director,
Arabic Research Program

Foreword to the Georgetown Classics Edition

This Moroccan reference grammar, published in 1962, is still the definitive study of the language. Dr. Richard Harrell's dialect research project produced materials in several dialects and all still stand as classics. Since Dr. Harrell's untimely death in 1964, he has truly never been replaced.

There are not many books that deal with Moroccan as a whole; notable titles include: Ernest Abdel-Massih, *Advanced Moroccan Arabic* (Ann Arbor: University of Michigan, 1974); Kristen Brustad, *The Syntax of Spoken Arabic* (Washington, D.C.: Georgetown University Press, 2000); Oliver Durand, *Introduzione ai Dialetti Arabi* (Milan: Centro Studi Camito-Semitici, 1995); Margaret Nydell, *From MSA to the Maghrebi Dialects, Moroccan and Algerian* (Arlington, Va.: DLS Press, 1993); and the unauthored *Moroccan Arabic* (Rabat: Peace Corps, 1994).

In the past twenty years there has been a steady stream of monographs and articles dealing with certain features of Moroccan that are readily available to specialists. This book is clear and thorough, and presents a useful overview of the Moroccan dialect. Two dictionaries were developed as part of the same project. The subjects discussed include pronunciation variables, the use of auxiliary words, verbal syntax, and terms of address.

It is gratifying to have this important book once again in print.

Margaret Nydell

Author's Preface

This book is designed to serve as a practical reference grammar for the student who has already had an introductory course in Moroccan Arabic. All that is attempted is an orderly cataloging of the principal grammatical facts of the language. No exercises or glossaries have been included since such things are primarily the function of an introductory textbook. Theoretical considerations and professional technical terminology have been held to an unavoidable minimum.

The form of Arabic described is that of the educated urban speakers of the northwestern part of Morocco. In actual fact, the author has worked exclusively with speakers from Fez, Rabat, and Casablanca. The works of my French predecessors in Moroccan Arabic, especially those of G.-S. Colin, Louis Brunot, and M.-T. Buret have been invaluable as source materials and guides (especially, Colin, *Chrestomathie marocaine* [Paris: Librairie d'amérique et d'orient, 1955]; Brunot, *Introduction à l'arabe marocain* [Paris: G.P. Maissonneuve et Cie, 1950]; *Textes arabes de Rabat* [Paris: Geuthner, I. Textes, 1931; II. Glossaire, 1952]; Buret, *Cours gradué d'arabe marocain* [Casablanca: Farairre, 1952]). The thorough and conscientious scholarship of these men is of the sort that commands both admiration and respect. Although I have in every case checked the material with Moroccan co-workers, I have drawn freely upon the work of these French scholars, both for insight as to procedure and for illustrations of grammatical points. Professor Colin's *Chrestomathie marocaine* has been an especially valuable source of primary text material. Without it my own task would have been much harder. To the experienced reader the influence not only of Professor Colin but of my other French colleagues as well will be abundantly evident in the following pages. They have my enduring gratitude and respect.

Thanks is also due to the many Moroccans who have worked with me. My principal collaborators in this country have been Mr. Mohamed Amin Saussane and his brother Mr. Majid Saussane, both of Casablanca; Mr. Allal Chraibi of Casablanca; and Mr. Mohamed Abou-Talib of Fez. It would be impractical to mention the names of all my Moroccan friends who helped me in so many ways during my stay in Rabat, but I cherish a warm memory of them, both individually and collectively.

My debt to various American colleagues is of the diffuse sort that defies precise acknowledgment. I would like, however, to single out the names of Thomas Fox and Mark Cowell, both of Georgetown University's Arabic Research Program, and William Stewart of the Center for Applied Linguistics, Washington, D.C. Mr. Fox read the entire manuscript, and Mr. Cowell and Mr. Stewart each read parts of it. All three of these colleagues offered many constructive criticisms.

Richard S. Harrell
Washington, D.C.
December, 1962

PART ONE
PHONOLOGY

NOTES

I. THE INDIVIDUAL SOUNDS

1. **Consonants:** Moroccan Arabic has thirty-one consonants. The table below lists them according to their articulatory positions.

	Bilabial	Labiodental	Apical	Palatal	Velar	Uvular	Pharyngeal	Glottal
Voiceless Stops:			*t ṭ*		*k*	*q*		*ʔ*
Voiced Stops:	*b ḅ*		*d ḍ*		*g*			
Voiceless Fricatives:		*f*	*s ṣ*	*š*		*x*	*ḥ*	*h*
Voiced Fricatives:			*z ẓ*	*ž*		*ġ*	*ε*	
Nasals:	*m ṃ*		*n*					
Lateral:			*l ḷ*					
Flap-Trill:			*r ṛ*					
Semi-Vowels:	*w*			*y*				

(a) **The Individual Consonants:** The labials *b, f,* and *m* are essentially the same as in English. Some examples:

bibi	'turkey'
sebbeb	'to cause'
šabb	'young man'

fas	'mattock'
kif	'marihuana'
leff	'to wrap up'
mmellka	'engaged' (fem. sg.)
semma	'to name'
ma-ši	'not'
ḥlem	'to dream'

A slight difference is that *b* is sometimes voiceless before a voiceless stop or fricative, e.g. *l-ḥebs* 'the prison', in which case it is like the "p" in English "naps".

The apical stops and fricatives differ from the corresponding English sounds in that the tip of the tongue touches or approaches the back surface of the upper front teeth. Corresponding sounds in English are made with the tip of the tongue touching or approaching the gum ridge above the upper front teeth. Some examples:

tani	'second'
ġeṭṭa	'to cover'
fas	'mattock'
keṛfeṣ	'to spoil, to mess up'
drari	'children'
ɛaṛeḍ	'to oppose, to contradict'
dezna	'we passed'
ẓaṛ	'to visit'

Some Moroccans pronounce the *t* with a noisy release which sounds similar to *s*, so that the consonant sounds similar to the consonant cluster *ts*, but even for such speakers *t* and *ts* are not pronounced exactly alike; compare *tsemma* 'to be named' and *temma* 'there'.

The consonants *š*, *ž*, *g*, and *h* are approximately as in English. The *š* is like the "sh" in "ship", the *ž* is like the "s" in "pleasure", the *g* is like the "g" in "go" or "geese", and the *h* is like the "h" in "hill". Unlike English, Moroccan *h* occurs after vowels and in consonant clusters. Some examples:

škaṛa	'satchel'

žwež	'to get married'
gles	'to sit down'
hbeṭ	'to come down, to go down, to get down'
šafuh	'they saw him'
ma-šefnah-š	'we didn't see him'

An important difference between English and Moroccan is that the Moroccan voiceless stops *t, ṭ, k,* and *q* do not have a noticeable puff of air upon release as is often the case with the corresponding English "t" and "k" ("c"). Compare the initial "t" and "c" ("k") of English "tab", "Tom", "clabber", and "calm" with the initial *t, ṭ, k,* and *q* of the following Moroccan words:

tab	'to repent'
ṭab	'to become ripe'
klab	'dogs'
qam	'to rise, to get up'

Except for the puff of breath on release, the English "k" and the Moroccan *k* are approximately the same, but Moroccan *q* is pronounced further back in the throat, and practice is required for the English speaker to distinguish *k* and *q* properly. The *q* is similar to the *k* except that contact between the upper surface of the tongue and the roof of the mouth is further forward for *k* than for *q*. Compare:

kelb	'dog'
qelb	'heart'
klam	'word(s)'
qlam	'pen'
šekk	'to doubt'
šeqq	'to split'

The *x* and *ġ* are fricatives pronounced in approximately the same position as the *q*, with the rear of the tongue raised toward the roof of the mouth in the neighborhood of the uvula. The *x* is like the "ch" of German "Bach" or Scotch "loch", and the *ġ* is like the French "üvular r". The English speaker may approximate the sounds with a light gargle, but care must be taken to distinguish *x* as voiceless and *ġ* as voiced. Some examples:

xrež	'to go out'
xobz	'bread'
ṛxiṣ	'cheap'
bexxeṛ	'to steam'
ṭbex	'to cook'
ġṛeq	'to sink, to drown'
ġḷiḍ	'thick, heavy'
bġel	'mule'
mḍeġ	'to chew'

The *ḥ* and the *ɛ* are different from anything in English. Careful practice with a native speaker or with recordings is necessary for the English speaker to acquire a proper pronunciation of these phonemes. These sounds are articulated by a simultaneous raising of the larynx and a movement of the root of the tongue toward the back wall of the throat. The compression of the throat in this way gives rise to the particular sound quality of these two phonemes.

Since *ɛ* is voiced and the friction noise accompanying it is small, the English speaker is likely to hear it as being somewhat similar to the "a" of "father". In many environments, the English speaker is apt to fail to hear the *ɛ* completely. The *ḥ* on the other hand is easy for the English speaker to hear but difficult to reproduce properly. Its closest equivalent in English is an "h" pronounced in a loud stage whisper. Especial care is necessary for the English speaker properly to hear or pronounce the difference between Moroccan *ḥ* and *h* since he has a tendency to identify them both with English "h". Some examples:

ɛaṛ	'shame'
ḥar	'to be perplexed'
haṛaž	'uproar, hubbub'
ɛid	'feast, holiday'
ḥit	'when, since'
himan	'wandering'
ɛud	'wood'
ḥudud	'boundaries'

huma	'they'
ɛbid	'slaves'
ḥbib	'maternal uncle'
hbil	'crazy, insane'
baɛ	'to sell'
baḥ	'to reveal' (a secret)
bnah	'he built it'

The glottal stop, symbolized by *ʔ*, is as rare in Moroccan as in English. It is the break between vowels as heard in the exclamation "uh oh". The "tt" in such a word as "bottle" is also commonly pronounced as a glottal stop in some varieties of New York English ("Brooklynese") or Scotch English. A pair of examples:

l-ʔislam	'Islam'
ʔeddeb	'to instruct, to educate'

Like the other apicals, *n*, *l*, and *ḷ* are pronounced with the tip of the tongue against the back of the upper front teeth rather than against the gum ridge above them. The *l* is like the French, Spanish, and Italian "l" rather than like the English "l" in that it is pronounced with the tongue further forward in the mouth and without the back of the tongue being raised toward the back of the roof of the mouth. The *ḷ* on the other hand (cf. p. 8 below, the discussion of the emphatic consonants) shares the characteristic of English "l", for example as in "full", with respect to the raising of the back of the tongue although the tip of the tongue still touches the back of the upper front teeth rather than the gum ridge above them. Some examples:

nbi	'prophet'
ban	'to appear'
tenber	'postage stamp'
limun	'orange(s)'
lbes	'to put on, to wear'
fil	'elephant'
tkellmu	'they talked'

ḷḷah	'God, Allah'
theḷḷa	'to take care of'
ḍeḷma	'darkness'

The Moroccan *w* and *y* are similar to English "w" and "y" when they are initial, although they are more softly articulated; e.g., *wella* 'he became', *yeddi* 'my hand'. After vowels, Moroccan *w* and *y*, especially when double, are likely to strike the English ear as being similar to the vowels of "who" and "he" respectively; e.g., *ma-nemšiw-š* 'we won't go', *ḥawel* 'to try', *luwwel* 'first', *ɛayen* 'to wait', *siyyeb* 'to throw', *myatayn* 'two hundred'.

The single *r* is a flap of the tip of the tongue past the gum ridge above the upper front teeth, like the "r" in Spanish "para" ('for') or the "t" in the usual American pronunciation of such words as "water" and "butter"; e.g., *bir* 'well'. The double *rr* is a trill; e.g., *derri* 'child', exactly comparable to a Spanish double "rr", as in "perro" ('dog'), but unlike any English sound.

(b) The Emphatic Consonants: The emphatic consonants are written with a subscript dot under the symbol for the corresponding plain consonants. There are eight emphatic consonants, *ḅ, ṃ, ṭ, ḍ, ṣ, ẓ, ḷ,* and *ṛ*. These sounds are lower in pitch than their non-emphatic counterparts. They are pronounced with greater muscular tension in the mouth and throat and with a raising of the back and root of the tongue toward the roof of the mouth. The English speaker can notice this contraction of the throat very easily by prolonging the "l" in "full", since this English "l" is exactly like Moroccan *ḷ* except for the place of the tip of the tongue (cf. p. 7 above). After having acquired conscious control of the movement of the back and root of the tongue with *ḷ*, the English speaker can proceed to practice combining it with the other articulatory features of *ḅ, ṃ, ṭ, ḍ, ṣ, ẓ,* and *ṛ*. In addition to lower pitch and the contraction of the throat, *ṭ* differs from *t* by being released without any friction noise whereas the *t* usually has some.

The emphatics *ṭ, ḍ,* and *ṣ* are quite common, with or without other emphatic consonants in the words in which they occur. The *ṛ* also occurs widely in words without the presence of any other emphatic consonants, but it is limited to the neighborhood of the vowels *e* and *a* unless a *ṭ, ḍ,* or *ṣ* also occurs in the word. The occurrence of *ḅ, ṃ, ẓ,* or *ḷ* in words where no *ṭ, ḍ, ṣ,* or *ṛ* occurs is quite rare. Contrariwise, there is no occurrence of a plain *b* or *m* in a word in which one of the other emphatics occurs.

In order to avoid the repetition of subscript dots, the transcription employed here is to write *ḅ* and *ṃ* only if no other emphatic occurs in the word; e.g., *ḅḅaha* 'her father'. Otherwise only *b* and *m* are written although they are to be interpreted as *ḅ* and *ṃ* if another emphatic consonant occurs in the word where they are found; e.g., *ṭḷeb* 'to request', where *b* is written although *ḅ* is pronounced, and *mḍeġ* 'to chew', where *m* is written although *ṃ* is pronounced. For the relation of *ḅ* and *ṃ* to labialization, see p. 9 below.

The pronunciation of the vowels differs greatly depending on whether they occur with plain or emphatic consonants (cf. p. 10 below, the discussion of the vowels). Due to the nature of the English consonant and vowel system, the English speaker easily hears the variation in Moroccan vowels, but has difficulty in hearing the distinction between the Moroccan plain and emphatic consonants. Some examples:

ṭaṛ	'to fly'
taṛ	'vengeance'
ḍaṛ	'house'
dar	'to do'
ṣbeɛ	'finger'
sbeɛ	'lion'
ẓaṛ	'to visit'
zad	'to advance, to continue'
ḷḷah	'God, Allah'
lla-ġedda	'day after tomorrow'

(c) **The Labialization of Consonants:** The consonants *b, m, f, k, g, q, x,* and *ġ* are labialized in a limited number of positions. Labialization consists of pronouncing a consonant with a simultaneous rounding of the lips accompanied by a fleeting "w" at the release of the consonant. Labialization is indicated by a small rounded stroke over the consonant in question; e.g., *m̂ṃ̂i* 'my mother'.

Labialized *b̂, m̂,* and *f̂* occur only as initial doubled consonants, that is as *b̂b̂-, m̂m̂-,* and *f̂f̂-*. In almost all words which begin with *b̂b̂-, m̂m̂-,* and *f̂f̂-*, many speakers have *bw-, mw-,* and *fw-* instead. Some examples:

b̂b̂iyyet or *bwiyyet*	diminutive of *bit* 'room'
ḃ̂ḃ̂ax or *bwax*	'steam'
m̂m̂iha or *mwiha*	diminutive of *ma* 'water'
m̂m̂alfa or *mwalfa*	'habit, custom'
f̂f̂ad or *fwad*	'viscera'

With labialized *b̂b̂-* and *m̂m̂-*, emphasis varies from speaker to speaker. Some speakers regularly make all cases of *b̂b̂-* and *m̂m̂-* emphatic as well as labialized; e.g., *m̂m̂alin* or *ṃ̂ṃ̂alin,* plural of *mul* 'master, owner, person concerned'. For the speakers who use *bw-* and *mw-* rather than *b̂b̂-* and *m̂m̂-*, the *b-* and *m-* are always non-emphatic. Thus *m̂m̂alin* or *ṃ̂ṃ̂alin,* either with non-emphatic *m̂m̂-* or emphatic *ṃ̂ṃ̂-*, but only *mwalin,* with non-emphatic *m-*.

There are only two words in which labialized *b̂b̂*– and *m̂m̂*– are never replaced by *bw*– and *mw*–. These are the inherently possessed (see p. 141) kinship terms *b̂b̂a* 'my father' and *m̂m̂i* 'my mother'. These two items have some further peculiarities. The use of *b̂b̂a* shows, from speaker to speaker, the expected variation between non-emphatic *b̂b̂*– and emphatic *ḅ̂ḅ̂*–, but an emphatic non-labialized form is also common with many speakers. Thus such variations as *b̂b̂a, ḅ̂ḅ̂a,* and *ḅḅa* 'my father', *b̂b̂ak, ḅ̂ḅ̂ak,* and *ḅḅak* 'your (sg.) father', etc., are heard.

On the other hand, the various forms for 'mother' are consistently both emphatic and labialized; e.g., *m̂m̂i* 'my mother', *m̂m̂ek* 'your (sg.) mother', *m̂m̂u* 'his mother', *m̂m̂ha* 'her mother', etc.

A closely similar pair which contrasts the difference between labialized emphatic *m̂m̂*– and non-emphatic non-labialized *mm*– is *m̂m̂na* 'our mother' and *mmnuƐ* (pronounced *memnuƐ* by some speakers) 'forbidden'.

The convention adopted here is to write *m̂m̂*– in all forms of 'mother', *ḅḅ*– in all forms of 'father', and *bw*–, *mw*–, and *fw*– elsewhere in view of the free interchange between these sequences and *b̂b̂*–, *m̂m̂*–, and *f̂f̂*–.

The occurrence of labialized *k̂, ĝ, q̂, x̂,* and *ġ̂* is almost entirely limited to their occurrence as the first member of initial consonant clusters; e.g., *k̂baṛ* 'big' (pl.), *ġ̂ṛab* 'crow'. As such, labialization with these consonants is of little functional importance in the structure of the language since many speakers use non-labialized consonants in these clusters; i.e., the pronunciations *kbaṛ* 'big' (pl.) and *ġṛab* 'crow' with non-labialized *k* and *ġ* are as common as the pronunciations with labialized *k̂* and *ġ̂*.

There are only a very few words where these initial labialized consonants are not interchangeable with the corresponding plain consonants, and in these cases there is an alternate form of the word with an initial *o*–. The only common such word is *x̂ṛa*[1] or *oxṛa* 'other' (fem. sg.). The convention adopted here is not to write labialization at all in such initial consonant clusters and to write *o*– in such cases as *oxṛa* 'other' (fem. sg.) where the plain consonant is usually not used.

There is also a variation between –*kk*– and –*k̂k̂*– medially before *a;* e.g., *ḥak̂k̂a* 'thus, so'. Labialized –*k̂k̂*– in this case is always interchangeable with non-labialized –*kk*–, and a regular indication of labialization in the transcription is not necessary.

2. Vowels: Moroccan Arabic has six vowels, three stable vowels and three variable vowels. The stable vowels *i, a,* and *u* occur in all positions within words, occur in combination with all consonants, and are never affected by elision and inversion (see p. 17). The variable vowels *e, ă,* and *o* never occur finally, occur only rarely initially or in open syllables, and are limited in terms of combination with consonants. The stable vowels are relatively long except at the end

[1] Cf. the taboo word *xṛa* 'feces' ('s--t'), with a non-labialized *x*–. Some speakers also say *xṛa* for 'other' (fem. sg.), but considerably to the embarrassment of those speakers who pronounce the two words differently.

of words, where they are short. The variable vowels on the other hand are always quite short.

The stable vowel *i* has two main pronunciations. In the neighborhood of most consonants, it is like the "i" of French "vite" ('quick'), similar to the vowel of English "beet" but without the glide that is usually heard with the English vowel. Before or after an emphatic consonant or the uvular and pharyngeal consonants *q, x, ġ, ḥ,* and *ع,* the *i* has a sound like the "é" of French "été" ('summer'), similar to the vowel of English "bait" but without the glide that is heard with the English vowel. Some examples:

bit	'room'
fti	'tender, soft'
žina	'we came'
sif	'sword'
bġit	'I want'
ṛfiع	'nice'
ṣif	'summer'
xil	'horse(s)'
nqi	'clean'
ḥiṭan	'walls'

The stable vowel *u* likewise has varying pronunciations. In the neighborhood of most consonants, it is like the "ou" of French "vous" ('you'), similar to the vowel of English "boot" but without the glide that is usually heard with the English vowel. Before or after an emphatic consonant or the *q,* the pronunciation of *u* is like the "ô" of French "tôt" ('soon'), similar to the vowel of English "boat" but without the glide that is usually heard with it. When at the end of a word or next to the uvular and pharyngeal consonants *x, ġ, ḥ,* and *ع,* the *u* has a sound intermediate between the vowels of French "vous" ('you') and "tôt" ('soon'). Some examples:

mut	'death'
huma	'they'
lun	'color'
ṭuḷ	'length'
ka-iqul	'he says'

xud!	'take!' (msc. sg.)
Ɛud	'wood'
šeftu	'I saw him'

The stable vowel *a* has three main pronunciations. Initially or medially where it does not occur next to an emphatic consonant or one of the uvular and pharyngeal consonants *q, x, ġ, ḥ,* and *Ɛ,* the *a* is pronounced like the vowel of English "mad". Some examples:

atay	'tea'
mat	'to die'
wad	'river'
kas	'(drinking) glass'
šaf	'to see'
hadi	'this' (fem. sg.)

Before or after the uvular and pharyngeal consonants as well as finally, the *a* has a pronunciation intermediate between the vowel of "mad" and the "a" of "father". Some examples:

qal	'to say'
xaf	'to be afraid'
ġaba	'forest'
baƐ	'to sell'
filaḥa	'agriculture'
mra	'to polish'

In the neighborhood of the emphatic consonants, the *a* is approximately like the "a" of English "father". Some examples:

ṭaṛ	'to fly'
ṭebbax	'cook'
ẓaṛ	'to visit'

mṛa	'woman, wife'
ḷḷah	'God, Allah'

The unstable vowel *o* is of relatively rare occurrence. In the neighborhood of the emphatic, the uvular, and the pharyngeal consonants, it is similar to the vowel of English "boat" but much shorter and without any off-glide. Elsewhere the *o* is similar to the vowel of English "put". Some examples:

moɛtabaṛ	'excellent'
oxṛa	'other' (fem. sg.)
koll	'all'
šefthom	'I saw them'

The *e* is the most frequently occurring of all Moroccan vowels and has a wide variety of different pronunciations. In environments where there are no emphatic, uvular, or pharyngeal consonants present, the *e* is approximately like the "e" in English "glasses". Some examples:

fe-s-setta	'at six o'clock'
bent	'girl'
šeftek	'I saw you' (sg.)
gerr	'to confess'

In the neighborhood of *q, x, ġ,* or one of the emphatic consonants, the *e* is like the "u" of English "butter". Some examples:

qeddem	'to present'
žḅen	'cheese'
hbeṭ	'to get down, to come down'
ṣebbaṛ	'patient'
mḍeġ	'to chew'
xedma	'work'
ġedda	'tomorrow'

In the environment of *ḥ* and *ɛ*, the *e* is similar to the "e" of English "bet". The vowel *e* is of limited occurrence before or after *ḥ* and *ɛ*. Some examples:

ɛers	'wedding'
ḥetta	'when, until'
beɛt	'I sold'

The variable vowel *ă* occurs very commonly before or after *ḥ* or *ɛ*. Except next to one of these two consonants, there are only a limited number of words in which *ă* occurs. The pronunciation of the variable vowel *ă* is like that of the stable vowel *a*, with the difference that *ă* is always quite short. Some examples:

ḥăbs	'jail'
ɛăbd	'slave'
băɛd	'after'
băɛḍ	'some'

There is only limited contrast between *e* and *ă*, and it is unnecessary to use both symbols for a practical transcription. Since *e* rarely occurs next to *ḥ* or *ɛ*, and since *ă* occurs only rarely other than next to *ḥ* or *ɛ*, it is possible to use only the symbol '*e*' for both phonemes with little ambiguity. The symbol *ă* is consequently not used in the remainder of this book.

The contrast between *e* and *ă* in Moroccan has a limited importance similar to the contrast made by some speakers of English between the last syllable of "heavens" and the last syllable of the proper name "Evans". Many speakers of English rhyme these two words, while others make a difference in the last syllables similar to the difference between "bit" and "but". Of the speakers of English who pronounce the last syllables of "heavens" and "Evans" alike, some make the vowel more similar to the vowel of "bit" and others make it more similar to the vowel of "but". Similarly in Moroccan, some speakers make a difference between *ḥăll* 'he opened' and the imperative *ḥell!* 'open!' (sg.). Other speakers pronounce the forms exactly alike.

In the examples cited in the remainder of the book, the symbol '*e*' next to *ḥ* or *ɛ* is thus a cover symbol for both *e* and *ă*. The practical student may adopt either pronunciation in such cases, or even vary freely from one pronunciation to another.

3. Diphthongs: The most commonly occurring diphthongs are *ay* and *aw*. The *ay* has a pronunciation intermediate between the vowels of English "buy" and "bay" and is relatively long; e.g., *fayn* 'where', *ɛaynu* 'they waited'. The *aw* is similar to the vowel of English "how"; e.g., *ḥawlu* 'they tried', *žawbu* 'they answered'.

The diphthongs *ey* and *ew* are of less frequent occurrence. The *ey* is similar to the vowel of English "bite" but is always very short; e.g., *ɛeynu* 'his eye', to be compared with the longer *ay* of *ɛaynu* 'they waited'. After *ḥ* or *ɛ*, the *ew* is like a very short pronunciation of the vowel of English "how"; e.g., *ɛewdu* 'his horse', to be compared with the longer *aw* of *ɛawdu* 'they repeated'. Elsewhere, the *ew* is similar to the vowel of "bet" followed by the vowel of "who", in quick succession and without any intervening break; e.g., *newṣeḷ,* 'I arrive'.

II. THE INTERCHANGE OF SOUNDS WITHIN WORDS

1. Consonants: The consonants *s, z, š, ž, q, g,* and *ʔ* are involved in a few minor variations.

From speaker to speaker, there is a free interchange of *s* with *š* and *z* with *ž* if any of these sounds occurs in a word with a *ž* following somewhere further on. Both pronunciations are generally acceptable. Some examples:

zuž or *žuž*	'two'
sžen or *šžen*	'to imprison'
seṛžem or *šeṛžem*	'window'
mzuwwež or *mžuwwež*	'married'

Many speakers, especially in the south of Morocco, replace *q* with *g;* e.g., *gal* instead of *qal* 'to say', *begṛa* instead of *beqṛa* 'cow'. The forms with the *q* are preferred in educated speech. In Fez, many speakers regularly replace the *q* with *ʔ;* e.g., *ʔam* instead of *qam* 'to rise, to get up'.

2. Semi-Vowels: There is a wide-spread variation between *ye-* and *i-* initially before consonant clusters; e.g., *yeddi* or *iddi* 'my hand', *yemmah* or *immah* 'his mother'. Pronunciations with *i-* predominate at ordinary conversational speed. There is a similar variation between *wo-* and *u-;* e.g., *wožda* or *užda,* a Moroccan city.

Many speakers also make no difference between *-y-* and *-yy-* or between *-w-* and *-ww-* in most environments. For example some speakers make a distinction between *liyen* 'soft, smooth' and *liyyen* 'to make soft, smooth', whereas other speakers have only the pronunciation *liyyen* for both meanings. Similarly, some speakers contrast a single *-w-* with a double *-ww-,* as for example *huwa* 'he' as opposed to *luwwa* 'to roll up, to twist'. This variation occurs before consonants as well as between vowels; e.g., some speakers contrast the sequence *-biytu* in *zeṛbiytu* 'his carpet' with *biyytu* 'he put him up over night, he lodged him for the night'.

The only place where *-y-* is consistently distinguished from *-yy-* and *-w-* from *-ww-* is when they are preceded by *e* after *ḥ* or *ɛ;* e.g., *ɛeynu* 'his eye' and *ɛeyynu* 'he appointed him', *ɛewdu* 'his horse' and *ɛewwdu* 'they accustomed'.

3. Vowels and Diphthongs: After *w*, there is a common interchange between *e* and *o* from speaker to speaker; e.g., some speakers say *weld* and some speakers say *wold* 'child, boy'. There is a similar interchange between *e* and *u* before *w;* e.g., some speakers say *žewžu* and some speakers say *žuwžu* 'they got married'.

There is a limited amount of variation between *i* and *ey* and between *u* and *ew* after *ɛ* and *ḥ;* e.g., some speakers say *ḥeyṭ* 'wall' and *ɛeyn* 'eye' while others say *ḥiṭ* and *ɛin,* some speakers say *ḥewma* 'quarter' (of a town) and *ɛewža* 'crooked' (fem. sg.) while others say *ḥuma* and *ɛuža*. For some speakers the variation also occurs in environments other than around *ḥ* and *ɛ;* e.g., *ġeyṭa* or *ġiṭa,* a kind of Moroccan oboe. Not all cases of *i* and *u* after *ḥ* and *ɛ* alternate with *ey* and *ew* nor do all cases of *ey* and *ew* after *ḥ* and *ɛ* alternate with *i* and *u*. The particular words in which these variations occur must be learned as individual lexical items.

4. Final Syllable Variation: There are a large number of words in Moroccan which end in the sequence *-aCeC;* e.g., *bellarež* 'stork', *waqef* 'standing', *kayen* 'there is' *ɛawen* 'to help'. In all such words the *e* is often dropped in rapid conversation; i.e., *bellarž* instead of *bellarež,* etc. If the last two consonants of the word are identical or similar in place of articulation (e.g., both *n* and *t* are articulated with the tip of the tongue), the dropping of the *e* is especially common; e.g., the pronunciation *ṣaff* 'to line up, to put in line' is more common than the pronunciation *ṣafef,* similarly with *kant* and *kanet* 'she was' or *qalt* and *qalet* 'she said'. The *e* is likewise especially commonly dropped when the consonant preceding it is *w* or *y;* e.g., the pronunciation *kayn* is more common than the pronunciation *kayen* 'there is', and *ɛawn* is more common than *ɛawen* 'to help'.

In order to avoid confusion with words where there is never an *e* between the last two consonants, as in *ma-qam-š* 'he didn't rise', the transcription adopted here has been always to write the *e* in such words as *bellarež* 'stork', *kanet* 'she was', etc.

A similar variation occurs when the stable vowels *i* or *u* occur in the syllable preceding the *e,* but examples are less common; e.g., *ɛurež* 'crooked' (pl.) or *ɛurž*. As with the cases where *a* appears in the syllable preceding the *e,* the convention adopted here is always to write the *e*.

5. Elision and Inversion of Variable Vowels: Variable vowels usually occur only before two or more consonants or before a single consonant at the end of a word; e.g., *ketbet* 'she wrote', where the first *e* is followed by the consonant cluster *-tb-* and the second *e* is followed by *-t* at the end of the word, or *ma-šeft-š* 'I didn't see', where the *e* is followed by three consonants.

The occurrence of a variable vowel in an open syllable, that is, before a single consonant followed by a vowel, is excluded by this pattern. The addition of a vowel suffix to a word ending in a single consonant preceded by a variable vowel would bring about the occurrence of a variable vowel in an open syllable, but various morphological changes occur which exclude such a sequence, for example *yakol* 'he eats', but *yaklu* 'they eat', with the loss of the variable vowel *o*. There are three such morphological changes. These are **elision, inversion,** and **base alteration.** The variable vowel involved is usually *e,* more rarely *o*.

(a) Elision: Elision is the simplest of the three morphological changes which exclude the occurrence of a variable vowel in an open syllable. The variable vowel in question is dropped. Some examples:

ṣifeṭ	'he sent'
ṣifṭu	'he sent him'
naxod	'I take'
naxdu	'we take'
bayeƐ (msc. sg.)	'having sold'
bayƐa (fem. sg.)	'having sold'
bayƐin (pl.)	'having sold'
ṛažel	'man, husband'
ṛažli	'my husband'

The only exception to this pattern of elision is when a sequence of three identical consonants would occur. In such cases elision may occur regularly or the variable vowel may be retained in the open syllable; e.g., *semmem* 'to poison', and either *semmmu,* with a triple *-mmm-,* or *semmemu,* with *e* in an open syllable, 'they poisoned'.

(b) Inversion: If a variable vowel is preceded by a cluster of two consonants and is then elided, a variable vowel is inserted between the two consonants. Inversion is especially common in the verbal system.[1] The inserted vowel is usually *e,* but if the elided vowel is *o,* the inserted vowel is sometimes *o* also. Some examples:

žbeṛ	'he found'
žebṛu	'they found'
šƐel	'he lit'
šeƐlet	'she lit'
ktef	'shoulder'
ketfi	'my shoulder'

[1] In Measures I and Ia of sound verbs, see p. 42.

ṣġoṛ	'childhood'
ṣoġṛi	'my childhood'
idxol	'he enters'
idexlu	'they enter'

When the inversion of a variable vowel would bring a preceding vowel into an open syllable, the preceding variable vowel is dropped. Practically, this double elision is limited to the prefix *me-*, for example *meslem* (msc. sg.), *mselma* (fem. sg.) 'Moslem', and *mselmin* (pl.) 'Moslems'.

(c) **Base Alteration:** Base alteration is limited to the third person feminine singular ending *-et* of the perfect tense, as in *šafet* 'she saw'. In Measure I hollow verbs (See p. 51) such as *šaf* 'to see', the *e* of the *-et* ending is either elided or the final *-t* is doubled. Some speakers use one form and other speakers use the other. Thus:

šafet	'she saw'
šafettu or *šaftu*	'she saw him'

With all other verb types, the *e* is either replaced by *a* or the *-t* is doubled. Some speakers use one form and other speakers use the other. Some examples:

žebṛet	'she found'
žebṛettu or *žebṛatu*	'she found him'
qeddmet	'she presented'
qeddmettu or *qeddmatu*	'she presented him'
ṣifṭet	'she sent'
ṣifṭettu or *ṣifṭatu*	'she sent him'

NOTES

PART TWO
MORPHOLOGY

NOTES

I. GENERAL MORPHOLOGICAL NOTIONS

1. **The Root and the Pattern:** Most Moroccan words are built up on a basic consonantal skeleton called the **root**. This root occurs in **patterns** with various vowels and additional, non-root consonants. The two concepts of root and pattern are fundamental to the structure of Moroccan words. The root usually has some fundamental kernel of meaning which is expanded or modified by the pattern.

An example of a root is the consonant sequence *KTB,* which always has something to do with the concept of "writing". For example:

KTeB	'he wrote'
iKeTBu	'they write'
KaTeB	'having written'
meKTuB	'written'
KTaB	'book'
KTuB	'books'
mKeTBa	'writing desk'

Another example is the root *QTL,* always having something to do with the concept of "killing". Examples of the root *QTL* in various patterns are:

QTeL	'he killed'
QTaL	'carnage, slaughter'
QTiL	'(action of) killing'
QTiLa	'murder, assassination'
QeTTaL	'killer, murderer; deadly'

2. **Types of Roots:** There are three basic root types, **triliteral**, **quadriliteral**, and **atypical**. Roots having three constituent elements are called triliteral; e.g., the *KTB* of *ktab* 'book' and *kteb* 'he wrote'. Roots with four constituent elements are called quadriliteral; e.g., the *ṬṚŽM* of *ṭeṛžem* 'he translated' and *ṭoṛžman* 'translator, interpreter'. Roots with fewer than three or more then four

constituent elements are called atypical, as in the words *ma* 'water' and *merdedduš* 'marjoram'.

Triliteral and quadriliteral roots are further classified as **strong** and **weak.** Those which are composed entirely of consonants are referred to as strong; e.g., triliteral *KTB* and quadriliteral *ṬṚŽM* of the examples above. Those which have a vowel element, usually variable and often alternating with *w* or *y*, are called weak; e.g., the root *Š(V)F* of *šaf* 'he saw' and *ka-išuf* 'he sees', the root *SQṢ(V)* of *seqṣa* 'he asked' and *ka-iseqṣi* 'he asks', the root *Z(V)N* of *mezyan* 'good'.

Strong triliteral roots are further called **sound** if all three constituent consonants are different; e.g., the *HṚB* of *hṛeb* 'he fled, ran away'; and **doubled** if the second and third consonants are identical; e.g., the *ŽDD* of *ždid* 'new' and the *ƐḌḌ* of *Ɛeḍḍ* 'he bit'. The vowel of the weak triliteral root occurs either as the second element, as in the *Š(V)F* of *ka-išuf* 'he sees', or as the third element, as in the *QṚ(V)* of *ka-iqṛa* 'he studies'.

Strong quadriliteral roots in which the last two consonants are a repetition of the first two are called **reduplicated**; e.g., the *ŽṚŽṚ* of *žeṛžeṛ* 'he dragged'. The vowel of weak quadriliteral roots is generally limited to either the second element, as in the *S(V)GR* of *suger* of 'he insured', or the fourth element, as in the *SQṢ(V)* of *seqṣa* 'he asked'.

The following table summarizes the different root types:

A. Triliteral

1. Strong

   (a) Sound; e.g., *KTB* of *kteb* 'he wrote', *XBZ* of *xobz* 'bread'

   (b) Doubled; e.g., *ŠMM* of *šemm* 'he smelled', *KLL* of *koll* 'all'

2. Weak

   (a) Middle-weak; e.g., *Š(V)F* of *šaf* 'he saw', *X(V)F* of *xuf* 'fear'

   (b) Final-weak; e.g., *MR(V)* of *mra* 'he polished', *ḤD(V)* of *ḥda* 'near, beside'

B. Quadriliteral

1. Strong; e.g., *ṬṚŽM* of *ṭeṛžem* 'he translated', *TNBR* of *tenber* 'postage stamp'
   Reduplicated; e.g., *ŽṚŽṚ* of *žeṛžeṛ* 'he dragged'

2. Weak

   (a) Second element weak; e.g., *Ṣ(V)FṬ* of *ṣifeṭ* 'he sent'

   (b) Fourth element weak; e.g., *SQṢ(V)* of *ka-iseqṣi* 'he asks'

C. Atypical, as in *ža* 'he came', *f-* 'in', *merdedduš* 'marjoram'

3. Types of Patterns: A simple pattern, strictly defined, consists of none, one, or two vowels inserted among the consonants of a root. A pattern is completely defined by specifying which vowel or vowels occur and between which two consonants they occur; e.g., the pattern of *kteb* 'he wrote', root *KTB*, is no vowel between the first and second consonants, a vowel between the second and third consonants, specific vowel *e*.

A pattern joined with an affix is called a **pattern complex**; e.g., *mketba* 'writing desk', where the pattern *e* before the first two consonants of the root *KTB* occurs in conjunction with the prefix *m-* and the suffix *-a*.[1] Affixes which combine with patterns to form pattern complexes are limited in number. There are two infixes. One consists of a *t* inserted after the first consonant of a triliteral root; e.g., *ḥtaž* 'he needed', with the root *Ḥ(V)Ž*. The other consists of doubling the middle consonant of a triliteral root; e.g., *qeddem* 'he presented', with the root *QDM*.

For all practical purposes, there is only one prefix and two suffixes which occur in pattern-complexes. The prefix is *m-*, followed by various vowels, and the two suffixes are *-an* and *-a*; e.g., root *Z(V)N* with *m-* in *mezyan* 'good', root *ZRB* with *-an* in *zerban* 'hurrying, in a hurry', root *WḤL* with *-a* in *weḥla* 'difficulty, troublesome situation'.

4. Root Structure and Word Derivation: There is a close relation between the various word classes and the various root types. Verbs are almost exclusively triliteral and quadriliteral, although there are a few which are atypical; e.g., *ža* 'he came'. Adjectives are also almost exclusively triliteral, as in *kbir* 'big' with root *KBR*, and it is difficult to cite a useful example of an adjective with either a quadriliteral or an atypical root.

Nouns largely have triliteral or quadriliteral roots; e.g., *weld* 'boy' with root *WLD* and *seksu* 'couscous' with root *SKS(V)*. Nouns with atypical roots are, however, not uncommon; e.g., *oxt* 'sister' with root *XT* and *ɛenkbut* 'spider web', with a long root not found in any other word.

The other parts of speech are mostly atypical with roots of fewer than three elements; e.g., *f-* 'in'. Only a few triliteral roots are to be found among the particles; e.g., *BƐD* in *beɛd* 'after', *KLL* in *koll* 'all'.

5. Stems and Affixes: A stem is a root already combined with a pattern or a pattern-complex to which, taken as a whole, a prefix or a suffix is added. For example the form *qeddem* 'to present', the pattern-complex of which shows a doubled middle consonant with *e* inserted both before and after it, serves as the stem for the prefix *t-* in the form *tqeddem* 'to advance, to progress'.

Stems are usually ordinary verbs, nouns, adjectives, and particles, the various forms and types of which are discussed in the following chapters. The number of affixes is quite small. In summary the principle ones are:

[1] The combination of a pattern-complex with a root must be distinguished from the addition of a suffix to a stem. See below, **5. Stems and Affixes.**

(a) The personal prefixes and suffixes of the imperfect tense of the verb; e.g., the *n-* of *nšuf* 'I see'; see p. 45ff.

(b) The personal suffixes of the perfect tense of the verb; e.g., the *-et* of *kanet* 'she was'; see pp. 41-42.

(c) The prefix *m-* of various noun, adjective, and verbal derivations; e.g., *mṣafeṛ* 'traveler'; see pp. 58-59, 102, 104, 111.

(d) The feminine *-a* suffix; e.g., *kbira* 'big' (fem. sg.); see pp. 65, 78-80, 95-100.

(e) The plural ending *-(a)t;* e.g., *ḥkayat* 'stories'; see pp. 107-113.

(f) The plural suffix *-in;* e.g., *feṛḥanin* 'happy' (pl.); see pp. 102-105.

(g) The nisba ending *-i;* e.g., *fṛanṣawi* 'French'; see pp. 67-74.

(h) The suffixed pronoun endings; e.g., the *-k* of *mɛak* 'with you' (sg.); see pp. 134-142.

6. **The Symbolization of Root and Word Structure:** It is often convenient to refer to root, pattern, and affix structure in the abstract without reference to any particular root. For triliteral roots this is done by using the three letter sequence *F-Ɛ-L,* with the *F* standing conventionally for the first element of a triliteral root, *Ɛ* standing for the second element, and *L* standing for the third element. In writing formulas, ordinary small letters are used to represent specific phonemes. According to this convention, the following five verb forms are all of the *FƐeL* form:

kteb	'he wrote'
šṛeb	'he drank'
mḍeġ	'he chewed'
lbes	'he wore, he put on'
qbel	'he accepted'

The characterization *FƐeL* is simply a formulaic way of saying that all five forms have strong triliteral roots with no vowel between the first and second consonants and the vowel *e* between the second and third consonants.

A form *FƐiL* is illustrated by such words as:

kbir	'big'
ktir	'much'
ɛbid	'slaves'
šṛib	'(the action of) drinking'

A form *FeƐLan* is illustrated by such words as:

ḍeṛban	'porcupine'
ṣeḷṭan	'sultan'
benyan	'building'
ṭefyan	'(the action of) extinction, putting out'
feṛḥan	'happy'

A form *meFƐaL* is illustrated by such words as:

medbal	'faded'
meḍḷam	'dark'
meṣwab	'polite, courteous'
mezyan	'good'

For doubled roots, the identity of the second and third consonants of the root can be indicated by repeating the *Ɛ* as the third consonant of the root and writing *F–Ɛ–Ɛ* instead of *F–Ɛ–L*. Thus *mešquq* 'split, chopped' is of the general pattern *meFƐuL* but more specifically of the pattern *meFƐuƐ*. The variable element of weak roots is indicated by the symbol *(V)*. Thus *mra* 'he polished', *Ɛdu* 'enemy', and *bni* 'building' are of the general form *FƐ(V)*, while each is respectively of the specific form *FƐa, FƐu,* and *FƐi*. Such a word as *bin* 'between' is of the general form *F(V)L* and the specific form *FiL*, etc.

Quadriliteral roots are symbolized by adding a final capital *C* to *F–Ɛ–L* to symbolize the fourth consonant of the root; e.g., the following words are all characterized as being of the form *FeƐLeC:*

festeq	'pistachio'
fendeq	'hotel'
melmel	'to move' (something)
ġerbel	'to sift'
ferkel	'to squirm, to writhe'

It is also sometimes convenient to have a general formula for vowels. In such cases $\breve{V}$ is used to stand for any variable vowel and the symbol $\bar{V}$ is used to stand for any stable vowel. Thus the words *kteb* 'he wrote' and *dxol!* 'enter!' (msc. sg.) are both of the general form *FƐ*$\breve{V}$*L*, while the words *sxun* 'hot', *kbir* 'big', and *žmal* 'camels' all have the same general form *FƐ*$\bar{V}$*L*.

In cases where it is convenient to speak of general consonant-vowel form without reference to specific root-pattern structure,[2] a capital *C* can be used to stand for any consonant, along with the symbols $\breve{V}$ for any variable vowel and $\bar{V}$ for any stable vowel. Thus both *mekteb* 'office' and *fendeq* 'hotel' have the same general consonant-vowel form *C*$\breve{V}$*CC*$\breve{V}$*C* (or *CeCCeC*), but *mekteb* has the specific root-pattern structure *meFƐeL* while *fendeq* has the specific root-pattern structure *FeƐLeC*. Their plurals, *mkateb* 'offices' and *fnadeq* 'hotels' are likewise identical in terms of general consonant-vowel form; i.e., *CC*$\bar{V}$*C*$\breve{V}$*C* (or *CCaCeC*), while *mkateb* is of the specific root-pattern structure *mFaƐeL* and *fnadeq* is of the specific root-pattern structure *FƐaLeC*.

[2]For example in the discussion of noun plurals, see p. 113ff.

II. THE VERB — DERIVATION

Moroccan verb stems have only a limited number of clearly defined shapes. These verb stems are built up on the basic root consonants plus a small number of patterns. There are ten such patterns for verbs with triliteral roots, and they are conventionally referred to as the **Measures** of the triliteral verb. There are only two different varieties of verbs with quadriliteral roots, and they may be conveniently referred to as the base form and the derived form.

1. **The Ten Measures of the Triliteral Verb:** Of the ten measures of the triliteral verb, only four, namely Measures I, Ia, II, and IIa(V), are found with a large number of verbs. The other six, namely Measures III, IIIa(VI), VII, VIII, IX, and X, are each represented by only a limited number of verbs.

Since most students of a spoken dialect of Arabic eventually come into greater or lesser contact with written Arabic, the written Arabic measure numbering system is followed as closely as possible in this description of the Moroccan verb in order to avoid possible later confusions. Deviations are made from the system of written Arabic only in the case of Moroccan Measure IIa (written Arabic Measure V) and Moroccan Measure IIIa (written Arabic Measure VI), and in these cases the written Arabic measure number is given in parentheses after the Moroccan number.

Moroccan has no equivalent for written Arabic Measure IV, and this number has consequently not been used in referring to Moroccan verb measures. In similar fashion, there is no written Arabic equivalent for Moroccan Measure Ia. Except for Measure Ia, the various Moroccan measures correspond directly to similarly numbered measures of written Arabic.[1]

1. Measure I

Measure I is the most frequently encountered type of verb stem. The pattern differs for each of the different root types. For sound roots the pattern is *FεeL*. Some examples of Measure I verbs with sound roots:

kteb	'to write'
šṛeb	'to drink'

[1]Although in a strictly technical sense Moroccan Arabic Measure IX corresponds more closely to written Arabic Measure XI than to written Arabic Measure IX.

kber	'to grow'
ṛžeɛ	'to come back, to go back'
lɛeb	'to play'
fṛeḥ	'to rejoice, to be happy'

For doubled roots the pattern is usually *Feɛɛ* although there are occasional examples of *Foɛɛ*. Measure I verbs with doubled roots are commonly referred to as **doubled verbs**. Some examples of doubled verbs:

medd	'to hand over, to give'
šedd	'to close'
ḥekk	'to rub'
ɛeḍḍ	'to bite'
koḥḥ	'to cough'

For middle-weak roots the pattern is uniformly *FaL*. Triliteral Measure I verbs with middle-weak roots are conventionally referred to as **hollow verbs**. Some examples of hollow verbs:

daz	'to pass'
qal	'to say, to tell'
šaf	'to see'
xaf	'to be afraid'
žab	'to bring'

The pattern for final-weak roots is uniformly *Fɛa*. Measure I triliteral verbs with final-weak roots are conventionally referred to as **defective verbs**. Some examples of defective verbs:

bṛa	'to get well'
mša	'to go, to walk'
šra	'to buy'
ḥba	'to crawl'

2. Measure II

All Measure II verb stems have the common characteristic of a medial doubled consonant. The pattern for strong roots, both sound and doubled, is *FeƐƐeL*. Some examples:

beƐƐed	'to move aside, to make distant'
beddel	'to change'
feṛṛeq	'to divide, to distribute'
melles	'to make smooth'
Ɛelleq	'to hang up'
dellel	'to sell at auction'
xeffef	'to lighten'
ḥedded	'to limit; to iron' (clothes)
Ɛeddeb	'to oppress, to mistreat'

The Measure II pattern for middle-weak roots is similar to that of sound and doubled roots. The medial doubled consonant is *-yy-* for some roots, *-ww-* for others,[2] and the medial doubled consonant is both followed and preceded by a vowel. Whether the medial doubled consonant is *-yy-* or *-ww-* varies from root to root. The vowel after the medial doubled consonant is always *e*, and the vowel which precedes the medial doubled consonant is determined by the consonants in the root.

Middle-weak roots of which Measure I verb stems take *i* in the imperfect[3] take *-yy-* in Measure II; e.g., Measure I *faq* 'to wake up, to become awake', imperfect *ifiq*, with Measure II verb stem *fiyyeq* 'to wake (someone) one'. Middle-weak roots of which Measure I verb stems take *u* in the imperfect take *-ww-* in Measure II; e.g., Measure I *naḍ* 'to arise, to get out of bed', imperfect *inuḍ*, with Measure II verb stem *nuwweḍ* 'to cause (someone, something) to stand up, to get out of bed'. Middle-weak roots of which Measure I verb stems take *a* in the imperfect are unpredictable as to whether Measure II takes *-yy-* or *-ww-*; e.g.,

Root *B(V)N*	Root *X(V)F*
Measure I stem *ban* 'to appear'	Measure I stem *xaf* 'to be afraid'
Imperfect *iban*	Imperfect *ixaf*

---

[2]See pp. 24, 32, 57-58, 63-64 for the alternation of *w* and *y* with vowels in weak roots.

[3]For the inflection of hollow verbs in the imperfect tense, see pp. 49-50.

Measure II *biyyen* 'to indicate, to show'

Measure II *xuwwef* 'to frighten'

The vowel before the medial *-yy-* or *-ww-* varies somewhat according to dialect. After an initial *ḥ* or *ɛ* the vowel is *e*. Otherwise the most general pattern is to have *i* before *-yy-* and *u* before *-ww-* although it is not uncommon to find *e* before the medial *-ww-* regardless of whether or not the initial consonant is *ḥ* or *ɛ*. Some examples:

siyyeb	'to throw'
zuwwel	'to remove'
ḥewweṣ	'to steal'
ɛeyyeṭ	'to call'

The general pattern for Measure II of final-weak roots is *Feɛɛa,* although the same kind of vowel variation before medial *-yy-* and *-ww-* is found as with middle-weak roots. Some examples:

ġeṭṭa	'to cover'
ḥella	'to sweeten'
ɛeyya	'to make tired'
luwwa	'to twist'
qiyya	'to make vomit'

3. Measure III

There are relatively few verbs which have the pattern of Measure III. The pattern is *FaɛeL*[4] for sound, doubled, and middle-weak roots.[5] The medial consonant of middle-weak roots is either *-y-* or *-w-*.[6] For final-weak roots the pattern is *Faɛa,* with a final *a* corresponding to the final *-eL* of the other root types. Some examples:

---

[4]See p. 17 for the tendency of *e* to drop out in such an environment; e.g., both *ṣafef* and *ṣaff* 'to put in line, to line up' are heard.

[5]Care must be taken to distinguish Measure III of sound and doubled roots and middle-weak roots with *-y-* from the Measure I active participle of the same root. The patterns are identical; see p. 57.

[6]The occurrence of *-y-* and *-w-* in Measure III is exactly parallel to *-yy-* and *-ww-* in Measure II; see p. 31.

ṣafeṛ	'to travel'
saɛef	'to heed the advice of, to listen to'
ṣafef, ṣaff	'to put in line, to line up'
žaweb	'to answer'
ɛayen	'to wait'
qaḍa	'to finish'

4. Measures Ia, IIa(V), and IIIa(VI)

The stems of these measures are derived by prefixing *tt-* or *t-* to the stems of Measures I, II, and III. There is no distinction to be made for the different kinds of roots in these measures. The single *t-* is always used in deriving Measures IIa(V) and IIIa(VI) from Measures II and III; e.g.,

II *ġeṭṭa* 'to cover'	IIa(V) *tġeṭṭa* 'to be covered'
III *ṣafef, ṣaff* 'to put in line'	IIIa(VI) *tṣafef, tṣaff* 'to line (oneself) up, to get into line'

For Measure Ia, some speakers use the double *tt-*, others use the single *t-*; e.g., Measure I *šaf* 'to see', Measure Ia *ttšaf* or *tšaf* 'to be seen'. The usage with *tt-* is more common. In the case of Measure I stems beginning with a consonant cluster (i.e., those with sound and final-weak roots), an *e* is inserted between the prefix and the following consonant cluster; e.g., Measure I *ḍṛeb* 'to hit' with Measure Ia *tteḍṛeb* 'to be hit', and Measure I *dḥa* 'to dismiss, to fire' with Measure Ia *ttedḥa* 'to be dismissed, to be fired'. If the consonant cluster begins with *w*, there is a variation between *e* and *u* in the prefix; e.g., Measure I *wled* 'to bear, to give birth to' with Measure Ia *ttewled* or *ttuwled* 'to be born', depending on the dialect of the speaker. The question of prefixing *tte-* to a consonant cluster beginning with *y* does not arise.

If the first consonant of the root is one of the phoneme group *t, ṭ, d, ḍ, z, ž,* the prefixes *tt-* and *t-* usually assimilate both for voice and emphasis, and combinations which would bring about a sequence of *ttt-, ddd-,* or *ḍḍḍ-* are simplified to *tt-, dd-,* and *ḍḍ-* respectively. Some examples:

(1) An assimilation of voice, *dd-* instead of *tt-:* Measure I *zad* 'to add, to make greater', with Measure Ia *ddzad* 'to be added, to become greater; to be born'.

(2) An assimilation of emphasis, *ṭ-* instead of *t-:* Measure II *ṭehheṛ* 'to circumcise', with Measure IIa(V) *ṭṭehheṛ* 'to be circumcised'.

(3) An assimilation of both voice and emphasis, *ḍ-* instead of *t-:* Measure III *ḍayef* 'to receive as a guest, to give hospitality to', with Measure IIIa(VI) *ḍḍayef* 'to be received as a guest'.

(4) A simplification of three identical consonants to two, *ḍḍ-* instead of *ḍḍḍ-:* Measure I *ḍeṛṛ* 'to hurt, to injure', with Measure Ia *ḍḍeṛṛ* 'to be hurt, to be injured'.

If the root begins with *ẓ* there is an assimilation of voice, but not of emphasis; e.g., Measure II *ẓuwweṛ* 'to falsify', with Measure IIa(V) *dẓuwweṛ* 'to be falsified'. There is also no assimilation of emphasis before *ṣ-;* e.g., Measure I *ṣab* 'to find', with Measure Ia *ttṣab* 'to be found'.

The prefix *tte-,* when prefixed to a Measure I sound verb, undergoes exactly the same assimilatory changes when the addition of a suffix brings about an inversion[7] in the stem; e.g., Measure I *ḍṛeb* 'to hit', Measure Ia *tteḍṛeb* 'to get hit', inflected form of Measure Ia showing inversion, *ḍḍeṛbu* 'they got hit'. The form *ḍḍeṛbu* shows an assimilation of both voice and emphasis and a simplification of a sequence of three identical consonants to two.

For sound and defective Measure I verbs beginning with *z, ẓ,* and *ž,* the prefix sometimes takes the form *dd-;* e.g., Measure I *zreƐ* 'to sow, to plant' with Measure Ia *ttezreƐ* or *ddzreƐ* 'to be sown, to be planted'; root *ẒḶṬ* (there is no Measure I verb with this root), Measure Ia *tteẓḷeṭ* or *ddẓḷeṭ* 'to fall into misery'; Measure I *žbed* 'to pull (out)' with Measure Ia *ttežbed* or *ddžbed* 'to be pulled (out)'.

Some speakers, especially in slower and more deliberate speech, do not assimilate these prefixes before the phonemes *ṭ, d, ḍ, z, ẓ,* and *ž.* Instead the prefix is retained unchanged, and an ultra-short vowel[8] (not written in our transcription) is pronounced between the prefix and the following *ṭ, d, ḍ, z, ẓ,* or *ž.* For example Measure I *dar* 'to do' with Measure Ia *ddar* (usually) or *ttdar* (less often) 'to be done'; Measure II *ṭuwweḷ* 'to lengthen' with Measure IIa(V) *ṭṭuwweḷ* (usually) or *tṭuwweḷ* (less often) 'to be lengthened'.

5. Measures IV, VII, VIII, IX, and X

Moroccan Arabic has no verb Measure corresponding to Measure IV of written Arabic. In order to avoid confusion for the student who wishes to work with written Arabic also, this number is not used in this description of the Moroccan verb.[9] Measures VII, VIII, IX, and X occur with only a very limited number of verbs.

Measure VII is characterized by an *n-* prefixed to Measure I. It usually serves as a kind of passive for Measure I; e.g., Measure I *dfen* 'to bury' and Measure VII *ndfen* 'to be buried', Measure I *šmet* 'to cheat' and Measure VII *nšmet* 'to be cheated'. Measure VII is the rarest of all the verb measures, and many Moroccans do not use it at all. Measure VII for such speakers is regularly replaced by Measure Ia with the same meaning; e.g., Measure Ia *ttedfen* 'to be buried', Measure Ia *ttešmet* 'to be cheated'.

---

[7]For inversion see pp. 17-19.

[8]Similar to the first "o" in such an English word as "tomorrow" when pronounced at ordinarily rapid conversational speed.

[9]Cf. the discussion of the measure numbers, p. 29.

Measure VIII is characterized by the insertion of a *t* after the first consonant of the root. With doubled roots the vowel *e* is inserted between the *t* and the final doubled consonant; e.g., *htemm* 'to be concerned with'. With middle-weak roots, an *a* is placed between the inserted *t* and the final consonant of the root; e.g., *rtaḥ* 'to rest', *ḥtaž* 'to need'. Sound roots likewise have *a* after the inserted *t*, combined with *e* between the last two consonants of the root; e.g., *ḥtaṛem* 'to respect', *xtaṛeƐ* 'to invent, to imagine'.

The pattern of Measure IX is *FƐaL;* e.g., *sman* 'to become fat'. Middle-weak roots have either *y* or *w*[10] functioning as the second root consonant; e.g., root *Ɛ(V)Ž* with Measure IX verb stem *Ɛwaž* 'to become bent, twisted', and root *B(V)Ḍ* with Measure IX verb stem *byaḍ* 'to become white'. Due to their lack of a third consonant, there is no Measure IX stem definable for final-weak roots.

The pattern of Measure X combines the pattern of Measure I with the prefix *ste-* before stems beginning with two consonants and *st-* before stems beginning with consonant plus vowel; e.g., root *XBṚ* with Measure X verb stem *stexbeṛ* 'to make inquiries', and root *ġLL* with Measure X verb stem *stġell* 'to benefit (from), to enjoy'.

2. The Quadriliteral Verb: Quadriliteral verbs have only two forms, a base form and a derived form. For strong roots the pattern of the base form is *FeƐLeC;* e.g., *ṭeṛžem* 'to translate', *žeṛžeṛ* 'to drag', *feṛgeƐ* 'to make explode, to blow up'.

In weak quadriliteral verbs, the weak element is always the second or the fourth of the four constituent elements of the root. When the second element is weak, the stem vowel is *i* for some roots and *u* for others; e.g., *ṛitel* 'to pillage' and *suret* 'to lock'. When the fourth element is weak, the stem vowel is always *a;* e.g., *seqṣa* 'to ask'.

The derived quadriliteral verb is formed by prefixing *t-* to the base form; e.g., base form *ṣifeṭ* 'to send' and derived from *tṣifeṭ* 'to be sent'. The same assimilatory changes occur as were described above for Measures IIa(V) and IIIa(VI) of the triliteral verbs (See pp. 33-34); e.g., base form *ṭeṛžem* 'to translate' with derived form *ṭṭeṛžem* 'to be translated', and base form *žeṛžeṛ* 'to drag' with derived form *džeṛžeṛ* 'to be dragged'.

3. The Meaning of the Verb Patterns: Most of the patterns of verb stems, both the ten measures of the triliteral verb and the base and derived forms of the quadriliteral verb, have a specific pattern meaning which combines with the inherent meaning of the root. In addition to meaningful relations between pattern and root, there are meaningful relations among the various patterns one with another.

---

[10]On the occurrence of *y* and *w* in middle-weak roots, cf. the comments on p. 31.

(a) Colorless Patterns: The patterns of the base form of quadriliteral verbs and of Measures I, III, VIII, and X of the triliteral verb have no specific meanings attached to them. They are merely four different consonant-vowel shapes which are found to occur among Moroccan verbs. There is nothing predictable about the meaning of a given verb stem from the fact that its pattern is that of Measures I, III, VIII, X, or the quadriliteral base form.

(b) Measure II: Measure II is usually causative. It is derived widely from the roots of Measure I verbs, nouns, adjectives, and occasionally other parts of speech. Measure II is an open form in the sense that new verbs of this pattern are invented freely to fit new situations. Some examples:

Nouns		**Measure II**	
dheb	'gold'	*dehheb*	'to gild'
fwaṛ	'steam'	*fuwweṛ*	'to steam'
sebba	'reason, cause'	*sebbeb*	'to cause'
ṭbeḷ	'drum'	*ṭebbeḷ*	'to play the drum'
ġiṭa	'(kind of) oboe'	*ġiyyeṭ*	'to play the *ġiṭa*'
ḥedd	'border, boundary'	*ḥedded*	'to bound, to limit'

Adjectives		**Measure II**	
byeḍ	'white'	*biyyeḍ*	'to make white'
kḥel	'black'	*keḥḥel*	'to blacken'
ṣġiṛ	'small'	*ṣeġġeṛ*	'to make small, to reduce'
ṭwiḷ	'long'	*ṭuwweḷ*	'to lengthen'
ḥlu	'sweet'	*ḥella*	'to sweeten'
ɛali	'high'	*ɛella*	'to make higher'

Measure I		**Measure II**	
fhem	'to understand'	*fehhem*	'to make understand, to explain'
gles	'to sit'	*gelles*	'to seat, to set'
šṛeb	'to drink'	*šeṛṛeb*	'to water, to give water to'
bat	'to pass the night'	*biyyet*	'to lodge for the night'

ṭaḥ	'to fall'	*ṭiyyeḥ*	'to make fall, to throw down'
xaf	'to be afraid'	*xuwwef*	'to frighten'
ġla	'to (be in a) boil'	*ġella*	'to (make) boil'

(c) **Measure IX:** There are relatively few Measure IX verbs, probably not more than fifty at the most. They are all intransitive, they are related to adjectives, and they all have the sense of 'to become' with respect to the adjectives to which they are related. Measure IX verbs are particularly related to the adjectives of color and defect (See below, p. 87), but they are not limited to these adjectives. Some examples:

byaḍ	'to become white'
kḥal	'to become black'
ṛṭab	'to become soft'
sman	'to become fat'
ṭwaḷ	'to become long'
ḥmaq	'to become crazy'
ḥmaṛ	'to become red'
ɛwaž	'to become twisted, crooked'

(d) **Measures I and II as Related to Measures Ia and IIa(V):** Measures Ia and IIa(V) are the corresponding medio-passives of transitive verbs of Measures I and II; e.g., Measure I transitive verb *baɛ* 'to sell' with medio-passive Measure Ia *ttbaɛ* 'to be sold', Measure II *feṛṛeq* 'to distribute' with medio-passive Measure IIa(V) *tfeṛṛeq* 'to be distributed'.

The medio-passive Measures Ia and IIa(V) have several different but closely related meanings. The simplest is the pure passive; e.g., Measure I *ḍṛeb* 'to hit, to beat' and Measure Ia *tteḍṛeb* 'to be beaten'. The purely passive connotation is often accompanied by the idea of possibility or permissibility. For example *ttbaɛ*, according to context, means either 'to be sold' or 'to be for sale, susceptible of being sold', and *tteḍṛeb* may mean either simply 'to be beaten' or 'to be liable to be beaten'.

The two other commonest shades of meaning of the medio-passive Measures Ia and IIa(V) are those of a simple intransitive or of a reflexive intransitive. Measure Ia *ttfešš* (cf. Measure I *fešš* 'to disinflate') has more the connotation of 'to go flat, to become disinflated' rather than 'to be disinflated, to get disinflated'. The reflexive intransitive is illustrated by the medio-passive Measure IIa(V) *ḍḍuwweṛ* 'to turn (oneself) around', from Measure II *ḍuwweṛ* 'to turn (something) around, to make rotate'.

The medio-passives are never accompanied by an equivalent of English 'by', and when the agent of an action is stated in a Moroccan sentence, a directly transitive verb is used with the agent as its subject; e.g., such an English sentence as 'the house was sold by the merchant' is rendered in Moroccan as 'the merchant sold the house', *t-tažer baɛ ḍ-ḍaṛ*.

(e) **Measure IIIa(VI):** Sometimes, but only rarely, Measure IIIa(VI) stands as the medio-passive of Measure III; e.g., Measure III *qaḍa* 'to finish (something)', Measure IIIa(VI) *tqaḍa* 'to come to an end, to be finished'.

More commonly Measure IIIa(VI) verbs have a reciprocal meaning, and the non-reciprocal verbs which are semantically related to them are often of Measures I and II as well as of Measure III; e.g., Measure I *žra* 'to run' and Measure IIIa(VI) *džara* 'to vie in running, to race', Measure I *wedd* 'to give (as a gift)' and Measure IIIa(VI) *twaded, twadd* 'to give gifts to one another'.

The reciprocal aspect of Measure IIIa(VI) implies at least two parties. A consequence is that plural forms of Measure IIIa(VI) verbs are more common than singular forms, and when singular forms do occur they are usually accompanied by *mɛa* 'with' or some other preposition; e.g.,

tfahemt mɛaha	'I came to a (mutual) understanding with her'
tfahemna	'we came to a (mutual) understanding'
ddaɛa mɛahom	'he went to court with them, had a lawsuit with them'
ddaɛaw	'they sued each other, they contested a lawsuit with each other'

The most common reciprocal implication of Measure IIIa(VI) verbs is a mutually transitive action, as in many of the examples above or as in *tbawsu* 'they kissed each other' or *ḍḍaṛbu* 'they hit each other, they had a fight'. The concept of rivalry or competitive action also appears in Measure IIIa(VI), as in *džara* 'to compete in racing, to run a race (with)'.

(f) **The Derived Quadriliteral Form:** The derived quadriliteral verb form is the medio-passive of the base form. As such, it has the same relation to the base form as Measures Ia and IIa(V) have to Measures I and II. For example:

Base Form		**Derived Form**	
feṛgeɛ	'to (make something) explode'	*tfeṛgeɛ*	'to explode, to blow up'
keṛfeṣ	'to soil, to rumple, to mess up'	*tkeṛfeṣ*	'to get dirty, rumpled, messed up'

melmel	'to move (something)'	*tmelmel*	'to move, to be moved'
suger	'to insure'	*tsuger*	'to be insured, to take out insurance for oneself'
žeṛžeṛ	'to drag'	*džeṛžeṛ*	'to be dragged'

4. Exceptions to the Root and Pattern System of the Verbs: There are very few verbs which do not fit into the root-pattern system. Such verbs must be learned as individual lexical items. The only common ones are *dda* 'to take' and *ža* 'to come'. There are occasional more complex forms; e.g., *ttkel* 'to rely on; to be eaten, to be edible', which has approximately the meaning and function of a Measure Ia verb with reference to Measure I *kla* 'to eat'.

III. THE VERB — INFLECTION

I. General Characteristics

1. **Inflectional Categories:** There are two kinds of inflected verb forms in Moroccan Arabic, **finite** forms and **non-finite** forms. There are two non-finite forms, the **active participle** and the **passive participle.**[1] There are two types of finite forms, the **perfect tense** and the **imperfect tense.** The two tenses share the grammatical categories of person and number.

The three persons are defined by affixes to the verb and by the pronouns *ana* 'I' and *ḥna* 'we' for the first person, *nta* 'you' (msc.), *nti* 'you' (fem.), and *ntuma* 'you' (pl.) for the second person, and *huwa* 'he', *hiya* 'she', and *huma* 'they' for the third person. The two numbers, singular and plural, are defined by affixes to the verb and the singular pronouns *ana* 'I', *nta* 'you' (msc.), *nti* 'you' (fem.), *huwa* 'he', and *hiya* 'she' as opposed to the plural pronouns *ḥna* 'we', *ntuma* 'you' (pl.), and *huma* 'they'.

The two tenses also make a limited distinction between two genders, a masculine and a feminine, and two moods, an indicative and an imperative. The distinction between indicative and imperative occurs only in the second person of the imperfect. The gender distinction of masculine versus feminine occurs only in the third person singular (*huwa* 'he' as opposed to *hiya* 'she') of the perfect and the imperfect and, for some speakers only, in the second person singular of the imperfect; e.g., *tekteb* 'you (msc.) write' and *tketbi* 'you (sg.) write'. Most urban speakers do not make a gender distinction in the second person and use such forms as *tekteb* 'you (sg.) write' in addressing both men and women.

2. **Inflectional Forms:** A Moroccan Arabic verb form consists of a verb stem combined with an inflectional affix. Both prefixes and suffixes are used, sometimes combined with internal vowel changes in the stem. The imperfect is formed by a set of prefixes in the singular and by the same set of prefixes plus a set of suffixes in the plural. The perfect is formed by a set of suffixes.

3. **The Verb Stem:** The simplest form of the Moroccan verb is the third person singular masculine form of the perfect tense, for example *ẓreb* 'he hurried'. There is no characteristic suffix for the third person singular masculine form of

---

[1]The participles are treated as part of noun and adjective derivation. See pp. 57-59.

the perfect, and this form is defined as the verb stem. This form is taken as the basic form of the verb, and other inflected forms are treated as being derived from it.

The third person singular masculine of the perfect is also the one which is used for dictionary listings. For dictionary purposes, *zreb* is listed as meaning 'to hurry', and vice versa. This procedure is simply a short-hand device whereby the base form of the English verb and the base form of the Moroccan verb are identified for citation purposes. The actual translation meaning of *zreb* is 'he hurried'. There is no direct translation meaning for 'to hurry', since the Moroccan verb has no infinitive form.

II. The Inflection of the Perfect Tense

1. The Inflectional Suffixes: The following table shows the characteristic personal suffixes of the perfect.

	Singular		Plural	
First Person:	*-t*	'I'	*-na*	'we'
Second Person:	*-ti*	'you'	*-tiw, -tu*	'you'
Third Person:	(stem alone)	'he'	*-u, -w*	'they'
	-et, -at, -t	'she'		

(a) The Alternate Forms for 'she': The ending *-t* is used after stems ending in *-a*[2]; e.g., stem *mša* 'to go', *mšat* 'she went'. Stems ending in *-aC* (i.e., Measures I, Ia, and VIII of middle-weak roots; see pp. 30, 33, 35) take the ending *-et;* e.g., stem *daz* 'to pass' and *dazet* 'she passed', stem *ttzad* 'to be born' and *ttzadet* 'she was born', stem *xtaṛ* 'to choose' and *xtaṛet* 'she chose'.

For all other stems, the endings *-et* and *-at* are interchangeable. Some speakers use *-et* and others use *-at;* e.g., stem *ḥell* 'to open' and *ḥellet* or *ḥellat* 'she opened'.

Before the pronoun object endings *-ek* 'you' (sg.) and *-u* 'him',[3] the ending *-et* undergoes one of two further changes. In Measures I, Ia, and VIII of middle-weak verbs, where the ending *-at* 'she' is never used, either the *e* of *-et* is dropped or

[2]No vowel other than *-a* occurs at the end of stems, which otherwise end in consonants. The ending *-t* 'she' attached to a stem ending in *-a,* as in the example given above, is not to be confused with the ending *-at* 'she', which is attached only to stems ending in consonants.

[3]For the pronoun object endings see pp. 134-149.

else the *t* is doubled before these pronoun endings; e.g., *šafet* 'she saw' and *šafettu* or *šaftu* 'she saw him'. With verb stems where the endings *-et* and *-at* are interchangeable, the *t* of *-et* is doubled before these pronoun endings; e.g., *qeddmet* or *qeddmat* 'she presented' and *qeddmettu* or *qeddmatu* 'she presented him'.

(b) The Alternate Forms for 'you' (pl.) and 'they': The alternate forms *-tiw* and *-tu* 'you' (pl.) are interchangeable with one another. Some speakers say *ktebtiw* while others say *ktebtu* 'you (pl.) wrote', etc. The form *-tiw* is the most common urban usage.

The ending *-u* 'they' occurs after stems ending in consonants, while the ending *-w* occurs after stems ending in vowels; e.g., *mat* 'to die' and *matu* 'they died', *dda* 'to take' and *ddaw* 'they took'.

2. Verb Stem Classes: Certain regular stem changes take place with the addition of the suffixes of the perfect tense. There are four major kinds of stems, distinguished on the basis of different stem changes entailed by the addition of the inflectional endings.

(a) Stems Ending in *-eC*: These stems are unchanged with the addition of the endings of the first and second persons. With the addition of the endings *-et* or *-at* 'she' and *-u* 'they', Measures I, Ia, and X of sound roots show an inversion of the *e* while other stems in *-eC* show an elision of it.[4] Some illustrative paradigms:

ktebt	'I wrote'	*ktebna*	'we wrote'
ktebti	'you (sg.) wrote'	*ktebtiw*	'you (pl.) wrote'
kteb	'he wrote'	*ketbu*	'they wrote'
ketbet	'she wrote'		

ttexleɛt	'I got scared'	*ttexleɛna*	'we got scared'
ttexleɛti	'you (sg.) got scared'	*ttexleɛtiw*	'you (pl.) got scared'
ttexleɛ	'he got scared'	*ttxelɛu*	'they got scared'
ttxelɛet	'she got scared'		

qeddemt	'I presented'	*qeddemna*	'we presented'
qeddemti	'you (sg.) presented'	*qeddemtiw*	'you (pl.) presented'
qeddem	'he presented'	*qeddmu*	'they presented'
qeddmet	'she presented'		

siyyebt	'I threw'	*siyyebna*	'we threw'
siyyebti	'you (sg.) threw'	*siyyebtiw*	'you (pl.) threw'
siyyeb	'he threw'	*siyybu*	'they threw'
siyybet	'she threw'		

ɛayent	'I waited'	*ɛayenna*	'we waited'
ɛayenti	'you (sg.) waited'	*ɛayentiw*	'you (pl.) waited'
ɛayen	'he waited'	*ɛaynu*	they waited'
ɛaynet	'she waited'		

[4]For inversion and elision see pp. 17-19.

ġerbelt	'I sifted'	*ġerbelna*	'we sifted'
ġerbelti	'you (sg.) sifted'	*ġerbeltiw*	'you (pl.) sifted'
ġerbel	'he sifted'	*ġerblu*	'they sifted'
ġerblet	'she sifted'		

The verb *ttkel* 'to rely', although atypical in terms of the root and pattern system, shows inversion in the forms *tteklet* 'she relied' and *tteklu* 'they relied'. In Measure II of doubled roots, elision sometimes does not take place; e.g., *dellelu* or *delllu* 'they sold at auction'. For the assimilation of the prefix *tte-* of Measure Ia in inverted forms, see pp. 33-34.

(b) Stems Ending in *-aC*: Verb stems that fall into this category are Measures I and Ia of middle-weak roots (see pp. 30, 33), for example Measure I *bas* 'to kiss' and Measure Ia *ttbas* 'to be kissed'; Measure VIII of middle-weak roots (see p. 35), for example *xtaṛ* 'to choose'; and all verbs of Measure IX regardless of root type, for example *sman* 'to become fat'. These stems remain unchanged before the endings *-et* 'she' and *-u* 'they' but are subject to change before the endings *-t* 'I', *-na* 'we', *-ti* 'you' (sg.), and *-tiw, -tu* 'you' (pl.) of the first and second persons.

In Measure I verbs the medial *a* is regularly replaced by *e* before the endings of the first and second persons. A sample paradigm:

beƐt	'I sold'	*beƐna*	'we sold'
beƐti	'you (sg.) sold'	*beƐtiw*	'you (pl.) sold'
baƐ	'he sold'	*baƐu*	'they sold'
baƐet	'she sold'		

The two verbs *kan* 'to be' and *qal* 'to say, to tell' are slightly irregular in standard urban speech since both of them substitute *o* instead of *e* for the medial *a* in the first and second persons, thus:

kont	'I was'	*konna*	'we were'
konti	'you (sg.) were'	*kontiw*	'you (pl.) were'
kan	'he was'	*kanu*	'they were'
kanet	'she was'		
qolt	'I said'	*qolna*	'we said'
qolti	'you (sg.) said'	*qoltiw*	'you (pl.) said'

qal	'he said'	*qalu*	'they said'
qalet	'she said'		

In the speech of some Moroccans, these two verbs are conjugated regularly with *e* in the stem, but *g* is substituted for *q* in *qal;* e.g., *kent* 'I was', *gelt* 'I said', etc.

The other verb types whose stems end in *-aC,* Measure IX, and Measures Ia and VIII of middle-weak roots, follow three different inflectional patterns, depending on dialect and individual speaker. Some speakers insert *-i-* before the endings of the first and second persons, some speakers change the *a* of the stem to *e,* exactly as for such Measure I verbs as *baɛ* 'to sell', and other speakers add the endings directly without any stem change. For example:

ttbas	'to be kissed'
ttbasit, ttbest, or *ttbast*	'I was kissed'
xtaṛ	'to choose'
xtaṛit, xteṛt, or *xtaṛt*	'I chose'
sman	'to become fat'
smanit, sment, or *smant*	'I became fat'

(c) Stems Ending in a Double Consonant: This category is comprised of Measures I, Ia, X, and, for some speakers, Measures III and IIIa(VI) of doubled roots. An *-i-* is inserted between the stem and the endings of the first and second persons. Some examples:

šemmit	'I smelled'	*šemmina*	'we smelled'
šemmiti	'you (sg.) smelled'	*šemmitiw*	'you (pl.) smelled'
šemm	'he smelled'	*šemmu*	'they smelled'
šemmet	'she smelled'		
ttfekkit	'I got loose'	*ttfekkina*	'we got loose'
ttfekkiti	'you (sg.) got loose'	*ttfekkitiw*	'you (pl.) got loose'
ttfekk	'he got loose'	*ttfekku*	'they got loose'
ttfekket	'she got loose'		
stġellit	'I profited'	*stġellina*	'we profited'
stġelliti	'you (sg.) profited'	*stġellitiw*	'you (pl.) profited'
stġell	'he profited'	*stġellu*	'they profited'
stġellet	'she profited'		

In Measures III and IIIa(VI) from doubled roots, there is considerable variation from speaker to speaker as to whether an *e* is retained between the last two consonants[5]; e.g., Measure III *ṣafef* or *ṣaff* 'to line (something) up' and Measure IIIa(VI) *tṣafef* or *tṣaff* 'to line (oneself) up, to get in line'. For speakers who regularly have the *e* between the last two consonants these verbs are inflected in the usual way for verbs ending in *-eC* (See pp. 00-00 above); e.g., *tṣafeft* 'I got in line', *tṣaffu* 'they got in line', etc. For speakers who regularly omit the *e* between the last two consonants, an *-i-* is inserted between the stem and the endings of the first and second persons, like other verb stems ending in a double consonant; e.g., *tṣaffina* 'we got in line', etc.

(d) Stems Ending in *-a*: In these stems, regardless of Measure or root type, the final *-a* is changed to *i* before the endings of the first and second persons; e.g.,

bdit	'I began'	*bdina*	'we began'
bditi	'you (sg.) began'	*bditiw*	'you (pl.) began'
bda	'he began'	*bdaw*	'they began'
bdat	'she began'		

neqqit	'I cleaned'	*neqqina*	'we cleaned'
neqqiti	'you (sg.) cleaned'	*neqqitiw*	'you (pl.) cleaned'
neqqa	'he cleaned'	*neqqaw*	'they cleaned'
neqqat	'she cleaned'		

qaḍit	'I finished'	*qaḍina*	'we finished'
qaḍiti	'you (sg.) finished'	*qaḍitiw*	'you (pl.) finished'
qaḍa	'he finished'	*qaḍaw*	'they finished'
qaḍat	'she finished'		

The verbs *ža* 'to come' and *dda* 'to take', although atypical in terms of root and pattern, are completely regular in inflection; i.e., *žit* 'I came', *ddit* 'I took', *žiti* 'you (sg.) came', *dditi* 'you (sg.) took', etc.

III. The Inflection of the Imperfect Tense

1. The Inflectional Affixes: The following table shows the characteristic personal affixes of the imperfect.

---

[5]See p. 17 for the behavior of the variable vowel *e* between the last two consonants of a word when a stable vowel precedes.

Singular

First Person:	*n(e)–*	'I'
Second Person:	*t(e)–*	'you' (msc.)
	t(e)– + –i, –y	'you' (fem.)
Third Person:	*i–, y(e)–*	'he'
	t(e)–	'she'

Plural

First Person:	*n(e)– + –u, –w*	'we'
Second Person:	*t(e)– + –u, –w*	'you' (pl.)
Third Person:	*i–, y(e)– + –u, –w*	'they'

(a) **The Plural Forms:** The plural forms are derived from the corresponding singular forms by the addition of *–u* or *–w*. The *–u* is added to stems ending in consonants, and the *–w* is added to stems ending in vowels, for example *iḥell* 'he opens' and *iḥellu* 'they open', *nekmi* 'I smoke' and *nekmiw* 'we smoke'.

(b) **The First Person:** An *n–* is prefixed when the verb stem begins with consonant plus vowel; e.g., *nsedd* 'I close', *nseddu* 'we close', etc. As a general rule, *ne–* is prefixed when the verb stem begins with two or more consonants; e.g., *neƐmel* 'I do', *nebdaw* 'we begin', etc. However, before stems beginning with *n* or one of the apical stops *t, ṭ, d,* or *ḍ,* the first person prefix is always *n* regardless of whether the stem begins with a consonant cluster; e.g., *nnsa* 'I forget', *ntqeb* 'I pierce', *nṭḷeb* 'I request', *nddiw* 'we take', *nḍṛeḃ* 'I hit'. In ordinary conversation, *n–* rather than *ne–* is also prefixed to verb stems whose initial consonant clusters begin with *s, ṣ, š, z, ẓ,* or *ž;* e.g., *nskon* 'I live, reside', *nṣbeṛ* 'I keep patient', *nšri* 'I buy', *nzreb* 'I hurry', *nžbeṛ* 'I find', etc.

(c) **The Second Person:** The second person singular feminine form, for example *tketbi* 'you (fem.) write', is rarely used among urban speakers. The masculine form *tekteb* 'you write' is used for addressing both men and women. The *–i* is added to stems ending in a consonant while the *–y* is added to stems ending in *–a;* e.g., *tšoṛbi* 'you (fem.) drink', *teqṛay* 'you (fem.) read, study'. Verb stems which end in *–i* in the imperfect tense do not distinguish a separate feminine form; e.g., *tekmi* 'you (msc., fem. sg.) smoke'.

In general the second person prefix has the form *t–* before stems beginning with a consonant plus a vowel and the form *te–* before stems beginning with consonant clusters; e.g., *tšuf* 'you (msc. sg.) see', *tebda* 'you (msc. sg.) begin'. There are some exceptions to this pattern, however. Before a stem beginning with *t* plus a consonant, the prefix is *t–* rather than *te–;* e.g., stem *tkellem* 'to speak', *ttkellem* 'you (sg.) speak'. Before a stem beginning with *ṭ, d,* or *ḍ,* regardless of whether the next phoneme is a vowel or a consonant, the prefix is *ṭ-*, *d-*, and *ḍ-* respectively instead of *te-*; e.g.,

ṭuwweḷ	'to lengthen'	*ṭṭuwweḷ*	'you (sg.) lengthen'
ṭḷeb	'to request'	*ṭṭḷeb*	'you (sg.) request'
deqq	'to knock'	*ddeqq*	'you (sg.) knock'
dfen	'to bury'	*ddfen*	'you (sg.) bury'
ḍemmen	'to guarantee'	*ḍḍemmen*	'you (sg.) guarantee'
ḍṛeb	'to hit'	*ḍḍṛeb*	'you (sg.) hit'

In the special case of stems beginning with *tt-*, *ṭṭ-*, *dd-*, or *ḍḍ-*,[6] the prefix is *te-* in deliberately slow speech, but at ordinary conversational speed there is no prefix at all; e.g., *ttexleƐ* 'to get scared' and *(te)ttexleƐ* 'you (sg.) get scared', etc. Before stems beginning with *z*, *ž*, or *ẓ* plus a vowel, the second person prefix is *d-*; e.g., *dzerbu* 'you (pl.) hurry', *džebṛu* 'you (pl.) find', *dẓuṛ* 'you (sg.) visit', etc. At conversational speed, the same thing is true of stems beginning with *z*, *ž*, or *ẓ* plus a consonant, although for deliberately slow speech the prefix remains *te-*; e.g., *tezreb* or *dzreb* 'you (sg.) hurry', *težbeṛ* or *džbeṛ* 'you (sg.) find'. There is a similar variation between *te-* and *t-* before stems beginning with *s*, *ṣ*, or *š* plus a consonant; e.g., *teskon* or *tskon* 'you (sg.) live, reside', *teṣneƐ* or *tṣneƐ* 'you (sg.) manufacture, make', *tešri* or *tšri* 'you (sg.) buy'.

(d) **The Third Person:** The prefix for 'she', the third person feminine singular, is identical with the prefix for the second person and undergoes the same changes. The prefix for 'he' and 'they', the third person singular masculine and the third person plural, is usually *i-*; e.g., *iddi* 'he takes', *iddiw* 'they take', *išuf* 'he sees', *išufu* 'they see'. Before stems beginning with *w*, *h*, *Ɛ*, or *ḥ* plus a consonant, the prefix is usually *ye-*; e.g.,

yewṣeḷ	'he arrives'
yehḍeṛ	'he talks'
yehdiw	'they give (as a gift)'
yeḥmel	'he carries'
yeḥkiw	'they tell (as a story)'

[6] Stems beginning with such consonant clusters are limited almost entirely to the medio-passive Measures Ia, IIa(V), and IIIa(VI); see pp. 33-34.

yeƐbeṛ	'he measures'
yeƐṭiw	'they give'

In slower speech, especially for words pronounced in isolation, the prefix may take the form *ye–* before any consonant cluster, not merely those beginning with *w, h, Ɛ,* or *ḥ;* e.g., *yedxol* 'he enters', etc.

In the stem *ybes* 'to get dry', the prefixes *ne–* and *te–* often become *ni–* and *ti–;* e.g., *neybes* or *niybes* 'I get dry', etc. There is the usual variation between *i–* and *ye–* in the third person singular, *iybes* or *yeybes* 'he gets dry'.

In the two irregular verbs, *yaxod* 'he takes, gets', *yaxdu* 'they take, get', and *yakol* 'he eats', *yaklu* 'they eat', the prefix has the form *y–*. For stems beginning with ˀ followed by a vowel, some speakers drop the ˀ, in which case the prefix has the form *y–;* e.g., *ˀameṛ* 'to order', imperfect *iˀameṛ* or *yameṛ* 'he orders'.

2. **Verb Stem Classes:** As with the perfect tense, certain regular stem changes take place with the addition of the affixes of the imperfect tense. The stem changes of the imperfect are, however, different from those of the perfect. It is often the case that two verbs which belong to the same stem type in the inflection of the perfect belong to different stem types in the inflection of the imperfect, and vice versa. Five different stem types are to be recognized in the imperfect.

(a) **Stems Ending in** *–eC:* With the addition of the ending *–i* in the second person feminine singular and the plural ending *–u* for 'we', 'you' (pl.), and 'they', stems ending in *–eC* show the same patterns of inversion and elision as they do in the perfect tense with the addition of the endings *–u* 'they' and *–et* 'she'.[7] Some examples:

neṛbeṭ	'I tie'	*nṛebṭu*	'we tie'
teṛbeṭ	'you (msc.) tie'	*tṛebṭu*	'you (pl.) tie'
tṛebṭi	'you (fem.) tie'		
iṛbeṭ	'he ties'	*iṛebṭu*	'they tie'
teṛbeṭ	'she ties'		
nḥawel	'I try'	*nḥawlu*	'we try'
tḥawel	'you (msc.) try'	*tḥawlu*	'you (pl.) try'

[7]See pp. 17-19, 42-43.

tḥawli	'you (fem.) try'		
iḥawel	'he tries'	*iḥawlu*	'they try'
tḥawel	'she tries'		

nttexleƐ	'I get scared'	*nttxelƐu*	'we get scared'
(te)ttexleƐ	'you (msc.) get scared'	*(te)ttxelƐu*	'you (pl.) get scared'
(te)ttxelƐi	'you (fem.) get scared'		
ittexleƐ	'he gets scared'	*ittxelƐu*	'they get scared'
(te)ttexleƐ	'she gets scared'		

A limited number of Measure I sound verbs substitute an *o* for the *e* of the stem in the non-inverted forms in the imperfect; e.g., *dxel* 'to enter', imperfect:

ndxol	'I enter'	*ndexlu*	'we enter'
ddxol	'you (msc.) enter'	*ddexlu*	'you (pl.) enter'
ddexli	'you (fem.) enter'		
idxol	'he enters'	*idexlu*	'they enter'
ddxol	'she enters'		

The most commonly encountered verbs which substitute *o* for *e* in the non-inverted forms of the imperfect are *dxel* 'to enter', *sken* 'to live, reside', *sket* 'to be silent', *sxen* 'to be warm', and *xrež* 'to go out'.

One verb of this stem class has a dual stem. Some speakers say *ṣafeṭ* and other speakers say *ṣifeṭ* 'to send'. The imperfect is always *iṣifeṭ* 'he sends', *nṣifeṭ* 'I send', etc. The atypical verb *ttkel* 'to rely' shows inversion in the imperfect just as in the perfect; e.g., *ittkel* 'he relies', *itteklu* 'they rely', etc.

(b) Measure I Hollow Verbs: Most such verbs change the medial *a* of the stem to *i* or *u* in the imperfect. A few verbs retain the *a* and have an invariable stem in the imperfect. The imperfect stem vowels of hollow verbs must be learned individually for each verb since there is no way of predicting them. Some examples:

nžib	'I bring'	*nžibu*	'we bring'
džib	'you (msc.) bring'	*džibu*	'you (pl.) bring'
džibi	'you (fem.) bring'		

ižib	'he brings'	*ižibu*	'they bring'
džib	'she brings'		

nšuf	'I see'	*nšufu*	'we see'
tšuf	'you (msc.) see'	*tšufu*	'you (pl.) see'
tšufi	'you (fem.) see'		
išuf	'he sees'	*išufu*	'they see'
tšuf	'she sees'		

nban	'I appear'	*nbanu*	'we appear'
tban	'you (msc.) appear'	*tbanu*	'you (pl.) appear'
tbani	'you (fem.) appear'		
iban	'he appears'	*ibanu*	'they appear'
tban	'she appears'		

Some common verbs showing the change of medial *a* to *i* in the imperfect are *baε* 'to sell', *dar* 'to do', *faq* 'to wake up', *ṭaṛ* 'to fly', *ṭaḥ* 'to fall', and *zad* 'to go, to proceed'.

Some common verbs showing the change of *a* to *u* in the imperfect are *bal* 'to urinate', *bas* 'to kiss', *daz* 'to pass', *kan* 'to be', *mat* 'to die', *naḍ* 'to get up', *qal* 'to say, to tell', *saq* 'to drive', *ṣam* 'to fast', and *εad* 'to return'.

Some additional examples of verbs which retain the *a* in the imperfect are *bat* 'to spend the night', *sal* 'to be creditor to', and *xaf* 'to be afraid'. The two verbs *kal* 'to eat' and *xad* 'to take, to get' more usually have the stem forms *kla* and *xda*. Their imperfect forms are irregular and are listed below (pp. 52-53) under the discussion of stems ending in *-a*.

(c) Measures I and Ia of Doubled Roots: Most such verbs show no stem change in the imperfect; e.g., *sedd* 'to close', imperfect *isedd* 'he closes'. A few stems, however, show a substitution of *o* in the imperfect for the *e* of the stem. Usually these are Measure I verbs; e.g., *ḥekk* 'to rub' with imperfect *iḥokk* 'he rubs'. Some speakers also substitute *o* for *e* in the imperfect stem of a few Measure Ia verbs; e.g., stem *ttfekk* 'to get loose', imperfect *ittfokk* 'he gets loose' for some speakers although the more usual form is *ittfekk* with no stem change. A sample paradigm:

nḥell	'I open'	*nḥellu*	'we open'
tḥell	'you (msc.) open'	*tḥellu*	'you (pl.) open'

tḥelli	'you (fem.) open'		
iḥell	'he opens'	*iḥellu*	'they open'
tḥell	'she opens'		

(d) Stems Ending in *-a*: This is the class of verbs with final-weak roots. The medio-passive forms Measures Ia, IIa(V), IIIa(VI), and the derived form of the quadriliteral verb show no stem change in the imperfect; e.g., *tεešša* 'to have supper', imperfect *itεešša* 'he has supper'. An illustrative paradigm:

ntεešša	'I have supper'	*ntεeššaw*	'we have supper'
ttεešša	'you (msc.) have supper'	*ttεeššaw*	'you (pl.) have supper'
ttεeššay	'you (fem.) have supper'		
itεešša	'he has supper'	*itεeššaw*	'they have supper'
ttεešša	'she has supper'		

Measures II and III and the base form of the quadriliteral verb change the final *-a* to *-i* in the imperfect; e.g., *ġeṭṭa* 'to cover', *qaḍa* 'to finish', *seqṣa* 'to ask'. An example of a full paradigm:

nġeṭṭi	'I cover'	*nġeṭṭiw*	'we cover'
tġeṭṭi	'you (sg.) cover'	*tġeṭṭiw*	'you (pl.) cover'
iġeṭṭi	'he covers'	*iġeṭṭiw*	'they cover'
tġeṭṭi	'she covers'		

Verbs of Measures I and X are unpredictable. Some verbs retain the final stem *-a* in the imperfect and some change it to *-i*; e.g., *qṛa* 'to read, to study' with imperfect *iqṛa* 'he reads, he studies', and *kma* 'to smoke' with imperfect *ikmi* 'he smokes'. An illustration of the full paradigm:

neqṛa	'I read'	*neqṛaw*	'we read'
teqṛa	'you (msc.) read'	*teqṛaw*	'you (pl.) read'
teqṛay	'you (fem.) read'		
iqṛa	'he reads'	*iqṛaw*	'they read'
teqṛa	'she reads'		

nekmi	'I smoke'	*nekmiw*	'we smoke'
tekmi	'you (sg.) smoke'	*tekmiw*	'you (pl.) smoke'
ikmi	'he smokes'	*ikmiw*	'they smoke'
tekmi	'she smokes'		

Three verbs only change the final *-a* to *-u* in the imperfect. These are *ɛfa* 'to have mercy on, to deliver', *ḥba* 'to crawl', and *xṭa* 'to progress', with imperfects *yeɛfu, yeḥbu,* and *yexṭu* respectively. The verb *ɛfa* is used mostly in the third person singular with *ḷḷah* 'God' as the subject; e.g., *ḷḷah yeɛfu ɛlih men...* 'May God deliver him from...' There is considerable variation from speaker to speaker in the inflection of *ḥba* 'to crawl'. The second person feminine singular is *teḥbi* 'you (fem.) crawl', and the plural forms show a variation among the endings *-uw, -aw,* and *-iw;* e.g., *neḥbuw, neḥbaw,* or *neḥbiw* 'we crawl'.

The two atypical verbs *ža* 'to come' and *dda* 'to take' have *-i* in the imperfect. The paradigms are:

nži	'I come'	*nžiw*	'we come'
dži	'you (sg.) come'	*džiw*	'you (pl.) come'
iži	'he comes'	*ižiw*	'they come'
dži	'she comes'		

nddi	'I take'	*nddiw*	'we take'
teddi[8]	'you (sg.) take'	*teddiw*[8]	'you (pl.) take'
iddi	'he takes'	*iddiw*	'they take'
teddi[8]	'she takes'		

The two verbs *kla* 'to eat' and *xda* 'to take, to get' have parallel irregular forms in the imperfect and are unlike any other verb in the language. The forms are:

nakol	'I eat'	*naklu*	'we eat'
takol	'you (msc.) eat'	*taklu*	'you (pl.) eat'
takli	'you (fem.) eat'		

[8] The initial *te-* is often not present in connected conversation or after a prefix; e.g., *ka-teddi* or *ka-ddi* 'she takes, is taking'.

yakol	'he eats'	*yaklu*	'they eat'
takol	'she eats'		

naxod	'I take'	*naxdu*	'we take'
taxod	'you (msc.) take'	*taxdu*	'you (pl.) take'
taxdi	'you (fem.) take'		
yaxod	'he takes'	*yaxdu*	'they take'
taxod	'she takes'		

(e) **Invariable Stems:** Measures Ia and VIII of middle-weak roots and Measure IX undergo no stem changes in the imperfect. For example Measure Ia *ttšaf* 'to be seen' with imperfect *ittšaf* 'he is seen', Measure VIII *xtaṛ* 'to choose' with imperfect *ixtaṛ* 'he chooses', and Measure IX *sman* 'to become fat' with imperfect *isman* 'he becomes fat'.

IV. The Inflection of the Imperative

The imperative has a special inflectional form only in the second person. The four verbs *mša* 'to go', *ža* 'to come', *kla* 'to eat', and *xda* 'to take, to get' have irregular imperatives. The forms are:

mša 'to go'

Imperative:	*sir!*	(msc.)	'Go!'
	siri!	(fem.)	
	siru!	(pl.)	

ža 'to come'

Imperative:	*aži!*	(sg.)	'Come!'
	ažiw!	(pl.)	

kla 'to eat'

Imperative:	*kul!*	(msc.)	'Eat!'
	kuli!	(fem.)	
	kulu!	(pl.)	

xda 'to take, get'

Imperative:	*xud!*	(msc.)	'Take!'
	xudi!	(fem.)	
	xudu!	(pl.)	

There is one common imperative which has no corresponding perfect or imperfect forms:

aṛa!	(msc.)	'Give, hand over!'
aṛi!	(fem.)	
aṛaw!	(pl.)	

In all other cases, the form of the imperative is identical with the form of the second person of the imperfect minus the imperfect prefix. A set of illustrative examples follows, paralleling the examples given to illustrate the forms of the imperfect. The second person imperfect forms are listed in the left hand column, and the corresponding imperatives are given in the right hand column.

(a) Stems Ending in *-eC*:

teḥseb	(msc.)	'you count'	*ḥseb!*	'Count!'
tḥesbi	(fem.)		*ḥesbi!*	
tḥesbu	(pl.)		*ḥesbu!*	
teskot	(msc.)	'you are quiet'	*skot!*	'Be quiet!'
tsekti	(fem.)		*sekti!*	
tsektu	(pl.)		*sektu!*	
ṭṭeṛžem	(msc.)	'you translate'	*ṭeṛžem!*	'Translate!'
ṭṭeṛžmi	(fem.)		*ṭeṛžmi!*	
ṭṭeṛžmu	(pl.)		*ṭeṛžmu!*	

(b) Measure I Hollow Verbs:

tfiq	(msc.)	'you wake up'	*fiq!*	'Wake up!'
tfiqi	(fem.)		*fiqi!*	
tfiqu	(pl.)		*fiqu!*	

tsuq	(msc.)	'you drive'	*suq!*	'Drive!'
tsuqi	(fem.)		*suqi!*	
tsuqu	(pl.)		*suqu!*	
txaf	(msc.)	'you are afraid'	*xaf!*	'Be afraid!'
txafi	(fem.)		*xafi!*	
txafu	(pl.)		*xafu!*	

(c) Measures I and Ia of Doubled Roots:

tmess	(msc.)	'you touch'	*mess!*	'Touch!'
tmessi	(fem.)		*messi!*	
tmessu	(pl.)		*messu!*	
tḥokk	(msc.)	'you rub'	*ḥokk!*	'Rub!'
tḥokki	(fem.)		*ḥokki!*	
tḥokku	(pl.)		*ḥokku!*	
(te)ttfekk	(msc.)	'you get loose'	*ttfekk!*	'Get loose!'
(te)ttfekki	(fem.)		*ttfekki!*	
(te)ttfekku	(pl.)		*ttfekku!*	

(d) Stems Ending in *-a*:

tekmi	(sg.)	'you smoke'	*kmi!*	'Smoke!'
tekmiw	(pl.)		*kmiw!*	
teqṛa	(msc.)	'you study'	*qṛa!*	'Study!'
teqṛay	(fem.)		*qṛay!*	
teqṛaw	(pl.)		*qṛaw!*	
ttƐešša	(msc.)	'you have supper'	*tƐešša!*	'Have supper!'
ttƐeššay	(fem.)		*tƐeššay!*	
ttƐeššaw	(pl.)		*tƐeššaw!*	

(te)ddi	(sg.) 'you take'	*ddi!*	'Take!'
(te)ddiw	(pl.)	*ddiw!*	
tseqşi	(sg.) 'you ask'	*seqşi!*	'Ask!'
tseqşiw	(pl.)	*seqşiw!*	

(e) Invariable Stems:

textaṛ	(msc.) 'you choose'	*xtaṛ!*	'Choose!'
textaṛi	(fem.)	*xtaṛi!*	
textaṛu	(pl.)	*xtaṛu!*	

IV. NOUN AND ADJECTIVE DERIVATION

I. The Participles

The participles are adjectives derived from verbs. They are inflected for both gender and number but not for person or tense. Transitive Measure I verbs have two participles, an active participle and a passive participle. Intransitive Measure I verbs have only an active participle. Other verb stems, of whatever root and pattern form, have only one participle. For transitive verbs, this one participle functions both as active and passive. For intransitives it functions only as active.

1. **The Active Participle of Measure I:** The general pattern is *FaƐeL,* for example *kteb* 'to write' with active participle *kateb* 'having written'. Doubled verbs regularly omit the *e* between the last two consonants, for example *ḥell* 'to open' with active participle *ḥall* 'having opened', and hollow verbs have *y* as the second consonant of the pattern, for example *baƐ* 'to sell' with active participle *bayeƐ* 'seller'. In defective verbs the final *-eL* of the pattern is replaced by *-i,* for example *šra* 'to buy' with active participle *šari* 'having bought'. The following table summarizes the forms:

Verb Stem		**Active Participle**	
kteb	'to write'	*kateb*	'having written'
ḥell	'to open'	*ḥall*	'having opened'
baƐ	'to sell'	*bayeƐ*	'having sold'
šra	'to buy'	*šari*	'having bought'

2. **The Passive Participle of Measure I:** The general pattern is *meFƐuL,* for example *mektub* '(having been) written'. In hollow verbs a *y* appears as the second consonant of the root, for example *mbyuƐ*[1] '(having been) sold', although many hollow verbs do not usually form passive participles, for example *šaf* 'to see'. In defective verbs the final *-uL* of the pattern is replaced by *-i,* for example *mešri* '(having been) bought'. The table summarizes the forms:

[1] The prefix is usually *m-* rather than *me-* if the following consonant is *b* or *m;* e.g., *mneƐ* 'to forbid', passive participle *memnuƐ* or *mmnuƐ* 'forbidden'.

Verb Stem		**Passive Participle**	
kteb	'to write'	*mektub*	'(having been) written'
ḥell	'to open'	*meḥlul*	'open, (having been) opened'
baƐ	'to sell'	*mbyuƐ*	'(having been) sold'
šra	'to buy'	*mešri*	'(having been) bought'

3. **Verbs With Only One Participle:** Verbs other than those of Measure I have only a single participle. This participle is formed by prefixing *m-* to stems beginning with a consonant plus a vowel, *me-* to stems beginning with consonant clusters. The final *-a* of final-weak stems is changed to *-i*. For transitive verbs, this one participle is used both as an active and a passive participle. For intransitive verbs it is only active. Some examples:

Verb Stem		**Participle**	
xeḍḍeṛ	'to garnish'	*mxeḍḍeṛ*	'having garnished; (having been) garnished'
ġeṭṭa	'to cover'	*mġeṭṭi*	'having covered; (having been) covered'
ṣafeṛ	'to travel'	*mṣafeṛ*	'traveling'
rtaḥ	'to rest'	*mertaḥ*	'resting'
qeṛṭeṣ	'to wrap up'	*mqeṛṭeṣ*	'having wrapped up; (having been) wrapped up'

4. **Limitations of Participle Formation:** Measure IX verbs, for example *byaḍ* 'to become white', do not have participles. Measure Ia verbs also do not have participles. Measure Ia is the medio-passive of Measure I (See pp. 37-38), and consequently the passive participle of Measure I serves as the participle of the corresponding Measure Ia, for example Measure I *ḍṛeb* 'to beat', Measure Ia *tteḍṛeb* 'to be beaten', passive participle *meḍṛub* '(having been) beaten'. Exactly the same relation holds for the base and derived form of the quadriliteral verb, for example base form *ṭeṛžem* 'to translate', derived form *ṭṭeṛžem* 'to be translated', participle *mṭeṛžem* 'having translated, (having been) translated'.

A similar, but not identical, relation holds for Measures II and III with respect to Measures IIa(V) and IIIa(VI). Since Measure IIa(V) is the medio-passive of Measure II, the participle formed from the stem of Measure II is usually used for both, and participles formed from the stem of Measure IIa(V) are rare; e.g., Measure II *xebba* 'to hide (something)', Measure IIa(V) *txebba* 'to be hidden, to hide oneself', common participle *mxebbi* 'having hidden, (having been) hidden, having hidden oneself'. The same relation holds for Measures III and IIIa(VI) when Measure

IIIa(VI) is the medio-passive of a corresponding Measure III verb; e.g., Measure III *dawa* 'to take care of', Measure IIIa(VI) *ddawa* 'to be taken care of, to take care of oneself', common participle *mdawi* 'having cared for, (having been) cared for, having taken care of oneself'. Measure IIIa(VI) verbs which have specialized or reciprocal meanings, however, usually form their own participles; e.g., Measure IIIa(VI) *tḥaṛeb* 'to wage war', participle *metḥaṛbin* (pl.) 'waging war (with one another)'.

5. **Classicized Participles:** There are an increasing number of participles in use in Moroccan Arabic whose form is an approximation of the form of written Arabic participles. These participles are almost always used as simple nouns and are distinguished by having the prefix *mu-* and either an *i* or an *a* between the last two consonants of stems other than those of Measure I verbs; e.g., *mufettiš* 'inspector', *muweḍḍaf* 'employe'. Classicizations of Measure I participles are limited to the active participle and are characterized by having *i* instead of the *e* of the usual Moroccan pattern; e.g., *katib* 'secretary, editor'. The classicized participles *mufettiš* 'inspector' and *katib* 'secretary' may be compared with the regular Moroccan participles from the corresponding verbs, *mfetteš* 'having inspected, (having been) inspected', and *kateb* 'having written'.

6. **Irregular Participles:** A few verbs have irregular participles. The most common are listed below.

Verb Stem		**Participles**		
kla	'to eat'	*wakel*	(active)	'having eaten'
		muwkul	(passive)	'(having been) eaten'
xda	'to take'	*waxed*	(active)	'having taken'
		muwxud	(passive)	'(having been) taken'
dda	'to take'	*dday*[2]	(active)	'having taken'
		meddi	(active, passive)	'having taken, (having been) taken'
ža	'to come'	*maži, žay*[3]		'coming'

II. The Adjective Pattern *FeƐLan*:

The adjective pattern *FeƐLan* is mostly derived from intransitive Measure I verbs, occasionally from nouns. In hollow verbs an *i* takes the place of the *eƐ* of

---

[2]Formally *dday* is an adjectival derivative equivalent to the *FeƐƐaL* pattern, see pp. 66-67.

[3]The form *maži* is more common than *žay*. In the feminine and plural forms, the final *y* is doubled, fem. *žayya*, pl. *žayyin*.

the pattern, and in defective verbs a *y* is added to serve as the third consonant of the root.

Adjectives of this pattern refer almost exclusively to human beings and to inherently temporary physical or mental states. Measure I verbs from which a *FeƐLan* form is derived usually have no active participle of the *FaƐeL* pattern. The number of *FeƐLan* adjectives is not large. Some of the most common are:

Base		**Derived Adjective**	
bred	'to be cold'	*berdan*	'(feeling) cold'
dheš	'to be astonished'	*dehšan*	'astonished'
fṛeḥ	'to be happy, to rejoice'	*feṛḥan*	'happy'
hṛeb	'to run away, to flee'	*heṛban*	'running away, in flight'
(nil)		*keslan*	'lazy'
sxef	'to be tired, to be out of breath'	*sexfan*	'out of breath, winded'
sker	'to get drunk'	*sekran*	'drunk'
zreb	'to hurry'	*zerban*	'in a hurry, hurrying'
ġḍeb	'to get angry'	*ġeḍban*	'angry'
ḥar	'to be perplexed'	*ḥiran*	'perplexed, puzzled'
Ɛra	'nudity'	*Ɛeryan*	'naked'
Ɛṛeq	'to sweat'	*Ɛeṛqan*	'sweating'
Ɛṭeš	'to become thirsty'	*Ɛeṭšan*	'thirsty'
Ɛya	'to become tired'	*Ɛeyyan*	'tired, ill'

III. The Verbal Noun

Most verbs have a corresponding verbal noun; e.g., *ḍṛeb* 'to hit', verbal noun *ḍṛib* '(the action of) hitting'. The regular meaning of the verbal noun is the activity or state indicated by the verb from which it is derived. However, verbal nouns also often refer to the result of the activity indicated by the parent verb; e.g., *ẓaṛ* 'to visit', verbal noun *ẓyaṛa* '(the action of) visiting' or '(a) visit'. This aspect of the Moroccan verbal noun has parallels in English; e.g., such a word as "organization" refers either to the action of organizing or to the result of the action of organizing.

The idea of the action of the verb is the consistently regular and predictable meaning of the verbal noun. The specific meaning of result which often attaches to verbal nouns is not entirely predictable; e.g., *l-makla u-š-šṛab* 'eating and drinking' or 'food and drink', from the verbs *kla* 'to eat' and *šṛeb* 'to drink'.

Measure I verbs and verbs which fall outside the root-pattern system usually have irregular verbal nouns which must be learned as vocabulary items. The other measures of the verb, as well as quadriliteral verbs, are usually consistent in having either no verbal noun or a regular verbal noun pattern. The details are as follows.

1. **Measure I:** Transitive Measure I verbs with sound roots regularly form their verbal noun on the pattern of *FƐiL*. Some examples:

dbeġ	'to tan'	*dbiġ*	'(the action of) tanning'
knes	'to sweep'	*knis*	'sweeping'
qṣem	'to divide'	*qṣim*	'division, partition'
ṛbeṭ	'to tie'	*ṛbiṭ*	'tying'
ġsel	'to wash'	*ġsil*	'washing'
ḥmel	'to carry'	*ḥmil*	'carrying'

A few transitive Measure I verbs with sound roots do not form a verbal noun on the pattern of *FƐiL*; e.g., *rkeb* 'to mount, to ride', verbal noun *rkub* '(the action of) mounting, riding'. Such exceptions must be learned as vocabulary items.

Most of the verbs with the verbal noun pattern *FƐiL* have two (and occasionally three) verbal nouns, the regular *FƐiL* and another form which must be learned as a vocabulary item. Sometimes the two verbal nouns are exactly the same in meaning; e.g., *qṭeƐ* 'to cut', verbal noun *qṭiƐ* or *qṭuƐ* '(the action of) cutting'. Usually, however, the different verbal nouns have separate shades of meaning. The *FƐiL* pattern consistently has the abstract meaning of the action of the verb from which it is derived, while the second verbal noun usually has a more specific meaning in addition to the predictable abstract meaning regularly associated with a verbal noun. Some examples:

qbeḍ		'to seize'
	qbiḍ	'(the action of) seizing'
	qebḍ	'seizing; seizure, arrest'
šṛeb		'to drink'
	šṛib	'drinking'

	šṛab	'drinking; beverage; alcoholic beverage'
	šeṛb	'drinking; love of alcoholic drink'
ḥṣeḍ		'to harvest'
	ḥṣiḍ	'harvesting'
	ḥṣaḍ	'harvesting; harvest (material harvested)'

Other commonly found Measure I verbal noun patterns are *FeƐL, FƐeL, FƐaL, FƐaLa, FƐuL, FƐuLa,* and *FeƐLan*. The most commonly met with of these patterns is *FeƐL,* which is the verbal noun pattern for a large number of verbs with sound and doubled roots. Some examples:

ḍṛeb	'to hit'	*ḍeṛb*	'hitting'
ḍḥek	'to laugh'	*ḍeḥk*	'laughing, laughter'
ṭṛeẓ	'to embroider'	*ṭeṛẓ*	'embroidering, embroidery'
ġešš	'to cheat'	*ġešš*	'cheating, trickery'

For hollow verbs the pattern corresponding to the *FeƐL* of sound and doubled verbs has a medial *i* or *u;* e.g., *baƐ* 'to sell', verbal noun *biƐ* 'selling', and *xaf* 'to fear', verbal noun *xuf* 'fear'. No defective verbs have verbal nouns of this pattern.

After *FeƐL,* the most frequently encountered verbal noun patterns are *FƐaL* and *FeƐLan*. Most verbal nouns of the *FƐaL* pattern come from sound verbs; e.g., *ṭḷeq* 'to turn loose, to let go', verbal noun *ṭḷaq* 'divorce'. Hollow verbs with verbal nouns on the pattern of *FƐaL* have *y* or *w* as their second consonant; e.g., *dam* 'to endure' with verbal noun *dwam* 'duration', *ṣam* 'to fast' with verbal noun *ṣyam* 'fast(ing)'. Doubled verbs very rarely have verbal nouns of the *FƐaL* pattern; e.g., *fekk* 'to save, to rescue', verbal noun *fkak* 'deliverance, rescue'. There are no verbal nouns on the pattern of *fƐaL* from defective verbs.

Verbal nouns of the *FeƐLan* pattern come mostly from doubled verbs; e.g., *ḥell* 'to open', verbal noun *ḥellan* '(the action of) opening'. Verbal nouns of this sort from defective verbs have *y* as their third consonant; e.g., *ṭfa* 'to extinguish, to put out', with verbal noun *ṭefyan* 'extinction, action of putting out'. Defective verbs which have *w* as their second consonant show *u* instead of *ew* in this verbal noun pattern; e.g., *ṭwa* 'to fold', verbal noun *ṭuyan*. Hollow verbs substitute an *i* or *u* for the medial *eƐ* of this pattern. Verbal nouns with *i* correspond to hollow verbs which have *i* in the imperfect, and verbal nouns with *u* correspond to hollow verbs which have *u* in the imperfect; e.g., *sal* 'to flow' with imperfect *isil* and verbal noun *silan,* and *šaf* 'to see' with imperfect *išuf* and verbal noun *šufan*. Sound verbs only rarely have verbal nouns on the pattern of *FeƐLan* although some do occur; e.g., *bṭeḷ* 'to cease' with verbal noun *beṭḷan* 'cessation'.

Other verbal noun patterns for Measure I verbs are less frequently met with and show little or no consistent derivational regularity. They must be learned as individual vocabulary items.

2. **Measure II:** For verbs with sound, doubled, and hollow roots, the verbal noun of Measure II has either the pattern *teFƐiL* or *teFƐaL*. These forms are usually interchangeable and have no difference in meaning. Whether a given speaker uses the *teFƐiL* pattern or the *teFƐaL* pattern depends on what part of Morocco he is from. Some examples:

biyyeḍ	'to whiten, to whitewash'
tebyiḍ, tebyaḍ	'whitening, whitewashing'
ḍuwweṛ	'to (make) turn, to (make) revolve'
teḍwiṛ, teḍwaṛ	'turning, revolving'
fetteš	'to inspect'
teftiš, teftaš	'inspection'
ṭuwweḷ	'to lengthen'
teṭwiḷ, teṭwaḷ	'lengthening'
žedded	'to renew'
težd id, težd ad	'renewing, renewal'
ġiyyeṛ	'to change'
teġyiṛ, teġyaṛ	'changing, change'

For verbs with final-weak roots the pattern is *tFeƐya;* e.g., *feḍḍa* 'to finish, to terminate' with verbal noun *tfeḍya* 'termination', *ṣeffa* 'to purify' with verbal noun *tṣefya* 'purification', etc.

3. **Measure III:** The verbal noun of Measure III has the pattern *mFaƐLa*. For verbs with final-weak roots, the *L* of the pattern is *y*. Some examples:

bala	'to care for, to attend to'	*mbalya*	'care, attention'
dawem	'to (make) continue'	*mdawma*	'continuation'
ṛažeɛ	'to review'	*mṛažɛa*	'review, reviewing'
sameḥ	'to pardon, to excuse'	*msamḥa*	'pardon, pardoning'
ɛawed	'to repeat'	*mɛawda*	'repetition'

4. Measures Ia, IIa(V), and IIIa(VI): These measures have no verbal noun patterns of their own. Instead, the corresponding verbal noun patterns of Measures I, II, and III respectively are used. If a given root happens to occur in both Measures I and Ia, II and IIa(V), or III and IIIa(VI), as is often the case, then the two verbs of the pair share a common verbal noun. Some examples:

Verb		**Verbal Noun**
bna	'to build'	*bni*
ttebna	'to be built'	*bni*
dfen	'to bury, to inter'	*dfin*
ttedfen	'to be buried'	*dfin*
ddexxem	'to live pleasantly, richly'	*tedxim*
theḷḷa	'to take care of, to look after'	*theḷya*
qeddem	'to present, to advance'	*teqdim*
tqeddem	'to be presented, to progress'	*teqdim*
tfafa	'to be embarrassed, confused'	*mfafya*
tɛaneq	'to embrace, to hug (one another)'	*mɛanqa*
ɛawen	'to help'	*mɛawna*
tɛawen	'to help one another'	*mɛawna*

5. Measures VII, VIII, IX, and X: Measure IX does not form a verbal noun, and Measures VII, VIII, and X are too rare for any useful statement of pattern to be made about them.

6. **The Quadriliterals:** The verbal noun of quadriliteral verbs is usually formed by inserting *i* between the last two consonants of the derived quadriliteral form. Where a quadriliteral root exists both in the primary and the derived form, the two verbs have a common verbal noun. Some examples:

Verb		**Verbal Noun**
fer̥geƐ	'to (make) explode'	*tfer̥giƐ*
tfer̥geƐ	'to explode, to be exploded'	*tfer̥giƐ*
ferkel	'to writhe, to flounder'	*tferkil*
suger	'to insure'	*tsugir*
tsuger	'to be insured'	*tsugir*
žer̥žer̥	'to drag'	*džer̥žir̥*
džer̥žer̥	'to be dragged'	*džer̥žir̥*

In the relatively infrequent case of quadriliterals which end in *a,* the verbal noun is made from the derived form by inserting *y* before the final *a;* e.g., *seqṣa* 'to ask', verbal noun *tseqṣya* '(the action of) asking, interrogation'. Occasionally quadriliteral verbs have irregular verbal nouns; e.g., *ṭer̥žem* 'to translate', verbal noun *ṭer̥žama* 'translation'.

IV. The Noun of Instance

The noun of instance is a sub-class of the verbal noun. The verbal noun refers to an action in general whereas the noun of instance refers to a single act. Only Measures I and II and the quadriliteral verb form separate nouns of instance.

The noun of instance of Measure I almost always has the form *FeƐLa,* regardless of the form of the verbal noun; e.g., *ḍḥek* 'to laugh', verbal *ḍeḥk* '(the action of) laughing, laughter', noun of instance *ḍeḥka* 'a laugh'. Defective verbs have *y* as the third consonant of the pattern; e.g., *šra* 'to buy', verbal noun *šra* '(the action of) buying', noun of instance *šerya* 'a purchase'. Hollow verbs have a medial *i* or *u* in the noun of instance, paralleling the *i* or *u* in the verbal noun and the imperfect of the verb (See pp. 49-50, 62); e.g., *baƐ* 'to sell', imperfect *ibiƐ,* verbal noun *biƐ* '(the action of) selling', noun of instance *biƐa* 'a sale'; *bas* 'to kiss', imperfect *ibus,* verbal noun *busan* '(the action of) kissing', noun of instance *busa* 'a kiss'. Doubled verbs follow the same pattern as the sound verbs; e.g., *deqq* 'to hit, to strike', verbal noun *deqq* '(the action of) hitting, striking', noun of instance *deqqa* 'a blow'.

It is only rarely that the noun of instance of Measure I verbs has a form other than *FeƐLa,* although such cases do occur; e.g., *qtel* 'to kill', verbal noun *qtil* '(the action of) killing', noun of instance *qtila* 'a killing, a murder'; *ẓar̥* 'to visit', verbal noun and noun of instance *ẓyar̥a* '(the action of) visiting, a visit'.

The noun of instance of Measure II and the quadriliteral verb is derived from the verbal noun by the addition of a final *-a*. For Measure II verbs, the verbal noun pattern *teFƐiL,* and never *teFƐaL,* is the base from which the noun of instance is derived. Some examples:

bexxeṛ	'to steam (food), to fumigate'
tebxiṛ, tebxaṛ	'(the action of) steaming, fumigation'
tebxiṛa	'a steaming, a fumigation'
feṛgeƐ	'to (make) explode'
tfeṛgeƐ	'to explode, to be exploded'
tfeṛgiƐ	'(the action of) explosion'
tfeṛgiƐa	'an explosion'
kerkeb	'to (make something) roll, tumble over'
tkerkeb	'to roll over, to tumble over'
tkerkib	'(the action of) rolling, tumbling over'
tkerkiba	'a rolling; a tumble, a fall'

V. The Noun-Adjective of Profession and Personal Characteristic

There are two similar forms, both having the overall pattern *CeCCaC.* The pattern *FeƐƐaL,* with the doubled middle consonant, is derived from triliteral roots, usually from Measure I verbs or from nouns. The pattern *FeƐLaC* is derived from quadriliteral verbs and nouns. As is usual, *ww* and *yy* function as the medial consonants of middle-weak roots, and *y* functions as the final consonant of final-weak roots.

Semantically this form bears a close relationship to the nisba of profession and personal characteristic.[4] By referring to an inherent or habitual activity, it contrasts with adjectives of the *FeƐLan* pattern, which usually refer to a temporary or momentary state.[5]

---

[4]For the nisba of profession and personal characteristic, see pp. 74-78.

[5]Compare *ġeḍban* 'angry' and *ġeḍḍab* 'easily irritated, irascible', both from *ġḍeb* 'to become angry'; likewise, *Ɛeṛqan* 'sweating' and *Ɛeṛṛaq* 'given to sweating', both from *Ɛṛeq* 'to sweat'.

These forms refer almost exclusively to human beings and indicate either professional or habitual activity with respect to the meaning of the base from which they are derived. Some examples:

Base		**Noun-Adjective**	
bgeṛ	'cattle'	*beggaṛ*	'cattle-keeper, -raiser'
bka	'to weep'	*bekkay*	'weeper, whiner'
(nil)		*beqqal*	'grocer'
dheb	'gold'	*dehhab*	'gilder, worker in gold inlay'
gezra	'butchered animal'	*gezzar*	'butcher'
kdeb	'to lie'	*keddab*	'liar'
kma	'to smoke'	*kemmay*	'(excessive) smoker'
keṛfeṣ	'to spoil, to ruin' (by handling roughly, clumsily)	*keṛfaṣ*	'clumsy'
nsa	'to forget'	*nessay*	'forgetful'
nḥel	'bee(s)'	*neḥḥal*	'bee-keeper'
nžeṛ	'to trim, to cut, to hew'	*nežžaṛ*	'carpenter'
sif	'sword'	*siyyaf*	'swordsman, executioner'
ṣbeṛ	'to wait, to be patient'	*ṣebbaṛ*	'patient'
xobz	'bread'	*xebbaz*	'baker'
xeṭṭ	'line; hand-writing'	*xeṭṭaṭ*	'calligrapher'
ḥdid	'iron'	*ḥeddad*	'blacksmith'
ġḍeb	'to become angry'	*ġeḍḍab*	'easily irritated, irascible'
Ɛṛeq	'to sweat'	*Ɛeṛṛaq*	'given to sweating'

VI. The Nisba

1. The Nisba Suffix: The nisba is characterized by the ending *-i* attached to a stem; e.g., *ˀislam* 'Islam', nisba *ˀislami* 'Islamic'. The common automatic stem changes of inversion and elision occur regularly in the nisbas; e.g., nisba *dehbi* 'golden, gilded' from *dheb* 'gold', showing inversion, and nisba *tunsi* 'Tunisian' from *tunes* 'Tunisia', showing elision. Other stem changes are rare and follow no set pattern; e.g., collective noun *qoṣṭaḷ* 'chestnut tree(s)', nisba *qoṣṭḷi* 'chestnut brown'.

When a nisba is formed from a singular noun which ends in *-a,* the usual procedure is for the *-a* to drop or for *w* to be inserted between the *-a* and the nisba ending; e.g., *qehwa* 'coffee' with nisba *qehwi* 'coffee colored', and *fṛanṣa* 'France' with nisba *fṛanṣawi* 'French'. In a few cases an *n* rather than a *w* is inserted; e.g., *šehwa* 'taste, appetite, desire', with nisba *šehwani* 'gluttonous, greedy'. Monosyllables in *-a* regularly take *w,* as in *ma* 'water' with nisba *mawi* 'watery, juicy', although there is one common exception, *nqa* 'cleanness' with nisba *nqi* 'clean'. Items of three or more syllables regularly drop the *-a,* as in *filaḥa* 'agriculture' with nisba *filaḥi* 'agricultural'. The two-syllable verbal noun of Measures III and IIIa(VI) regularly drops its final *-a* in forming the nisba, as in *mdabza* 'quarrel, fight' with nisba *mdabzi* 'quarrelsome, quarreler', but other two-syllable nisba bases ending in *-a* are unpredictable as to whether *-a* is dropped or *w* is inserted, as in the above quoted nisbas *qehwi* 'coffee colored' and *fṛanṣawi* 'French', from *qehwa* 'coffee' and *fṛanṣa* 'France' respectively.

There are a few examples of *aw* being inserted between the nisba *-i* and a noun ending in a consonant; e.g., *ġeṛb* 'Gharb' (the part of Morocco located, roughly, between Rabat and Meknes, of an indefinite north-south extension), nisba *ġeṛbawi* 'native to the Gharb'. This item may be contrasted with *ġeṛb* 'west', which has the normal nisba pattern *ġeṛbi* 'western'.

A small number of nisbas, of which only a dozen or so occur frequently, show the ending *-ani,* characterized by *-ni* being added to stems which end in *-a* and *-ani* to stems which end in a consonant. For the small group of adverbial-prepositional particles indicating spatial relations, *-ani* is the regular nisba ending. The only exception is *qoddam* 'in front of, up ahead' (preposition, adverb), nisba *qoddami* 'facing, lying ahead or in front' (adjective). Other stems which take *-ani* as the nisba ending must be memorized as lexical items. For the adverbial-prepositional particles of spatial relation, see pp. 71, 211 below. Some examples of the ending *-ani* from other stems:

Base		**Nisba**	
(l)uwwel	'first'	*(l)uwwlani*	'first'
lexxer	'last'	*lexxrani*	'last'
(cf. *ṛebbi* 'God')		*ṛebbani*	'pious'
šehwa	'desire, appetite'	*šehwani*	'gluttonous, greedy'
šib	'white, grey hair'	*šibani*	'white, grey haired' (with age)
ṭeṛf	'border, edge'	*ṭeṛfani*	'located on the border, edge'
ḥmeṛ	'red'	*ḥomṛani*	'reddish'

2. **Nisba Stems:** There are only a limited number of word types from which nisbas are derived. They are listed below. The first three types occur frequently as nisba stems. The remainder are limited in number.

(a) **From Singular Nouns:** Most nisbas are derived from singular nouns. The number of such nisbas is quite large. Some examples:

Noun		Nisba	
l-ʔandalus	'Andalusia'	*ʔandalusi*	'Andalusian'
din	'religion'	*dini*	'religious'
fas	'Fez'	*fasi*	'native to Fez'
fḍuḷ	'(unwarranted, excessive) curiosity, pushiness'	*fḍuḷi*	'annoyingly, imprudently curious, pushy'
kebrit	'sulfur'	*kebriti*	'sulfur colored, light yellow'
limun	'orange(s)' (in Fez 'lemon')	*limuni*	'orange colored' (in Fez 'lemon colored')
šheṛ	'month'	*šehṛi*	'monthly'
xrif	'fall, autumn'	*xrifi*	'autumnal'
yum	'day'	*yumi*	'daily' (adjective)
ɛsel	'honey'	*ɛesli*	'honey colored'

(b) **From Plural Nouns:** There are a fairly large number of nisbas formed from plural nouns. Most such nouns refer to concrete objects and have the broken plural pattern *CCaCeC*.[6] The only common examples of nisbas derived from plural nouns of a pattern other than *CCaCeC* are *muluki* 'royal' (*malik* 'king', pl. *muluk*), *ržali* 'manly, masculine' (*ṛažel* 'man', pl. *ržal*), and *ṛuṣi* 'headstrong, self-willed' (*ṛaṣ* 'head', pl. *ṛuṣ* 'heads'). Some examples of the regular pattern:

Noun		Nisba	
bermil	'barrel'	*bramli*	'barrel maker'
pl. *bramel*			
bḥira	'vegetable garden'	*bḥayri*	'vegetable gardener'
pl. *bḥayer*			

[6]For the broken plural pattern *CCaCeC*, see pp. 113-116.

fendeq	'hotel'	*fnadqi*	'hotel keeper'
pl. *fnadeq*			
gaẓiṭa	'newspaper'	*gwaẓṭi*	'journalist'
pl. *gwaẓeṭ*			
kaṛṭa	'playing card'	*kwaṛṭi*	'card player'
pl. *kwaṛeṭ*			
meḥṛat	'plow'	*mḥaṛti*	'plow maker'
pl. *mḥaṛet*			
nzaha	'picnic'	*nzayhi*	'picnic lover'
pl. *nzayeh*			
ġoṛbal	'sieve'	*ġ̂ṛabli*	'sieve maker'
pl. *ġ̂ṛabel*			

(c) **From the Pseudo-Plural Stem** *CCayC-*: The plural pattern *CCayeC*[7] is a common sub-pattern of the more general plural pattern *CCaCeC,* and there are a number of nisbas formed from such stems; e.g., *fluka* 'boat', pl. *flayek,* nisba *flayki* 'boatman'. The pattern *CCayC-* has, however, become generalized as a nisba stem, and a number of nouns which either have no plural or which have a plural of some form other than *CCayeC* derive their nisbas from a stem of pattern *CCayC-*. Some examples:

Noun		**Nisba**	
džaž	'chicken, fowl'	*džayži*	'fowl merchant'
pl. *džažat*			
mešṭa	'comb'	*mšayṭi*	'comb maker, merchant'[8]
pl. *mšaṭi*			
nefḥa	'pinch of snuff'	*nfayḥi*	'snuff taker'
noqṛa	'silver'	*nqayṛi*	'maker of silver jewelry'

[7]For the broken plural pattern *CCayeC,* see pp. 115-116.

[8]In Fez this word has acquired the meaning of 'briber'.

qobb	'wooden bucket'	*qbaybi*	'maker of wooden buckets and casks'
pl. *qbab*			
ṛxam	'marble'	*ṛxaymi*	'marble mason'
sella	'basket'	*slayli*	'basket maker'
pl. *slel*			
Ɛefyun	'opium'	*Ɛfayni*	'opium addict'

(d) From the Adverbial-Prepositional Particles of Spatial Relation: There are eight such particles. They and their nisbas are listed below. The stem change in the nisbas of *daxel* 'inside' and the ending *-i* instead of *-ani* in the nisba of *qoddam* 'facing, up ahead' constitute a slight deviation from the pattern shown by the other particles.

Particle		**Nisba**	
beṛṛa	'outside'	*beṛṛani*	'external, exterior; stranger'
daxel	'inside'	*dexlani*	'interior, internal'
fuq	'above, over'	*fuqani*	'upper'
(ḷ-) ḷuṛ	'(the) rear'	*ḷuṛani*	'last, rear, hindmost'
qoddam	'facing, up ahead'	*qoddami*	'lying ahead, in front'
teḥt	'below, under'	*teḥtani*	'bottom, nether, under' (adj.)
wṛa	'behind, after'	*wṛani*	'last, rear, hindmost'
woṣṭ	'middle, center'	*woṣṭani*	'middle, central'

(e) From Numerals: There is a group of eight nisbas with a special stem form based on the numerals from three through ten. The nisba based on *tlata* 'three' deviates from the pattern of the other members of this group. The forms are:

Numeral		**Nisba**	
tlata, telt 'three'		*telti*	'three-fold, composed of three elements'
ṛebƐa	'four'	*ṛbaƐi*	'four-fold, composed of four elements'
xemsa	'five'	*xmasi*	'five-fold, composed of five elements'

setta	'six'	*sdasi*	'six-fold, composed of six elements'
sebƐa	'seven'	*sbaƐi*	'seven-fold, composed of seven elements'
tmenya	'eight'	*tmani*	'eight-fold, composed of eight elements'
tesƐud	'nine'	*tsaƐi*	'nine-fold, composed of nine elements'
Ɛešra	'ten'	*Ɛšari*	'ten-fold, composed of ten elements'

(f) **Miscellaneous Stems:** Occasional nisbas are found from other kinds of stems than those listed above; e.g., adjective *ḥmeṛ* 'red', nisba *ḥemri* 'light soil of reddish color'.

(g) **Nisbas With Stems Which Do Not Exist Independently:** A number of nouns and adjectives which are nisbas both in terms of meaning and external form have stems which occur only in the nisba[9]; e.g., *beldi* 'native, local, indigenous'. Usually such nisbas have a stem which is comparable in form to common independently found nisba stems; e.g., both *beldi* 'native' and *dehri* 'atheist' have stems which are comparable in form to such a pair as *dheb* 'gold' with nisba *dehbi* 'golden, gilded'. Such a nisba as *ktatbi* 'secretary, editor' has a stem which, although it does not exist independently of the nisba form, is directly comparable to nisbas from plural noun stems such as *šeṭṭaba* 'broom', pl. *šṭaṭeb*, nisba *šṭaṭbi* 'broom maker'. Occasionally items which are formally classifiable as nisbas are found with stems which neither occur independently nor follow any regularly found nisba stem pattern; e.g., *kotbi* 'bookseller'.

Most nisbas whose stems do not occur independently are nevertheless readily relatable to a root which occurs elsewhere, as in *ktatbi* 'secretary, editor' and *kotbi* 'bookseller', both of which are relatable to the root found in *kteb* 'to write'. Completely isolated items, such as *doxṛi* 'crude, boorish', neither the stem nor root of which is found elsewhere, are comparatively rare.

3. **The Nisba as a Relational Adjective:** With the exception of items which have the stem pattern *CCaCC–*,[10] the nisba is fundamentally a relational adjective, the meaning of which is directly predictable from the meaning of the stem.

---

[9]Compare such an English form as "uncouth". The stem "-couth" is found only with the prefix "un-".

[10]Regardless of whether the *CCaCC–* stem is a broken noun plural, the pseudo-plural pattern *CCayC–*, or whether the stem is not found independently of the nisba form. See below, pp. 74-78, **4. The Nisba of Professional Activity or Permanent Personal Characteristic.**

Such a straight forward derivational pair as *ḍaṛuṛa* 'necessity', nisba *ḍaṛuṛi* 'necessary' is typical. Examples of this type of nisba may be multiplied indefinitely, and new ones are formed readily from singular nouns.

Geographical place names are a common source of nisbas. Some typical examples:

Place Name		**Nisba**	
l-ʔandalus	'Andalusia'	*ʔandalusi*	'Andalusian'
fas	'Fez'	*fasi*	'native to Fez'
l-hend	'India'	*hendi*	'Indian'
maṣeṛ	'Egypt'	*meṣṛi*	'Egyptian'
l-meġṛib	'Morocco'	*meġṛibi*	'Moroccan'
ṛ-ṛbaṭ	'Rabat'	*ṛbaṭi*	'native to Rabat'
r-rif	'the Rif'	*rifi*	'Rifian'
s-sudan	'the Sudan'	*sudani*	'Sudanese'
š-šam	'Syria'	*šami*	'Syrian'
tunes	'Tunisia'	*tunsi*	'Tunisian'

In many cases the meaning of the nisba is either metaphorical or else focused upon some specific aspect of the meaning of the parent stem. The exact meaning of such nisbas is not directly predictable from the meaning of their stem source and must consequently be learned as a lexical item. One of the most common kinds of specialized meaning among nisbas is reference to the color of some concrete object. Some typical examples:

Noun		**Nisba**	
kebrit	'sulfur'	*kebriti*	'sulfur colored, light yellow'
limun	'orange(s)'	*limuni*	'orange colored'
mešmaš	'apricot(s)'	*mešmaši*	'apricot colored'
nḥas	'copper'	*nḥasi*	'copper colored'
nila	'indigo'	*nili*	'indigo blue'
ṛmaḍ (also *rmad*)	'ash(es)'	*ṛmaḍi* (also *rmadi*)	'gray, ash colored'
ṛṣaṣ	'lead'	*ṛṣaṣi*	'gray, lead colored'

tben	'straw'	*tebni*	'straw colored'
xux	'peach(es)'	*xuxi*	'peach colored'
ɛsel	'honey'	*ɛesli*	'honey colored'

Such a nisba of color as *mdadi* 'violet', from *mdad* 'ink', shows an even greater degree of specialization in meaning than the examples quoted above. Specialization in terms of color is not the only sort which occurs; e.g., *beṛṛa* 'outside', nisba *beṛṛani,* which in addition to its original meaning of 'exterior' also means 'stranger' or 'foreigner'. Nisbas which involve a metaphorical extension of the meaning of the term from which they are derived follow no predictable pattern and must be learned as individual items; e.g., *adam* 'Adam' (the Biblical first man), nisba *adami,* which means not only 'human (being)' but also 'polite, agreeable, courteous'.

4. The Nisba of Profession and Personal Characteristic: Nisbas of this sort refer only to human beings. This category includes all nisbas with the stem pattern *CCaCC-,*[11] including the pseudo-plural pattern *CCayC-,* and a very few nisbas derived from other stem types.

The nisbas referring to professional activity are nouns. Many of them are based on broken plurals referring to objects of hand manufacture and refer to the artisan who manufactures and sells the object in question.[12] In the case of musical instruments and such like, the nisba refers equally to the artist who uses the instrument. Some typical examples referring to artisans:

Noun		**Nisba**	
bendir	'tambourine'	*bnadri*	'tambourine maker, seller, player'
pl. *bnader*			
berdɛa	'pack-saddle'	*bradɛi*	'pack-saddle maker'
pl. *bradeɛ*			
meḥṛat	'plow'	*mḥaṛti*	'plow maker'
pl. *mḥaṛet*			
qeršal	'carding-brush'	*qrašli*	'carding-brush maker'
pl. *qrašel*			

[11]For the nisba stem *CCaCC-,* see pp. 69-71 above.

[12]In Moroccan society the artisan himself usually merchandises the wares which he manufactures.

škaṛa	'satchel'	*škayṛi*	'satchel maker'
pl. *škayeṛ*			
šeṭṭaba	'broom'	*šṭaṭbi*	'broom maker'
pl. *šṭaṭeb*			
ġoṛbal	'sieve'	*ġṛabli*	'sieve maker'
pl. *ġṛabel*			
ḥṣiṛa	'(straw) mat'	*ḥṣayṛi*	'mat maker'
pl. *ḥṣayeṛ*			

Many nisbas with the pseudo-plural stem *CCayC–*[13] also refer to artisans. The pseudo-plural nisba stem *CCayC–* is formed only in those cases where the corresponding noun either has no plural or else has a plural of some pattern other than *CCaCeC*. Some examples:

Noun		**Nisba**	
džaž	'chicken(s)'	*džayži*	'fowl merchant'
pl. *džažat*			
mešṭa	'comb'	*mšayṭi*	'comb maker'
pl. *mšaṭi*			
noqṛa	'silver'	*nqayṛi*	'maker of silver jewelry'
rbab	'rebec'	*rbaybi*	'rebec maker, seller, player'
pl. *rbabat*			
sella	'basket'	*slayli*	'basket maker'
pl. *slel*			

A wide range of professional activities other than those of artisans is indicated by nisbas with the stem pattern *CCaCC–*. These nisbas are almost always derived from a plural noun, and the meaning of the nisba is usually inferrable from the meaning of the noun. In the case of nouns which do not have plurals or which have plurals of a pattern other than *CCaCeC*, a special *CCaCC–* nisba stem is formed from the singular. Some examples:

[13]For the pseudo-plural nisba stem *CCayC–*, see pp. 70-71.

Noun		Nisba	
bḥiṛa	'vegetable garden'	*bḥayṛi*	'vegetable gardener'
pl. *bḥayeṛ*			
dendna	'music'	*dnadni*	'musician'
fluka	'boat'	*flayki*	'boatman'
pl. *flayek*			
fendeq	'hotel'	*fnadqi*	'hotel keeper'
pl. *fnadeq*			
feṛṛan	'furnace'	*fṛaṛni*	'furnace tender'
pl. *fṛaṛen*			
gnaza	'funeral'	*gnayzi*	religious personnage who recites prayers at funerals
pl. *gnayez*			
gaẓiṭa	'newspaper'	*gwaẓṭi*	'journalist'
pl. *gwaẓeṭ*			
mellaḥa	'salt works'	*mlalḥi*	'salt worker'
qadus	'pipe'	*qwadsi*	'plumber'
pl. *qwades*			
qeṭṛan	'tar'	*qṭaṛni*	'tar seller'
zelliž	'tile(s)'	*zlayži*	'tile maker, setter'

Many nisbas with a *CCaCC-* stem pattern refer to habitual personal characteristics rather than strictly professional activity. Some examples:

Noun		Nisba	
flus	'money'	*flaysi*	'covetous, venal'
kaṛṭa	'playing card'	*kwaṛṭi*	'card player'
pl. *kwaṛeṭ*			
leƐba	'game'	*lƐaybi*	'player'
pl. *leƐbat*			

naƐuṛa	'dirty trick'	*nwaƐṛi*	'sly, tricky'
pl. *nwaƐeṛ*			
sekra	'drunkenness'	*skayri*	'drunkard'
xṛafa	'story, (tall) tale'	*xṛayfi*	'story teller, windbag'
pl. *xṛayef*			
ḥsifa	'rancor, resentment'	*ḥsayfi*	'vindictive, resentful'
pl. *ḥsayef*			
ḥšiša	'marihuana'	*ḥšayši*	'marihuana addict'
Ɛefyun	'opium'	*Ɛfayni*	'opium addict'

Despite the usual regularity of meaning of this type of nisba, unpredictable specialized and metaphorical meanings also occur. Some examples:

Noun		**Nisba**	
bṭana	'sheep-skin'	*bṭayni*	'backbiter, evil-tongued' [14]
pl. *bṭayen*			
(cf. *din* 'debt')		*mdayni*	'creditor'
mexṭaf	'hook'	*mxaṭfi*	'hanger-on, parasite'
pl. *mxaṭef*			
nefḥa	'pinch of snuff'	*nfayḥi*	'snuff-taker'
pl. *nefḥat*			
nzaha	'picnic'	*nzayhi*	'picnic lover'
pl. *nzayeh*			
zerda	'party'	*zraydi*	'carouser, glutton'
pl. *zradi*			

Nisbas of professional activity or habitual personal characteristic from stems of a pattern other than *CCaCC–* are rare, although they do occur. Some examples:

[14] Compare the idiom *ntef-lu bṭantu* 'he talked maliciously about him behind his back', literally 'he plucked (the hair off) his skin for him'.

Noun		**Nisba**	
ʔala	'musical instrument'	*ʔali*	'musician, instrumentalist'
bḥeṛ	'sea, ocean'	*beḥri*	'sailor; maritime, marine'
kamanža	'violin'	*kamanži*	'violin player'
malik	'king'	*muluki*	'royal'
pl. *muluk*			
musiqa	'music'	*musiqi*	'musician'
ṛaṣ	'head'	*ṛuṣi*	'headstrong, self-willed'
pl. *ṛuṣ*			
ṛažel	'man'	*ṛžali*	'manly, masculine'
pl. *ṛžal*			
ṛžel	'foot, leg'	*režli*	'pedestrian, foot-soldier'
ṭaḥuna	'mill'	*ṭaḥuni*	'miller'

VII. Collectives

There are a number of nouns in Moroccan which are masculine singular in form but which have a collective meaning; e.g., *nmel* 'ant(s)', *xobz* 'bread'. To indicate one member of the general category referred to by the collective, a singular is formed by adding the feminine ending *-a;* e.g., *nemla* 'an ant', *xobza* 'a piece, loaf of bread'. In the rare cases where a collective ends in a vowel, the singular ending is *-ya;* e.g., *xizzu* 'carrot(s)', singular *xizzuya* 'a carrot'.

The singular in *-a* forms a regular plural by adding *-t,* and the collective form itself sometimes has a broken plural; e.g., collective *dellaḥ* 'watermelon(s)' with broken plural *dlaleḥ* 'watermelons', singular *dellaḥa* 'a watermelon' with plural *dellaḥat* 'watermelons'. These plural forms are used almost exclusively for counting.

Various animals and insects are commonly indicated by collective nouns. Among the larger animals where biological sex is immediately apparent, the singular in *-a* generally denotes the female of the species, the collective denotes the species as a whole, and there is sometimes (but not always) a separate word for the male of the species; e.g., *bgeṛ* 'cattle', *begṛa* 'a cow', *tuṛ* 'a bull'. In the cases where there is no separate word for the male of the species, the collective can be used in that sense; e.g., *bellarež* 'stork(s)', *bellarža* 'a (female) stork'. Some further examples of collectives referring to various members of the animal kingdom:

Collective		Singular	
babbuš	'snail(s)'	*babbuša*	'a snail'
beqq	'bug(s)'	*beqqa*	'a bug'
bṛek	'duck(s)'	*beṛka*	'a duck'
dbab	'gad-fly, -ies'	*dbaba*	'a gad-fly'
debban	'fly, flies'	*debbana*	'a fly'
džaž	'chicken(s)'	*džaža*	'a chicken, a hen'
cf. *dik* 'rooster'			
dud	'worm(s)'	*duda*	'a worm'
namus	'mosquito(es)'	*namusa*	'a mosquito'
nḥel	'bee(s)'	*neḥla*	'a bee'
ṛẓuẓi	'wasp(s)'	*ṛẓuẓiya*	'a wasp'
wezz	'goose, geese'	*wezza*	'a goose'
ḥut	'fish'	*ḥuta*	'a fish'
ɛleq	'leech(es)'	*ɛelqa*	'a leech'

Also frequent are collectives which refer to plants or plant products. Some examples:

Collective		Singular	
beṛquq	'plum(s)'	*beṛquqa*	'a plum'
bṣeḷ	'onion(s)'	*beṣḷa*	'an onion'
dreg	'cactus, cacti'	*derga*	'a cactus'
festeq	'pistachio(s)'	*festqa*	'a pistachio nut'
ful	'fava bean(s)'	*fula*	'a fava bean'
fžel	'radish(es)'	*fežla*	'a radish'
left	'turnip(s)'	*lefta*	'a turnip'
luz	'almond(s)'	*luza*	'an almond'
mešmaš	'apricot(s)'	*mešmaša*	'an apricot'
nxel	'date palm(s)'	*nexla*	'a date palm'

qṣeb	'reed(s)'	*qeṣba*	'a reed'
šuk	'thorn(s)'	*šuka*	'a thorn'
šžeṛ	'tree(s)'	*šežṛa*	'a tree'
xux	'peach(es)'	*xuxa*	'a peach'
zbib	'raisin(s)'	*zbiba*	'a raisin'
zitun	'olive(s)'	*zituna*	'an olive'
ɛdes	'lentil(s)'	*ɛedsa*	'a lentil'

Collective nouns are not limited to the categories of animals and plants. Collectives are found with a wide range of meaning, and their only consistently common element is the contrast between a general category and an individual member of the category. Some examples:

Collective		**Singular**	
biḍ	'egg(s)'	*biḍa*	'an egg'
hbeṛ	'boneless meat'	*hebṛa*	'a piece of boneless meat'
keḥk	'cooky, -ies'	*keḥka*	'a cooky'
luḥ	'board(s), plank(s)'	*luḥa*	'a board, a plank'
meṣṛan	'viscera'	*meṣṛana*	'an intestine'
sbib	'(animal) hair(s)'	*sbiba*	'a hair'
šqef	'shard(s)'	*šeqfa*	'a shard'
šɛeṛ	'hair'	*šeɛṛa*	'a hair'
talul	'wart(s)'	*talula*	'a wart'
ṭšaš	'spark(s)'	*ṭšaša*	'a spark'
ṭub	'brick(s)'	*ṭuba*	'a brick'
wqid	'match(es)'	*wqida*	'a match'
zelliž	'tiling'	*zelliža*	'a tile'
ḥṭeb	'fire wood'	*ḥeṭba*	'a piece of fire wood'
ḥžeṛ	'rock(s)'	*ḥežṛa*	'a rock'

VIII. The Diminutive

Diminutives are derived from a great variety of nouns and adjectives. The distinguishing characteristic common to all diminutives is an initial cluster of two consonants followed by *i*. There are several different classes of stem types, with a number of irregularities, and the exact meaning of the diminutive is not uniformly predictable from the meaning of the derivational base. The most commonly found forms are as follows.

1. **Monosyllables:** Monosyllables with triliteral roots usually form the diminutive by inserting *-iyye-* between the second and third consonants. Some examples:

Base		Diminutive
bṭen	'belly'	*bṭiyyen*
bğel	'mule'	*bğiyyel*
kelb	'dog'	*kliyyeb*
ṭeṛf	'piece'	*ṭṛiyyef*
xobz	'bread'	*xbiyyez*

Monosyllables with middle-weak triliteral roots usually have the diminutive pattern *FwiyyeL*, occasionally *FwiLa*. Some examples:

Base		Diminutive
bab	'door'	*bwiba*
bir	'well'	*bwiyyer*
buq	'horn, trumpet'	*bwiyyeq*
faṛ	'rat'	*fwiyyeṛ*

A few monosyllables with triliteral roots and the vowel *e* show the diminutive pattern *FƐiLa*. For example:

Base		Diminutive
bent	'girl, daughter'	*bnita*
ṛžel	'foot, leg'	*ṛžila*

yedd	'hand'	*ydida*
ɛsel	'honey'	*ɛsila*

Adjectives of color and defect[15] and many adjectives of the pattern *FɛiL* have diminutives of the pattern *FɛiɛeL,* showing a repetition of the second root consonant. Occasional other monosyllabic nouns also have diminutives of the pattern *FɛiɛeL*. Some examples:

Base		**Diminutive**
bden	'human body'	*bdiden*
bhel	'foolish, stupid'	*bhihel*
bkem	'mute, dumb'	*bkikem*
kḥel	'black'	*kḥiḥel*
mles	'smooth, soft'	*mliles*
ḥmeṛ	'red'	*ḥmimeṛ*
bxil	'miserly'	*bxixel*
kbir	'big'	*kbibeṛ*
mliḥ	'good, excellent'	*mlileḥ*
ṭwil	'tall, long'	*ṭwiwel*

There are two common exceptions in this category, diminutive *bwiweḍ* from *byeḍ* 'white' and diminutive *ṣġiweṛ* from *ṣġiṛ* 'small'.

2. The Stem Patterns *FeɛL–* and *FoɛL–* Plus a Vowel: The diminutive is usually formed by inserting *i* between the second and third consonants while retaining the final vowel. Some examples:

Base		**Diminutive**
bedwi	'bedouin'	*bdiwi*
begṛa	'cow'	*bgiṛa*
ḍeṛba	'a blow'	*ḍṛiba*
qedra	'pot'	*qdira*

[15]For the adjectives of color and defect, see p. 87.

woždi	'native to Oujda'	*wžidi*
ġenmi	'mutton'	*ġnimi*

In words of this sort, *-iyy-* instead of *-i-* between the second and third consonants is relatively rare; e.g., *bekra* 'virgin', diminutive *bkiyyra*.

3. Middle-Weak Stems With a Final Vowel: The diminutive pattern is the same as for stems *FeƐL-* and *FoƐL-* plus a vowel, cf. the section immediately above. A *w* is added as the second consonant of the diminutive form. Some examples:

Base		**Diminutive**
biru	'office'	*bwiru*
busa	'kiss'	*bwisa*
fasi	'native to Fez'	*fwisi*
ḥuta	'fish'	*ḥwita*

4. The Stem Patterns *FƐaLa* and *FƐiLa*:[16] The regular diminutive pattern is *FƐiyyLa*. Some examples:

Base		**Diminutive**
bḷaṣa	'place'	*bḷiyyṣa*
bniqa	'room, cell'	*bniyyqa*
bṭaṭa	'potato'	*bṭiyyṭa*
džaža	'chicken'	*džiyyža*
zbiba	'raisin'	*zbiyyba*

5. Words With Four Consonants: Regardless of their root and pattern structure, words with four consonants usually have the diminutive pattern *CCiCeC*. If such a word has a final vowel, the diminutive has the same final vowel, and the *e* before the last consonant of the diminutive pattern is dropped. Some examples:

[16] The pattern *FƐuLa* is too rare for consideration.

Base		**Diminutive**
bedƐiya	'vest'	*bdiƐya*
beḷḷaṛ	'crystal'	*bḷiḷeṛ*
berbri	'Berber'	*bribri*
dellaḥ	'watermelon(s)'	*dlileḥ*
keskas	'couscous pot'	*ksikes*
mbexṛa	'incense burner'	*mbixṛa*
meḍṛub	'out of luck, stricken by fate'	*mḍiṛeb*
meknasi	'native to Meknes'	*mkinsi*
mektub	'pocket'	*mkiteb*
sokkaṛ	'sugar'	*skikeṛ*

Occasionally diminutives with four consonants are found with *i* between the third and fourth consonants as well as between the second and third. Some examples:

Base		**Diminutive**
beṛquqa	'plum'	*bṛiqiqa*
ṭenžiya	'cooking pot'	*ṭnižiya*
xedduž	girl's name	*xdidiž*
ẓeṛbiya	'carpet, rug'	*ẓṛibiya*

The form *mziwen,* from *mezyan* 'good', shows the regular diminutive pattern, but with a substitution of *w* for *y*.

6. Three-Consonant Words With a Stable Vowel Between the First and Second Consonants: Words of this sort follow the same pattern as words with four consonants. A *w* is inserted as the second consonant of the diminutive pattern. Some examples:

Base		**Diminutive**
bakit	'package'	*bwiket*

buhali	'foolish, stupid'	*bwihli*
faṭma	girl's name	*fwiṭma*
ṛažel	'man'	*ṛwižel*
ṭabḷa	'table'	*ṭwibḷa*
Ɛafya	'fire'	*Ɛwifya*

Occasional diminutives with an additional *i* between the third and fourth consonants occur; e.g., *ṣiniya* 'tray', diminutive *ṣwiniya*. A few other forms are also encountered; e.g., *xadem* 'female servant, slave woman' with diminutive *xwidma; waseƐ* 'broad' with diminutive *wsiseƐ*.

7. **Miscellaneous:** Other diminutive types are relatively rare and not readily classifiable. Some examples:

Base		**Diminutive**
bṛa	'letter'	*bṛiyya*
ma	'water'	*mwiha*
omm	'mother'	*mwima*
mṛa	'woman'	*mṛiwa*
xu	'brother'	*xiyy*
bellarež	'stork'	*blilirež*
beṭṭaniya	'cover'	*bṭiṭna*
kyayfi	'marihuana seller'	*kwiyyfi*
mzuwweq	'ornamented, decorated'	*mziwweq*
mḥennša	kind of cake	*mḥinnša*

IX. The Comparative

Only a limited number of adjective types have a special comparative form, and within a given type not all examples take it. The exceptions must be learned as vocabulary items.

1. **The Patterns** *FƐiL, FƐuL,* **and** *FaƐeL*: Adjectives of these patterns have the comparative form *FƐeL*. Some examples:

Base		**Comparative**	
kbir	'big'	*kbeṛ*[17]	'bigger'
sxun	'hot'	*sxen*	'hotter'
tqil	'heavy'	*tqel*	'heavier'
bared	'cold'	*bred*	'colder'
waseƐ	'wide, roomy'	*wseƐ*	'wider, roomier'

2. **The Pattern** *FiyyeL*: Adjectives of this sort have the comparative pattern *FyeL* or *FweL*. Whether the comparative form has *y* or *w* as the second consonant is not predictable; e.g., *xiyyeṛ* 'good', comparative *xyeṛ*, and *žiyyed* 'noble, generous', comparative *žwed*.

3. **The** *FƐiL* **Pattern from Doubled Roots**: Adjectives of this sort, which have identical second and third consonants, usually vary in the comparative form. Some speakers use the comparative pattern *FƐeƐ* while others use the pattern *FeƐƐ*. Some examples: *bnin* 'delicious, tasty', comparative *bnen* or *benn; xfif* 'light', comparative *xfef* or *xeff; ždid* 'new', comparative usually only *žded*.

4. **The Final-Weak Patterns** *FƐi* **and** *FƐu*: Adjectives of this sort have the comparative form *FƐa*. For example: *nqi* 'clean', comparative *nqa; ḥlu* 'sweet', comparative *ḥla*.

5. **The Adjectives of Color and Defect**: The characteristic form of these adjectives is the same as that of most comparative forms, namely *FƐeL*.[18] They are used in the comparative sense without change of form; e.g., *kḥel* means both 'black' and 'blacker', *ḥmeq* means both 'crazy' and 'crazier', etc.

6. **Irregularities**: Occasional irregularities which do not fit any of the above listed patterns occur; e.g., *Ɛegzan* 'lazy', comparative *Ɛgez* 'lazier'.

---

[17] A final *r* regularly becomes emphatic *ṛ* in the comparative form. An additional example is *ktir* 'much, many', comparative *kteṛ* 'more'.

[18] See p. 87.

X. Adjectives of Color and Defect

There is a small group of adjectives with the characteristic pattern *FƐeL* for the masculine singular, *FeƐLa* for the feminine singular, and *FuƐeL* for the plural. Most of these adjectives share the semantic characteristic of referring to color or some sort of physical characteristic, often a defect. The most commonly occurring items are:

Msc.	Fem.	Pl.	
bhel	*behla*	*buhel*	'simple minded, foolish'
bkem	*bekma*	*bukem*	'mute'
byeḍ	*biḍa*[19]	*buyeḍ*	'white'
kḥel	*keḥla*	*kuḥel*	'black'
mles	*melsa*	*mules*	'soft, smooth'
ṛqeṭ	*ṛeqṭa*	*ṛuqeṭ*	'speckled'
ṣfeṛ	*ṣefṛa*	*ṣufeṛ*	'yellow'
ṭṛeš	*ṭeṛša*	*ṭuṛeš*	'deaf'
xḍeṛ	*xeḍṛa*	*xuḍeṛ*	'green'
ẓṛeq	*ẓeṛqa*	*ẓuṛeq*	'blue'
——	*ḥebla*	*ḥubel*	'pregnant'
ḥmeq	*ḥemqa*	*ḥumeq*	'crazy'
ḥṛeš	*ḥeṛša*	*ḥuṛeš*	'rough'
ḥwel	*ḥewla*	*ḥiwel*[20]	'cross-eyed'
Ɛma	*Ɛemya*	*Ɛumi*[20]	'blind'
Ɛṛež	*Ɛeṛža*	*Ɛuṛež*	'lame'
Ɛweṛ	*Ɛewṛa*	*Ɛiweṛ*,[20] *Ɛewṛin*	'one-eyed'

[19]The expected sequence *ey* appears as *i*.

[20]These represent the middle-weak and final-weak root variations of the general feminine and plural patterns *FeƐLa* and *FuƐeL*.

XI. The Abstract Noun of Profession and Personal Characteristic

The abstract noun of profession and personal characteristic is formed by prefixing *ta–* and suffixing *–t, –et, –yet,* or *–it* to a noun or adjective. The type of noun or adjective determines which suffix is used. The abstract noun names either the profession or the abstracted personal quality associated with the meaning of the stem from which it is derived.

The abstract noun of profession and personal characteristic is regularly derived from the verbal noun-adjective patterns *FeƐƐaL* and *FeƐLaC*[21] and from the nisbas of professional and personal characteristic.[22] For the verbal noun-adjective forms, the suffix is *–et,* while for the nisbas of profession and personal characteristic the suffix in all cases varies freely between *–t* and *–yet*. Some examples:

Base		**Abstract Noun**	
bennay	'mason'	*tabennayet*	'(profession, art of) masonry'
keddab	'liar'	*takeddabet*	'(excessive, habitual) lying'
nežžaṛ	'carpenter'	*tanežžaṛet*	'carpentry'
qeṭṭaƐ	'bandit'	*taqeṭṭaƐet*	'banditry'
šuwwaf	'fortune teller, diviner'	*tašuwwafet*	'fortune telling, divination'
wekkal	'glutton'	*tawekkalet*	'gluttony'
semsaṛ	'broker'	*tasemsaṛet*	'brokerage'
mwagni	'clock maker, watch maker'	*tamwagni–t, –yet*	'clock making, watch making'
kotbi	'bookseller'	*takotbi–t, –yet*	'book-selling'
ṛžuli	'manly'	*taṛžuli–t, –yet*	'manliness, virility'
zlayži	'tile-maker, tile-setter'	*tazlayži–t, –yet*	'(the profession, art of) tile-making, tile-setting'
ẓṛaybi	'carpet-maker'	*taẓṛaybi–t, –yet*	'carpet manufacture'

---

[21] For the patterns *FeƐƐaL* and *FeƐLaC,* see pp. 66-67.

[22] For the nisba of professional and personal characteristic, see pp. 74-78.

Abstract nouns of profession and personal characteristic are occasionally derived from other noun and adjective types, invariably referring to human beings. Nouns and adjectives ending in *i* vary freely between *-t* and *-yet* as the suffix form. Of nouns and adjectives ending in a consonant, the usual pattern is for *-et* to be added if a stable vowel precedes the final consonant, otherwise *-it*. Some examples:

Base		**Abstract Noun**	
ʔadami	'polite, courteous'	*taʔadami-t, -yet*	'politeness, courteousness'
bašawi	relative to, pertaining to a *baša*	*tabašawi-t, -yet*	function, role, duties of a *baša*
derri	'child'	*taderri-t, -yet*	'childishness'
kafer	'rascal; infidel'	*takafrit*	'rascality, dishonesty'
lamin	'syndic, receiver'	*talaminet*	duties, responsibilities of a syndic
mqeddem	'chief, foreman'	*tamqeddmit*	duties of a *mqeddem*
meslem	'Moslem'	*tamselmit*	behavior becoming or appropriate to a (good) Moslem
neṣṛani	'Christian, European'	*taneṣṛani-t, -yet*	Christian, European behavior, manner of living'
š-šiṭan	'the devil'	*tašiṭanet*	'devilry, wicked behavior'
xbaṛži	'spy, informer'	*taxbaṛži-t, -yet*	'espionage'
ɛezri	'bachelor'	*taɛezri-t, -yet*	'celibacy'

XII. Numerals

From one through twelve, Moroccan has separate forms for cardinal and ordinal numbers. From two through ten, there are separate fractional forms. From eleven on, fractions are not definable, and from thirteen on there is no distinction of form between cardinal and ordinal.

1. The Cardinals: There are individual forms for the numbers from one through nineteen, for the tens from twenty through ninety, for a hundred, for a thousand, for a million, and for a billion. The forms for these are given below. For the complex numbers, for example "three thousand, seven hundred and forty-six", which are expressed in terms of multiples and combinations of the basic forms, see p. 207.

(a) **The Cardinals From One Through Ten:**

Full Form		Short Form	
waḥed	(msc.)	(none)	'one'
weḥda	(fem.)		
weḥdin	(pl.)		
žuž		(none)	'two'
tnayn or *tnin*			
tlata		*telt*	'three'
ṛebƐa		*ṛbeƐ, ṛebƐ*	'four'
xemsa		*xems*	'five'
setta		*sett*	'six'
sebƐa		*sbeƐ, sebƐ*	'seven'
tmenya		*temn*	'eight'
tesƐud[23]		*tseƐ, tesƐ*	'nine'
Ɛešṛa		*Ɛešṛ*	'ten'

The numeral *waḥed* 'one' differs from all other numerals in being an adjective. It occupies the same place in the sentence as other adjectives and similarly agrees in gender with whatever noun it modifies;[24] e.g., *ktab waḥed* 'one book'.

For 'two', the form *tnayn* (or *tnin*) is used in compound numerals such as *tnayn u Ɛešrin* 'twenty-two', etc. Otherwise *žuž* is used; e.g., *žuž d-le-ktub* 'two books'.

The short forms of the numerals from three through ten are used only with a limited number of words which must be memorized as lexical items. In general they are the same as those items which also take the dual ending[25]; e.g., *telt šhuṛ* 'three months'. Usage differs somewhat from speaker to speaker.

---

[23] The form *tesƐa* is sometimes heard among rural speakers, but *tesƐud* is universal among urban speakers.

[24] For the function of adjectives, see pp. 204-205.

[25] For the dual, see pp. 100-101.

(b) The Cardinals From Eleven Through Nineteen:

ḥḍaš, -eṛ, -el	'eleven'
ṭnaš, -eṛ, -el	'twelve'
tleṭṭaš, -eṛ, -el	'thirteen'
ṛbeƐṭaš, -eṛ, -el	'fourteen'
xemṣṭaš, -eṛ, -el	'fifteen'
seṭṭaš, -eṛ, -el	'sixteen'
sbeƐṭaš, -eṛ, -el	'seventeen'
tmenṭaš, -eṛ, -el	'eighteen'
tseƐṭaš, -eṛ, -el	'nineteen'

When used directly before a noun in counting, these forms take the ending *-eṛ* or *-el;* e.g., *seṭṭašeṛ Ɛam* or *seṭṭašel Ɛam* 'sixteen years', *ṛbeƐṭašeṛ bent* or *ṛbeƐṭašel bent* 'fourteen girls', etc. Usage varies from speaker to speaker as to whether the form with *-eṛ* or *-el* is used.

(c) The Cardinal Decades:

Ɛešrin	'twenty'
tlatin	'thirty'
ṛebƐin	'forty'
xemsin	'fifty'
settin	'sixty'
sebƐin	'seventy'
tmanin	'eighty'
tesƐin	'ninety'

(d) The Hundreds:

mya	'one hundred'
myatayn, mitin	'two hundred'

telt-emya	'three hundred'
ṛbeƐ-mya, ṛebƐa-mya	'four hundred'
xems-emya	'five hundred'
sett-emya	'six hundred'
sbeƐ-mya, sebƐa-mya	'seven hundred'
temn-emya	'eight hundred'
tseƐ-mya, tesƐa-mya	'nine hundred'

When used directly before a noun, the various forms for the hundreds, except for the dual *myatayn, mitin* 'two hundred', add a *-t* ending; e.g., *myat ḥila* 'a hundred tricks', *telt-emyat metqal* 'three hundred metqals'.

(e) The Thousands:

alef	'one thousand'
alfayn	'two thousand'
telt-alaf	'three thousand'
ṛebƐ-alaf	'four thousand'
xems-alaf	'five thousand'
sett-alaf	'six thousand'
sebƐ-alaf	'seven thousand'
temn-alaf	'eight thousand'
tesƐ-alaf	'nine thousand'
Ɛešṛ-alaf	'ten thousand'

Above ten thousand, *alef* 'thousand' pl. *alaf* 'thousands' is counted as an ordinary noun[26]; e.g., *ḥḍašel alef* 'eleven thousand', *Ɛešrin alef* 'twenty thousand', etc.

[26] For the counting of nouns, see pp. 206-207.

(f) **Larger Numbers:** The units for 'million' *melyun* pl. *mlayen*, and 'billion', *melyaṛ* pl. *mlayeṛ* are morphologically nouns and are counted as such[27]; e.g., *tesƐud d-le-mlayen* 'nine million'.

2. **The Ordinals:** There are independent ordinal forms from one through twelve. The ordinal numerals are simple adjectives, both morphologically and syntactically.[28] Except for 'first' and 'second', which have special forms, they are all formed on the pattern *FaƐeL* from the first three consonants of the corresponding cardinal, with the form for 'sixth' showing an irregular set of consonants. The forms are:

luwwel	'first'
tani	'second'
talet	'third'
ṛabeƐ	'fourth'
xames	'fifth'
sades	'sixth'
sabeƐ	'seventh'
tamen	'eighth'
taseƐ	'ninth'
Ɛašeṛ	'tenth'
ḥaḍeš	'eleven'
ṭaneš	'twelfth'

The forms listed are the masculine singular. The feminine and plural forms are regular, formed with the endings *-a*[29] and *-in*[30] respectively.

---

[27] For the counting of nouns, see pp. 206-207.

[28] For adjectives, see pp. 204-205.

[29] For the feminine ending *-a*, see pp. 95-96.

[30] For the plural ending *-in*, see p. 103.

3. The Fractions: The fractions are simple nouns, both morphologically and syntactically. They are counted accordingly.[31] The forms are:

Singular	Plural	
neṣṣ	*nṣaṣ*	'half'
tulut	*tulutat*	'third'
ṛubuɛ	*ṛubuɛat*	'fourth'
ṛbeɛ	*ṛbaɛ*	
xumus	*xumusat*	'fifth'
xom̩s	*xmas*	
sudus	*sudusat, sdas*	'sixth'
subuɛ	*subuɛat*	'seventh'
sbeɛ	*sbaɛ*	
tumun	*tumunat*	'eighth'
tmen, tm̩en	*tman, tm̩an*	
tusuɛ	*tusuɛat*	'ninth'
ɛušuṛ	*ɛušuṛat, ɛšaṛ*	'tenth'

The fractions from three through ten show a considerable amount of variation. The use of the alternate forms differs from speaker to speaker and in different counting situations.

[31]For the counting of nouns, see pp. 206-207.

V. NOUN AND ADJECTIVE INFLECTION

Moroccan nouns and adjectives have two main grammatical features. There are two genders, a masculine and a feminine, and two numbers, a singular and a plural. Some nouns and adjectives ending in *-a* have a special combining form, and a few nouns show a dual number. Nouns also take the suffixed pronoun endings, which adjectives do not.

I. Gender

1. **The Adjective:** The base form of the adjective is the masculine singular, which must be learned as a lexical item. The feminine is formed by adding *-a* to the masculine. Some examples:

Masculine	Feminine	
feṛḥan	*feṛḥana*	'happy'
sxun	*sxuna*	'hot'
kbir	*kbira*	'big'
merr[1]	*merra*	'bitter'
ḥeyy	*ḥeyya*	'alive'

Participles which end in *-i*,[2] except for the passive participle of Measure I verbs,[3] change the *-i* to *-y* before adding the feminine *-a*. For example:

Masculine	Feminine	
maši	*mašya*	'walking, going'
mṛebbi	*mṛebbya*	'having raised, educated; having been raised, educated'

[1] Some speakers say *meṛṛ*, with an emphatic *ṛ*.

[2] Such participles arise from verbs with final-weak roots; see pp. 57-58.

[3] For the passive participle of Measure I, see pp. 57-58.

All other adjectives ending in *-i*, including the passive participle of Measure I verbs, add *y* before adding the feminine *-a*. There are a large number of adjectives of this sort.[4] Some examples:

Masculine	Feminine	
nqi	*nqiya*	'clean'
mešri	*mešriya*	'(having been) bought'
meṣṛi	*meṣṛiya*	'Egyptian'

The usual phenomena of elision and inversion are met with. Some examples:

Masculine	Feminine	
gales	*galsa*	'sitting'
miyyet	*miyyta*	'dead'
megder	*mgedra*	'strong, husky'
meslem	*mselma*	'Moslem'
xḍeṛ	*xeḍṛa*	'green'
ḥmeq	*ḥemqa*	'crazy'

There are only three common adjectives which fail to fit one of the general patterns listed above. These are:

Masculine	Feminine	
axoṛ	*oxṛa*	'other'
ḥlu	*ḥluwa*	'sweet'
ɛma	*ɛemya*[5]	'blind'

[4] Including all the nisba adjectives; see pp. 72-74.

[5] This word shows the final-weak root equivalent for the pattern illustrated by *xḍeṛ* 'green', which has a sound root.

2. **The Noun:** Nouns ending in *-a* are usually feminine, for example *leḥya* 'beard', while nouns not ending in *-a* are generally masculine, for example *ktab* 'book'. There are only a few exceptions to this pattern.

Nouns, unlike adjectives, usually have fixed gender, and most nouns are either inherently masculine or inherently feminine. Only for living beings, where there is a direct correspondence between gender and sex, is it possible to derive a feminine noun from a masculine noun by the addition of *-a*. Some examples:

Masculine	Feminine	
bġel	*beġla*	'mule'
dib	*diba*	'wolf'
dellal	*dellala*	'auctioneer'
ḍif	*ḍifa*	'guest'
fqi	*fqiha*[6]	'teacher'
hežžal	*hežžala*	'widower; widow'
malik	*malika*	'king; queen'
qerd	*qerda*	'monkey'
rbib	*rbiba*	'stepson; stepdaughter'
xal	*xala*	'maternal uncle; maternal aunt'
ġul	*ġula*	'ogre; ogress'
ɛemm	*ɛemma*	'paternal uncle; paternal aunt'
ɛewd	*ɛewda*	'horse; mare'

This process is of limited extension. For the more fundamental human male-female correspondences there are usually separate nouns for the male and female; e.g., *weld* 'boy' and *bent* 'girl', *ṛažel* 'man' and *mṛa* 'woman'. The same is true for animals; e.g., collective *bqeṛ* 'cattle', *beqṛa* 'cow', *tuṛ* 'bull', where the feminine *beqṛa* is derived from the collective *bqeṛ* rather than from the masculine singular *tuṛ*. Among animals, such sex-gender word pairs exist only for the larger and more common ones; e.g., *l-beṛṭaḷ wled tlata de-l-biḍat* 'the sparrow laid three eggs', where a grammatically masculine noun *beṛṭaḷ* refers to a biologically female living being.

[6] Note the change of the stem form, with the addition of *h*, in the feminine.

(a) **Feminine Nouns Not Ending in** *-a*: In general, names of towns and countries are feminine; e.g., *fas* 'Fez', *maṣeṛ* 'Egypt'. The exceptions to this rule must be learned as individual lexical items; e.g., *ṛ-ṛbaṭ* 'Rabat' is masculine. Nouns referring specifically to women, including personal names, are always feminine; e.g., *bent* 'girl, daughter', *xadem* 'female servant', the woman's name *zineb*. Nouns of the derivational pattern illustrated by *tafexxaṛet*[7] '(profession of) pottery making' are also feminine.

In addition to the categories mentioned above, there are a few feminine nouns not ending in *-a* which must be memorized as individual lexical items. The most common are:

blad	'town, country'	*ṣuf*	'wool'
ḍaṛ	'house'	*šemš*	'sun'
kerš	'belly'	*ṭṛiq*	'road, way'
left	'turnip(s)'	*wden*	'ear'
ḷeṛḍ	'earth'	*xatem*	'ring'
mut	'death'	*yedd*	'hand'
moġṛeb	'prayer (at sunset)'	*zit*	'oil'
naṛ	'fire, hell'	*žahennam*	'hell, gehenna'
nas[8]	'people'	*ġlem (ġnem)*	'sheep' (collective)
nefs	'soul, spirit, self-respect'	*ḥanut*	'shop'
rneb[9]	'hare'	*ɛegṛeb*	'scorpion'
ṛuḥ	'soul, spirit'	*ɛenkbut*	'spider web'
ržel	'foot, leg'	*ɛeyn*	'eye; spring (of water)'
ṣif[10]	'harvest'		

The following nouns are sometimes masculine and sometimes feminine, depending on the speaker.

[7] See pp. 88-89.

[8] Also plural, see

[9] Singular and collective.

[10] Masculine with the meaning 'summer'.

bab	'door'	*mus*	'knife, razor'
bit	'room'	*sekkin*	'large knife'
keṛmuṣ	'fig(s)'	*žameع*	'mosque'
lḥem	'meat'		

(b) **Masculine Nouns Ending in** *-a*: These nouns must be memorized as individual lexical items. The majority of them are short nouns on the pattern *CCa* from final-weak roots. The most common are:

baba	'father'	*ṛḍa*	'acquiescence'
baša	'pasha'	*ṛža*	'hope'
ḅḅa	'father'	*ṛwa*	'bouillon; rain'
bha	'beauty'	*sma*[11]	'sky'
bka	'(act of) weeping'	*šqa*	'difficulty, bother'
bla	'misfortune'	*šra*	'purchase, purchasing'
dra	'rust'	*ṭḷa*	'(action of) painting'
ḍṛa[11]	'maize'	*wfa*	'fidelity' (to promise)
fna	'annihilation'	*xa*	'brother'
gza	'right' (to the use of a piece of mortmain property)	*xlifa*	'caliph'
hna	'peace, tranquility'	*xṛa*	'feces' ('s--t')
hwa	'air'	*xṭa*	'fault, error'
lġa	'voice, sound'	*xwa*	'emptiness, nothingness'
ma	'water'	*zna*	'adultery'
msa	'evening'	*ġla*	'highness' (of prices)
nqa	'cleanness'	*ġna*	'song, singing'
nša	'starch'		
qḍa	'fate'		

[11] Also feminine.

ḥṣa	'counting, enumeration'	*Ɛra*	'nudity'
ḥya	'modesty, shame'	*Ɛwa*	'yelping'
Ɛma	'blindness'	*Ɛya*	'fatigue'

II. Number — The Dual

The dual is formed by adding the ending *-ayn* to the singular; e.g., *tulut* '(one) third', *tulutayn* 'two thirds'. In the case of feminine nouns ending in *-a*, the ending is added to the combining form of the noun[12]; e.g., *saƐa* 'hour', *saƐtayn* 'two hours'.

The dual ending is used only with the numerals *mya* '(one) hundred', and *alef* '(one) thousand', with the fraction pattern *FuƐuL*[13] from one third through one tenth, and with a limited number of nouns, all of which are units of measure of some sort, either of time, space, or quantity. The nouns to which the dual ending can be added must be memorized as individual lexical items. The most common are included in the list below.

Numerals and Fractions

alef	'(one) thousand'	*alfayn*	'two thousand'
mya	'(one) hundred'	*myatayn*	'two hundred'
tulut	'(one) third'	*tulutayn*	'two thirds'
ṛubuƐ	'(one) fourth'	*ṛubuƐayn*	'two fourths'
xumus	'(one) fifth'	*xumusayn*	'two fifths'
sudus	'(one) sixth'	*sudusayn*	'two sixths'
tumun	'(one) eighth'	*tumunayn*	'two eighths'
tusuƐ	'(one) ninth'	*tusuƐayn*	'two ninths'
Ɛušuṛ	'(one) tenth'	*Ɛušuṛayn*	'two tenths'

Nouns of Measure

nuba	'(one) time, once'	*nubtayn*	'twice, two times'
qṣem	'five minutes'	*qeṣmayn*	'ten minutes'

[12]For the combining form of the noun, see pp. 128-133.

[13]For the fractions, see p. 94.

ṛṭeḷ	'(one) pound'	*ṛeṭḷayn*	'two pounds'
saƐa	'(one) hour'	*saƐtayn*	'two hours'
šber	'(one) span'	*šebrayn*	'two spans'
šheṛ	'(one) month'	*šehṛayn*	'two months'
wqiya	'(one) ounce'	*wqiytayn*	'two ounces'
yum	'(one) day'	*yumayn*	'two days'
Ɛam	'year'	*Ɛamayn*	'two years'

III. Number — The Plural

There are two major plural types among Moroccan nouns and adjectives: **sound plurals** and **broken plurals**. Plurals formed by the addition of an ending without any basic change in the stem of the noun or adjective to which it is added are called sound plurals; e.g., *feṛḥan* pl. *feṛḥanin* 'happy', *neǆǆaṛ* pl. *neǆǆaṛa* 'carpenters', *qwilba* pl. *qwilbat* 'suppositories'. Plurals formed by an internal change in the stem, accompanied or not by the addition of an ending, are called broken plurals; e.g., *bermil* pl. *bramel* 'barrels', *bab* pl. *biban* 'doors'.

It is usually not possible to determine from the singular form whether a given word has a sound or a broken plural. Even given the general type, it is often ambiguous as to what sub-type of sound or broken plural is involved. It is not uncommon for a word to have two or more plurals, sometimes equivalent in meaning, sometimes different in meaning. For example the three plurals *xeddamin* 'working', *xeddama* 'workers', and *xdadem,* units of agricultural land measurement, have the common singular *xeddam*.

There are three sound plural endings: *-in, -a,*[14] and *-(a)t*. The usual phenomena of elision and inversion occur; e.g., *meslem* 'Moslem', pl. *mselmin*. With words ending in *-i,* the *-i* is changed to *y* or has *y* added to it according to the same patterns described for the addition of the feminine ending *-a*[15]; e.g., *šari* 'having bought' pl. *šaryin,* and *mešri* 'bought' pl. *mešriyin*.[16] There are a large number of broken plural patterns, many of which are not easily classifiable.

[14]This plural ending, although the same in form, is not to be confused with the feminine ending *-a,* for which see pp. 95-97.

[15]For the addition of the feminine ending *-a* to masculine forms ending in *-i,* see pp. 95-96.

Except for the forms outlined below, the various singular noun and adjective patterns are ambiguous as to plural type. For example both *bhima* 'beast' (of burden) and *rtila* 'spider' are of the pattern *FƐiLa,* but the plural of *bhima* is *bhayem* while the plural of *rtila* is *rtilat.*

1. **Sound Plurals With** ***-in:***[16] This ending occurs almost exclusively with adjectives or adjectives which have come to be used as nouns.[17] There are eleven word classes which take it. Only the first two of these classes, the participles and the nisbas, include a large number of words. The other nine classes have only about a hundred items each. The classes are:

(a) **The Participles Except Those of Measure I Used as Nouns:**[18] The following are some typical examples. Classicized participles[19] also form their plurals regularly according to this pattern.

Masculine Singular		**Plural**	
meḍṛub	(passive participle of *ḍṛeb* 'to hit, to beat')	*meḍṛubin*	'having been beaten'
kateb[20]	(active participle of *kteb* 'to write')	*katbin*	'having written'
mqeddem	(participle of *qeddem* 'to present'	*mqeddmin*	'having presented, having been presented; foreman, chief'
nasi	(active participle of *nsa* 'to forget')	*nasyin*	'having forgotten'
msemmi	(participle of *semma* 'to name')	*msemmyin*	'having named, having been named'

---

[16] When preceded by *y,* the plural ending *-in* is often replaced by *-en,* especially in rapid conversation; e.g., both *šaryen* and *šaryin* are heard as the plural of *šari* 'having bought', both *mešriyen* and *mešriyin* are heard as the plural of *mešri* 'bought', and both *ʔandalusiyen* and *ʔandalusiyin* are heard as the plural of *ʔandalusi* 'Andalusian'.

[17] For the use of adjectives as nouns, see p. 204.

[18] When used as nouns both the active and passive participles of Measure I verbs usually have broken plurals. See pp. 113-114, 122.

[19] For classicized participles, see p. 59.

[20] As a noun meaning 'secretary', *kateb* has the broken plural *kottab.*

mebni	(passive participle of *bna* 'to build')	*mebniyin*	'having been built'
mufettiš	(classicized participle of *fetteš* 'to inspect, to search')	*mufettišin*	'inspector'

(b) **All Nisba Adjectives and Some Nisba Nouns:**[21] As in the case of the feminine ending *-a,* a *y* is added to the stem before the ending *-in.*[22] Some examples:

Masculine Singular	Plural	
nefsi	*nefsiyin*	'self-respecting'
nqi	*nqiyin*	'clean'
žanubi	*žanubiyin*	'southern'
ʔali	*ʔaliyin*	'musician'
šṭaṭbi[23]	*šṭaṭbiyin*	'street-sweeper'

(c) **All Diminutive Adjectives:** For example, msc. sg. *ṣġiweṛ* pl. *ṣġiwṛin* 'little, small', msc. sg. *zwiwen* pl. *zwiwnin* 'nice, pretty', etc. In a few rare cases diminutive nouns referring directly to human males also take the plural ending *-in,* for example *ṛwižel* 'little man', pl. *ṛwižlin.*[24]

(d) **The Ordinal Numerals:** For example msc. sg. *talet* pl. *taltin* 'third', etc.

[21] As has been noted above, pp. 72-74, the nisba is basically an adjective, but a large number of nisbas have become specialized as nouns and as such often have broken plurals. Geographical nisbas commonly have separate plurals for the noun and adjective functions; e.g., *meṣṛi* 'Egyptian', adj. pl. *meṣṛiyin,* noun pl. *mṣaṛwa.*

[22] See p. 96, cf. footnote 16.

[23] Many speakers use this word only in the sense of 'broom maker', in which case it has the plural *šṭaṭbiya.*

[24] The regular plural ending *-at* of diminutive nouns (see p. 107) is also possible in such cases, thus *ṛwižlat* 'little men'.

(e) **Adjectives of the *FeƐLan* Pattern:**[25] There are not many adjectives of this sort. For example, msc. sg. *keslan* pl. *keslanin* 'lazy', msc. sg. *ḥešman* pl. *ḥešmanin* 'shy', etc.

(f) **Adjectives of the *FeƐƐaL* Pattern:**[26] For example, msc. sg. *heḍḍaṛ* pl. *heḍḍaṛin* 'talkative', msc. sg. *ṭemmaƐ* pl. *ṭemmaƐin* 'envious', etc.

(g) **Adjectives of the *meFƐaL* Pattern:**[27] For example, msc. sg. *mebrad* pl. *mebradin* 'cold-natured, sensitive to the cold', msc. sg. *mehrar* pl. *mehrarin* 'ticklish', etc.

(h) **Some Adjectives of the *FƐiL* Pattern:** There is no way of predicting from the form or meaning whether a given *FƐiL* adjective has a broken plural or a plural with *-in,* and the plurals of these words must be learned as vocabulary items; e.g., *ṛfiƐ* 'good, excellent', pl. *ṛfiƐin.* Many adjectives of the *FƐiL* pattern take either a broken plural or the plural in *-in,* with no difference in meaning; e.g., *bnin* 'delicious, tasty', pl. *bninin* or *bnan.*[28]

(i) **Verbal Adjectives of the *FeƐLaC* Pattern:** Such adjectives are from quadriliteral roots and bear the same relation to quadriliteral roots as the *FeƐƐaL* pattern bears to triliteral roots (see pp. 66-67). An example, *meṛmad* 'clumsy', pl. *meṛmadin.*

(j) **Adjectives on the Pattern *FiyyeL*:** There are only a few such adjectives. The most common are:

Masculine Singular	**Plural**	
hiyyen	*hiyynin*	'easy'
kiyyes	*kiyysin*	'clever, subtle'
liyyen	*liyynin*	'soft'
miyyet[29]	*miyytin*	'dead'

[25] Note, however, that not all words of the *FeƐLan* pattern are adjectives; e.g., the verbal noun *beṭlan* 'cessation'.

[26] Nouns of the *FeƐƐaL* pattern take either broken plurals or plurals in *-a;* e.g., *xeddam* with adj. pl. *xeddamin* 'working', noun pl. *xeddama* 'workers', noun pl. *xdadem* unit of measurement of agricultural land.

[27] There are not many such adjectives. Nouns, as opposed to adjectives, of the *meFƐaL* pattern take broken plurals; e.g., *mexṭaf* 'hook' pl. *mxaṭef.*

[28] For the broken plural of *FƐiL* adjectives, see p. 117.

[29] As a noun *miyyet* has the plural *muta* 'corpses, dead ones'.

(k) **Non-Patterned:** There are a small number of adjectives and nouns with a plural in *-in* and no consistent common singular pattern. These words must be learned as vocabulary items. The most common are:

Masculine Singular	**Plural**	
axoṛ	*oxṛin*	'other'
merr (or *meṛṛ*)	*merrin* (*meṛṛin*)	'bitter'
messus	*messusin*	'tasteless, insipid'
ṛžel	*režlin*	'foot, leg'
sxun[30]	*sxunin*	'hot'
(*waled*)[31]	*waldin*	'parents'
wden	*wednin*	'ear'
yedd	*yeddin*	'hand'
zin	*zinin*	'pretty'
ḥaṛṛ	*ḥaṛṛin*	'hot, spicy'
ḥlu	*ḥluwin*	'sweet'
ḥoṛṛ[32]	*ḥoṛṛin*	'free'
ḥeyy	*ḥeyyin*	'alive'
ɛwež[33]	*ɛewžin*	'crooked, twisted'
ɛeyn	*ɛeynin*	'eye'

2. **Sound Plurals With *-a*:** This ending occurs only with a limited number of nouns and never with adjectives. There are three classes which take it. All three classes consist entirely of nouns referring to persons engaged in either a professional or a habitual activity. Nouns of the first two categories which take

[30] *sxun* also has the plural form *sxan*.

[31] Actually the active participle of *wled* 'to bear, to give birth to'. A classicized singular *walid* is used in the sense of 'father'.

[32] As a noun, *ḥoṛṛ* has the plural *ḥṛaṛ* 'free ones, free people'.

[33] *ɛiwež* is more commonly heard than *ɛewžin* as the plural of *ɛwež*.

the plural *-a* are common while the third category is represented by only a handful of items. The classes are as follows.

(a) The *FeƐƐaL* Noun Pattern of Professional or Habitual Activity:[34] Some typical examples of this pattern:

Masculine Singular	Plural	
bennay	*bennaya*	'mason'
beqqal	*beqqala*	'grocer'
keddab	*keddaba*	'liar'
nežžaṛ	*nežžaṛa*	'carpenter'
ṭeḷḷab	*ṭeḷḷaba*	'beggar'

(b) Nouns Ending in *-i*, Other Than Participles, Which Refer to Professional or Habitual Activity:[35] These nouns are mostly nisbas formed from a broken plural base; e.g., *bramel* 'barrels', nisba *bramli* 'barrel maker', plural *bramliya*. There are also occasional examples of nisbas from a singular noun; e.g., *bḥeṛ* 'sea', nisba *beḥri*[36] 'sailor', plural *beḥriya*. A few foreign borrowings complete the list; e.g., *bombi* 'fireman', plural *bombiya,* from French "pompier", 'fireman'. Nouns of this sort add *y* to the stem before the plural ending *-a*. Some examples:

Masculine Singular	Plural	
bnadri	*bnadriya*	'tambourine player'
dmanži	*dmanžiya*	'helmsman'
dnadni	*dnadniya*	'musician'
flayki	*flaykiya*	'boatman'

[34] Other nouns of this pattern usually have broken plurals; e.g., *berrad* 'teapot', pl. *brared;* see pp. 113-114 for such broken plurals. Adjectives of this pattern have a plural in *-in,* cf. p. 104.

[35] Cf. pp. 74-78, **The Nisba of Profession and Personal Characteristic.** Measure I participles, whether ending in *i* or not, which are used as nouns usually have broken plurals; e.g., *šareb* 'lip', pl. *šwareb*. Other nouns and adjectives, including participles, ending in *i* take either a broken plural or a plural in *-in;* e.g., *muḥami* 'lawyer', pl. *muḥamiyin*.

[36] As an adjective meaning 'maritime, marine', the plural of *beḥri* is *beḥriyin,* as is regular for nisba adjectives, see p. 103.

ṣwabni	*ṣwabniya*	'soap vendor'
šṭaṭbi[37]	*šṭaṭbiya*	'broom maker'

(c) **The Quadriliteral Noun Pattern** *FeƐLaC*: This is the quadriliteral equivalent of the triliteral *FeƐƐaL* pattern. There are very few nouns of this sort. The most common is *ṣemṣaṛ* pl. *ṣemṣaṛa* 'broker, agent, go-between' (in a business transaction).

3. **Sound Plurals With** *-(a)t*: This ending is common with nouns but occurs only rarely with adjectives. The form varies from *-t* to *-at* depending on the stem to which the ending is attached. Stems ending in a consonant take *-at,* for example *žwab* 'answer' pl. *žwabat,* and those ending in *-a* take *-t,* for example *Ɛemma* 'paternal aunt' pl. *Ɛemmat.* Stems ending in a vowel, usually *i* or *u* but occasionally *a,* add a *y* or a *w* before the ending; e.g., *kilu* 'kilogram, kilometer', plural *kiluyat.*

The plural ending *-(a)t* is scarcely used with adjectives. Of the adjectives which form a sound plural, the form with *-in* is usually used for both masculine and feminine plural nouns; e.g., *wlad oxṛin* 'other boys' and *bnat oxṛin* 'other girls'. Theoretically any feminine adjective in *-a* forms a plural by adding *-t,* but the only circumstances where this plural is used is with a preceding feminine noun which also has the plural ending *-at,* for example *ši-ḥkayat meġṛibiyat* 'some Moroccan stories', *le-Ɛyalat l-meƐṛudat* 'the invited women', *bnat fasiyat* 'girls from Fez'.

The classes of nouns which form their plural with the ending *-(a)t* are as follows.

(a) **All Diminutive Nouns:**[38] Some typical examples:

Singular	**Plural**	
bnita, from *bent*	*bnitat*	'little girl'
ydida, from *yedd*	*ydidat*	'little hand'
qdira, from *qedra*	*qdirat*	'little pot'
xwidem, from *xadem*	*xwidmat*	'little (girl) servant'

[37] Some speakers also have the meaning 'street sweeper' for *šṭaṭbi,* in addition to the meaning 'broom maker'. In the sense of 'street sweeper' the plural is *šṭaṭbiyin.*

[38] When a diminutive noun specifically refers to a human male, the plural ending *-in* is sometimes used as well; e.g., *ṛwižel* 'little man' pl. *ṛwižlin, xwidem* pl. *xwidmin* 'little (boy) servants'. For the diminutives, see pp. 81-85.

(b) **All Nouns of Unity from Collectives:**[39] Some typical examples:

Singular	**Plural**	
biḍa, coll. *biḍ*	*biḍat*	'egg'
beqqa, coll. *beqq*	*beqqat*	'bug'
beṛquqa, coll. *beṛquq*	*beṛquqat*	'plum'
ṭuba, coll. *ṭub*	*ṭubat*	'brick'
xuxa, coll. *xux*	*xuxat*	'peach'

(c) **Almost All Nouns Ending in** *-iya*: Some examples:

Singular	**Plural**	
ḍḥiya	*ḍḥiyat*	'sacrifice'
fuqiya	*fuqiyat*	type of garment
hdiya	*hdiyat*	'gift'
kommiya	*kommiyat*	'(curved) dagger'
namusiya	*namusiyat*	'bed'
šexṣiya	*šexṣiyat*	'personality'
ẓṛaybiya	*ẓṛaybiyat*	'(female) carpet maker'

There are very few exceptions to this pattern. None of the exceptions refer to living beings. The most common exceptions are listed below. All of them have the regular plural in *-(a)t* in addition to the broken plural listed here.

Singular	**Broken Plural**	
bestiliya	*bsatel*	'tub'
faṛažiya	*fwaṛež*	kind of tunic
fetqiya	*ftaqi*	'slat'
menṣuṛiya	*mnaṣeṛ*	kind of garment

[39]For collective nouns and the nouns of unity, see pp. 78-80.

mṣebḥiya	*mṣabeḥ*	kind of lamp
mexfiya	*mxafi*	kind of platter
meƐṣiya	*mƐaṣi*	act of disobedience, 'sin'
qaḍiya	*qaḍaya*	'affair, lawsuit'
qeṣṛiya	*qṣaṛi*	kind of large earthenware bowl
ṣṭeṛmiya	*ṣṭaṛem*	'(round) cushion'
teṛṛabiya	*tṛaṛeb*	kind of hamper
xeddiya	*xdadi*	'(square) cushion'
ẓeṛbiya	*ẓṛabi*	'carpet'
žebbaniya	*žbaben*	'bowl'

(d) **Almost All Nouns of the** *FeƐƐaLa* **Pattern Which Refer to Human Females:** The only common exceptions are *neggafa* pl. *ngagef,* a woman in charge of certain functions during family festivals such as weddings, etc., and *ṭiyyaba* 'masseuse', with pl. either *ṭyayeb* or *ṭiyyabat.* Some typical examples of the regular plural:

Singular	**Plural**	
dellala	*dellalat*	'woman auctioneer'
ṛebbaya	*ṛebbayat*	'governess'
xebbaza	*xebbazat*	'woman baker'
ġezzala	*ġezzalat*	'woman spinner'
ḥeṣṣaḍa	*ḥeṣṣaḍat*	'woman harvester'

Nouns of the *FeƐƐaLa* pattern which do not refer to human females are unpredictable as to plural. Some form their plural with *-(a)t,* for example *žeffafa* pl. *žeffafat* 'sponge', some have two plurals, one with the ending *-(a)t* and the other broken, for example *šeṭṭaba* pl. *šṭaṭeb* or *šeṭṭabat* 'broom', while others have only broken plurals, for example *sebbala* pl. *sbabel*[40] 'fountain'. Plurals of this sort have to be learned individually as lexical items.

(e) **Sex-Gender Pairs:** In pairs such as *malik* 'king' and *malika* 'queen', where the feminine noun is derived from the masculine noun by the addition of *-a*

[40]Some speakers also make a regular plural *sebbalat* for this word.

and where the grammatical difference of masculine-feminine corresponds to the biological difference of male-female,[41] the feminine noun usually forms its plural with *-(a)t*.[42] The only common exceptions are *šqiqa* '(full-blood) sister' pl. *šqayeq*, derived from *šqiq* '(full-blood) brother', and *Ɛguza* 'old woman' pl. *Ɛgayez* or *Ɛgużat*, derived from *Ɛguz* 'old man'. Some common examples of the regular plural with *-(a)t* are:

Singular		Plural	
hežžala		*hežžalat*	'widow'
hežžal	'widower'		
malika		*malikat*	'queen'
malik	'king'		
rbiba		*rbibat*	'stepdaughter'
rbib	'stepson'		
xṛufa		*xṛufat*	'lamb' (female)
xṛuf	'lamb' (male)		
ḥellufa		*ḥellufat*	'sow'
ḥelluf	'boar'		

In many cases the nouns treated under **(c)** and **(d)** immediately above, nouns ending in *-iya* and nouns on the pattern of *FeƐƐaLa* which refer to human females, are also logically members of the present category. Many nouns ending in *-iya* are the feminine-female member of noun pairs such as *slugi* '(male) greyhound' and *slugiya* '(female) greyhound'. The same is true of many nouns on the *FeƐƐaLa* pattern, for example *xeddam* '(male) worker' and *xeddama* '(female) worker'.

(f) The Nouns of Instance ***FeƐLa*** **and** ***teFƐiLa*****:**[43] Such nouns of instance are quite numerous, and only a few of them have broken plurals. Those which have broken plurals must be learned individually as lexical items. Some examples of the regular plural are:

---

[41] For the derivation of sex-gender pairs, see p. 97.

[42] The masculine member of such pairs almost invariably has a broken plural, for example *hežžal* 'widower', pl. *hžažel*.

[43] For the nouns of instance, see pp. 65-66. There are many nouns on the pattern of *FeƐLa* which are not nouns of instance. The plural form of such nouns is unpredictable, sometimes with *-(a)t* as in *žebha* pl. *žebhat* 'forehead', sometimes broken as in *leḥya* pl. *lḥi* 'beard', and sometimes either broken or with *-(a)t* as in *gebḍa* pl. *gebḍat* or *gbaḍi* 'handle'.

Singular	**Plural**	
defƐa, from *dfeƐ* 'to push'	*defƐat*	'push'
deqqa, from *deqq* 'to hit'	*deqqat*	'blow'
kedba, from *kdeb* 'to lie'	*kedbat*	'lie, falsehood'
ṛežƐa, from *ṛžeƐ* 'to return'	*ṛežƐat*	'return'
xedma, from *xdem* 'to work'	*xedmat*	'work'
ġesla, from *ġsel* 'to wash'	*ġeslat*	'washing'
tebsima, from *tbessem* 'to smile'	*tebsimat*	'smile'
tedƐima, from *deƐƐem* 'to stay, to support'	*tedƐimat*	'stay, support'
tešlila, from *šellel* 'to rinse'	*tešlilat*	'rinsing'

(g) All nouns of the Patterns *mFaƐLa, muFaƐaLa, tFeƐya,* **and** *tFeƐLiCa*: These are all verbal noun types.[44] Some examples:

Singular	**Plural**	
mdabza	*mdabzat*	'quarrel'
mlaqya	*mlaqyat*	'meeting'
mnaqša	*mnaqšat*	'discussion'
mšabha	*mšabhat*	'resemblance'
mwaƐda	*mwaƐdat*	'promise'
muḍahaṛa	*muḍahaṛat*	'(political) demonstration'
mušawaṛa	*mušawaṛat*	'consultation'
muƐahada	*muƐahadat*	'treaty'
tsenya	*tsenyat*	'waiting'
tƐezya	*tƐezyat*	'condolence'
tbehdila	*tbehdilat*	'humiliation'
tfernisa	*tfernisat*	'grin'

[44] *mFaƐLa* is also the pattern for the feminine participle of Measure III verbs. For verbal nouns, see pp. 60-65.

tleḥliḥa	*tleḥliḥat*	'flattery'
tṣeṛfiqa	*tṣeṛfiqat*	'slap'

(h) **All Feminine Participles Used as Nouns, Except the Active Participle of Measure I:**[45] Some typical examples:

Singular	Plural	
meṛfuda	*meṛfudat*	'vow'
metƐellma	*metƐellmat*	'maid servant'
mḥennša	*mḥennšat*	kind of cake
mƐeddya	*mƐeddyat*	'raft'

(i) **Most Nouns Ending in** *-u*: These nouns add *w* or *y* to the stem before adding *-at*. The usual pattern is to add *w*. There is also sometimes variation between *w* and *y* in the same word from speaker to speaker. Some examples:

Singular	Plural	
biru	*biruwat*	'office'
bnu	*bnuwat*	'tire'
gaṛṛu	*gaṛṛuwat, -yat*	'cigaret'
maryu	*maryuwat*	'wardrobe'
qbu	*qbuwat*	'niche'
ṭabḷu	*ṭabḷuwat*	'blackboard'

There are only a limited number of exceptions to this pattern. The most common are:

Singular	Plural	
bhu	*bhawat*	'(wall) niche'
bidu	*biduwat, bwada*	'can'

[45] Measure I feminine active participles used as nouns sometimes have broken plurals, for example *qabla* pl. *qwabel* 'midwife'.

dlu	*delwan, dlawi*	'bucket'
nimiru	*-wat, -yat, nwamer*	'number'
xu	*xut, xwan*	'brother'
ǯṛu	*ǯṛa*	'panther cub'
Ɛdu	*Ɛedyan*	'enemy'

(j) **Most Nouns on the Pattern of** *FƐa*: These nouns add *w* or *y* before the *-at* in the same manner as nouns ending in *-u*. For example, *bṛa* pl. *bṛawat* 'letter', *rwa* pl. *rwayat* 'stable', *sma* pl. *smawat* 'sky', *ġda* pl. *ġdawat* 'noon meal'. The most common exceptions are:

Singular	Plural	
dwa	*-yat, duyan, ʔadwiya*	'medicine'
qfa	*-wat, qfi*	'nape' (of neck)
ṣḷa	*-wat, ṣaḷawat*	'prayer'

(k) **Miscellaneous:** There are a large number of nouns which form their plural in *-(a)t* which are not readily classifiable according to form. Foreign words especially tend to take the plural ending *-(a)t*, for example *fabrika* pl. *fabrikat* 'factory', *tilifun* pl. *tilifunat* 'telephone', etc.

4. **The Broken Plural:** Most nouns, and many adjectives, have broken plurals. There are approximately forty different broken plural patterns. The four most common patterns include the great majority of all nouns and adjectives which take broken plurals, another dozen occur moderately often, while the remaining patterns are met with only occasionally. The most common broken plural patterns, along with the singular patterns to which they correspond, are listed below. The order of presentation corresponds approximately to the frequency of occurrence of the plural form. Note that a given broken plural pattern may come from several different singular patterns and that a given singular pattern may correspond to several different broken plural patterns.

(a) **The Plural Pattern** *CCaCeC*: This pattern accounts for about half of all broken plurals. It is typically the plural of four-consonant words, regardless of whether the four consonants come from a quadriliteral root or from a triliteral root with a consonantal affix. The four-consonant singulars which take this plural typically have patterns which begin with *CeCC-* or *CoCC-*, but the specific vowel which occurs between the third and fourth consonants or the presence of *-a*, *-i*, or *-iya* as an ending is of no importance with respect to the plural form. The following examples illustrate the wide variety of vowel patterns in four-consonant singular nouns which have the plural pattern *CCaCeC*.

Singular	Plural	
fendeq	*fnadeq*	'hotel'
medfeɛ	*mdafeɛ*	'canon'
šeṛžem	*šṛažem*	'window'
fekṛun	*fkaṛen*	'turtle'
melyun	*mlayen*	'million'
qenfud	*qnafed*	'hedgehog'
menšaṛ	*mnašeṛ*	'saw'
serwal	*srawel*	'(pair of) trousers'
ɛonwan	*ɛnawen*	'address'
berrad	*brared*	'teapot'
konnaš	*knaneš*	'notebook'
qeṛṛan	*qṛaṛen*	'cuckold'
mellasa	*mlales*	'trowel'
žellaba	*žlaleb*	king of garment
bermil	*bramel*	'barrel'
meskin	*msaken*	'poor'
beṛwiṭa	*bṛaweṭ*	'wheelbarrow'
zeɛlula	*zɛalel*	'(child's) swing'
mṭeṛqa	*mṭaṛeq*	'hammer'
mḍeḷḷ	*mḍaḷḷ* [46]	'umbrella'
žebbaniya	*žbaben*	'bowl'

Nouns with *ww* or *yy* as the two middle consonants of the singular usually have *u* before the *ww* and *i* before the *yy* but still allow plurals of this pattern; for example, *nuwwala* pl. *nwawel* 'hut', *ṭiyyaba* pl. *ṭyayeb* 'masseuse'. In a few cases one of the consonants of the singular is changed; e.g., *mḍemma* pl. *mḍayem* or *mḍamm* '(woman's) belt', *mxedda* pl. *mxayed* or *mxadd* 'cushion, pillow'.

[46] When the last two consonants are the same, the *e* between them is sometimes dropped out.

The plural pattern *CCaCeC* is also widely derived from singulars with three consonants; e.g., *ṛḍuma* 'bottle' pl. *ṛḍayem*. The typical case is for a *w* or *y* to be added to the three consonants of the singular noun to fill out the four consonants of the plural pattern, although there are occasional unpredictable exceptions; e.g., *ġobṛa* 'dust' pl. *ġbabeṛ* 'clouds of dust'. Most plurals of the sort which add a consonant to fill out the four consonants of the plural pattern derive from singular nouns which have an *a*, an *i*, or a *u* between their first and second consonants or between their second and third consonants, or both, for example *šareb* pl. *šwareb* 'lip', *nfula* pl. *nfayel* 'ticket', *zuhaga* pl. *zwaheg* 'earring', *faṛažiya* pl. *fwaṛež*, a kind of garment.

If an *a*, an *i*, or a *u* occurs after the first consonant of the singular, regardless of what vowels occur further in the word, the usual case is for the plural to be of the form *CwaCeC* if the singular has *a* or *u* after the first consonant and *CyaCeC* if it has *i*. Some examples:

Singular	Plural	
xatem	*xwatem*	'ring'
žameƐ	*žwameƐ*	'mosque'
kaṛṭa	*kwaṛeṭ*	'(playing) card'
luleb	*lwaleb*	'screw'
giṭun	*gyaṭen*	'tent'
nišan	*nyašen*	'target'

The plural pattern *CyaCeC* comes from no other kind of singular pattern. For the plural pattern *CwaCeC* to come from some other kind of singular pattern is rare, although there are a few examples, as *rneb* pl. *rwaneb* 'rabbit', *ṣemƐa* pl. *ṣwameƐ* 'minaret', *qiṛaṭ* pl. *qwaṛeṭ* 'carat'.

The other common plural of pattern *CCaCeC* from singular nouns with three consonants has the specific pattern *CCayeC*, with *y* being added between the second and third consonants of the singular to fill out the four consonants of the plural pattern, for example *msid* pl. *msayed* 'Koranic school'. This plural is usually formed from singular nouns which have no vowel between the first and second consonants and *a*, *i*, or *u* between the second and third consonants. Some examples:

Singular	Plural	
bḷaṣa	*bḷayeṣ*	'place'
bzim	*bzayem*	'belt-buckle'
fluka	*flayek*	'boat'
ftila	*ftayel*	'wick'

mṛaṛ	*mṛayeṛ*	'bile'
Ɛguz	*Ɛgayez*	'old man'

A few nouns on the pattern of *FeƐLa* also have the plural pattern *CCayeC,* for example *sebba* pl. *sbayeb* 'reason'. A few plurals on the pattern of *CCayeC* also come from singular nouns which have *a, i,* or *u* between the first and second consonants as well as between the second and third consonants of the singular,[47] for example *žarima* pl. *žrayem* 'crime'. For the plural pattern *CCayeC* to come from any other singular type is rare although there are a few cases, for example *ṭbeƐ* pl. *ṭbayeƐ* 'melody'.

There are occasional cases of a four-consonant plural pattern *CCaweC* coming from a singular noun with three consonants, for example *žnaḥ* pl. *žnaweḥ* 'wing'.

The plural pattern *CCaCeC* derived from singular nouns with more than four or fewer than three consonants is rare, and only a few examples can be found. Some common ones are:

Singular	Plural	
mṭeṛṛba	*mṭaṛeb*	'mattress'
riḥa	*rwayeḥ*	'odor'
saƐa	*swayeƐ*	'hour'
žiha	*žwayeh*	'side, direction'
ḥaža	*ḥwayež*	'thing; clothes' (pl. only)

(b) The Plural Pattern *FƐaL*: The plural pattern *FƐaL* corresponds to six different triconsonantal singular patterns. Of these, singulars of the patterns *FaƐeL* and *FƐuLi* only rarely have plurals in *FƐaL,* for example *ṣaḥeb* pl. *ṣḥab* 'friend', *slugi* pl. *slag* 'greyhound'. The other four patterns are:

(1) Singular Pattern *FeƐL, FoƐL*:

Singular	Plural	
bent	*bnat*	'girl, daughter'
kelb	*klab*	'dog'
moxx	*mxax*	'brain'

[47] Although broken plurals from this kind of singular usually have the pattern *CwaCeC* or *CyaCeC* rather than *CCayeC*. See above.

ṭeṛf	*ṭṛaf*	'piece'
ḥokk	*ḥkak*	'box'

One singular of this pattern alters one of its consonants in the plural, *fomm* pl. *fwam* 'mouth'.

(2) Singular Pattern *FƐiL*:[48]

Singular	Plural	
bƐid	*bƐad*	'far, distant'
mṛiḍ	*mṛaḍ*	'sick'
nsib	*nsab*	'brother-in-law' (wife's brother)
qdim	*qdam*	'old' (of things, not people)
smin	*sman*	'fat'

(3) Singular Pattern *FƐeL*, *FƐoL*:

Singular	Plural	
bġel	*bġal*	'mule'
mhed	*mhad*	'cradle'
šġol	*šġal*	'work'
žmel	*žmal*	'camel'

(4) Singular Pattern *FeƐLa*, *FoƐLa*:

Singular	Plural	
keƐba	*kƐab*	'ankle'
senna	*snan*	'tooth'

[48] Most adjectives of the pattern *FƐiL* have plurals in *FƐaL*, as in the examples given.

weṛqa	*wṛaq*	'paper'
ġorza	*ġraz*	'stitch' (in sewing)
ḥeyya	*ḥyay*	'viper'

The plural pattern *FƐaL* derived from singulars with fewer than three consonants always involves a *w* or a *y* as the second consonant of the plural pattern. There are two nouns with only one consonant each in the singular, *ma* pl. *myah* 'water', *ša* pl. *šyah* 'sheep'. All the other examples of this category are words which in the singular have a stable vowel between two consonants, either with or without the ending *-a*. Words with medial *a* are unpredictable as to whether the extra consonant of the plural is *w* or *y*, for example *xal* pl. *xwal* 'maternal uncle', *nab* pl. *nyab* 'fang'. Otherwise, a medial *i* usually implies *y* in the plural pattern, for example *dib* pl. *dyab* 'wolf', and a medial *u* implies *w* in the plural pattern, for example *ḍuw* pl. *ḍwaw* 'light'. The exceptional case of a *y* in the plural corresponding to a medial *u* in the singular is represented by *tub* pl. *tyab* 'cloth'. Some further examples:

Singular	Plural	
bir	*byar*	'well'
duḥ	*dwaḥ*	'cradle'
hul	*hwal*	'worry'
muža	*mwaž*	'wave'
naga	*nyag*	'female camel'
riḥ	*ryaḥ*	'wind'

(c) The Plural Pattern ***FƐaLi*****:** The majority of plurals of the pattern *FƐaLi* are derived from the singular pattern *FeƐLa, FoƐLa*. Some examples:

Singular	Plural	
deƐwa	*dƐawi*	'lawsuit'
noqṭa	*nqaṭi*	'point'
qebḍa	*qbaḍi*	'handle'
xenša	*xnaši*	'sack'
ḥofṛa	*ḥfaṛi*	'hole'

There are various examples of *FƐaLi* plurals from singular patterns other than *FeƐLa, FoƐLa*. A few show the same consonants in the plural as in the singular, for example:

Singular	Plural	
derri	*drari*	'boy' (in pl. 'children')
meṭwi	*mṭawi*	'tobacco pouch'
mexfiya	*mxafi*	kind of platter
seqqaya	*sqaqi*	'fountain'
ḥsiba	*ḥsabi*	'account, reckoning'

The example *dlu* pl. *dlawi* 'bucket' is anomalous. The words *škaya* pl. *škawi* 'complaint' and *tluya* pl. *tlawi* 'turning, twist' show a substitution of *w* in the plural for *y* in the singular. More regular are the sub-patterns *FwaLi* and *FyaLi* which show *w* or *y* as the second consonant of the plural pattern corresponding to *a, i,* or *u* after the initial consonant of the singular. Usually an *a* or a *u* in the singular implies *w* in the plural and an *i* in the singular implies a *y* in the plural, but the correspondence is not complete. Some examples:

Singular	Plural	
(with *Fa–*)		
dalya	*dwali*	'vine'
saqya	*swaqi*	'irrigation ditch, canal'
sarya	*swari*	'pillar, column'
ṭagiya	*ṭwagi*	'skullcap'
xamiya	*xwami*	'curtain' (in doorway)
ḥasi	*ḥwasi*	'well'
(with *Fi–*)		
lil(a)	*lyali*	'night'
mida	*myadi*	'table'
riḥiya	*rwaḥi*	'(woman's) slippers'
ṣiniya	*ṣwani*	'tray'

(with *Fu–*)

kuṛ(a)	*kwaṛi*	'ball'
zubya	*zwabi*	'brazier pit'

(d) **The Plural Pattern** *FƐuL*: This pattern bears a close relation with the following one *FƐuLa,* since a number of words form their plural indifferently in *FƐuL* or *FƐuLa,* for example *dik* pl. *dyuk* or *dyuka* 'rooster'. The plural pattern *FƐuL* is, however, more common than the pattern *FƐuLa.*

The two most common singular patterns are *FeƐL,* (or *FoƐL*) and *FƐeL,* for example *qelb* pl. *qlub* 'heart', *Ɛžel* pl. *Ɛžul* 'calf'. There are four other singular patterns with strong roots, all rare, as exemplified by *ḍeḷƐa* pl. *ḍḷuƐ* 'rib', *draƐ* pl. *druƐ* 'cubit', *mdina* pl. *mdun* 'city', and *šahed* pl. *šhud* 'witness'. Some further examples:

Singular	**Plural**	
xedd	*xdud*	'cheek'
xeṭṭ	*xṭuṭ*	'line'
želd	*žlud*	'skin'
qbeṛ	*qbuṛ*	'tomb'
žder	*ždur*	'root'
qlaƐ	*qluƐ*	'(boat) sail'
sfina	*sfun*	'ship'
Ɛadel	*Ɛdul*	'notary'

There are a few examples with middle-weak roots. The second consonant of the plural is *y,* corresponding to an *a* or an *i* after the initial consonant of the singular. Almost all the singulars are of the pattern *FiL.* Some examples:

Singular	**Plural**	
bit	*byut*	'room'
dik	*dyuk*	'rooster'
hiša	*hyuš*	'animal'
ṛaṣ	*ṛyuṣ*	'head'
sif	*syuf*	'sword'

ṣif	*ṣyuf*	'summer'
xiṭ	*xyuṭ*	'thread, cord'
ž ib	*ž yub*	'pocket'

(e) **The Plural Pattern** *FƐuLa*:

Singular	**Plural**	
(pattern *FƐeL*)		
bṭen	*bṭuna*	'belly'
ḍfeṛ	*ḍfuṛa*	'fingernail'
kfen	*kfuna*	'shroud'
ždeƐ	*žduƐa*	'colt'
(pattern *FeƐL, FoƐL*)		
derb	*druba*	'(dead-end) street'
moxx	*mxuxa*	'brain'
žeṛf	*žṛufa*	'cliff'
ḥenš	*ḥnuša*	'snake'
(pattern *CCeCC*)		
mqeṣṣ	*mquṣa*	'scissors'
(pattern *FiL*)		
dib	*dyuba*	'wolf, jackal'

(f) **The Plural Pattern** *FƐaLa*: This plural pattern comes almost exclusively from singulars of the pattern *FeƐLi, FoƐLi*. A rare exception is *neṣṛani* pl. *nṣaṛa* 'Christian, European'. Some examples of the usual singular pattern:

Singular	**Plural**	
ferdi	*frada*	'pistol'
korsi	*krasa*	'stool'
sebsi	*sbasa*	'pipe' (for smoking)

ḥewli	*ḥwala*	'sheep'
Ɛezri	*Ɛzara*	'batchelor'

There are also a few cases of the plural pattern *FƐaLa* deriving from singulars with middle-weak roots. These singulars regularly have an *a*, an *i*, or a *u* after the first consonant and *w* or *y* as the second consonant of the plural, with the *w* of the plural corresponding to the *a* and *u* of the singular and the *y* of the plural corresponding to the *i* of the singular. Some examples: *buži* pl. *bwaža* 'spark plug', *tali* pl. *twala* 'last', *ḥiṭi* pl. *ḥyaṭa* '(wall) tapestry'.

(g) **The Plural Pattern** *FoƐƐaL*: Most nouns of this pattern refer to human beings and the pattern is almost exclusively limited to the active participles of Measure I verbs when they are used as nouns rather than adjectives.[49] Some examples:

Singular	**Plural**	
kafer	*koffaṛ*[50]	'unbeliever'
kateb	*kottab*	'scribe, clerk'
rakeb	*rokkab*	'rider, passenger'
sareḥ	*sorraḥ*	'shepherd'
Ɛamel	*Ɛommal*	'governor'

In the case of defective verbs,[51] the active participles of which have the pattern *FaƐi*, for example *šra* 'to buy' with active participle *šari* 'having bought', a *y* appears as the final consonant of the plural pattern, for example *ḥaḍi* pl. *ḥoḍḍay* 'guardian'. In the case of middle-weak roots, the medial doubled consonant is sometimes *ww* and sometimes *yy*,[52] for example *nayeb* pl. *nuwwab*[53] 'representative', *qayed* pl. *qoyyad* 'judge'.

A few words which have the Measure I active participle pattern *FaƐeL* without actually being participles also take the plural pattern *FoƐƐaL*, for example *qayed*

---

[49]For Measure I verbs, see pp. 29-30, 57; for adjectives used as nouns, see p. 204.

[50]A final emphatic *ṛ* in the plural corresponding to non-emphatic *r* in the singular is common.

[51]For defective verbs, see pp. 30-57.

[52]For hollow verbs and the variation between medial *w* and *y*, see pp. 24, 30-33, 57-58, 63-64.

[53]The *o* of the plural pattern regularly becomes *u* before *w*.

pl. *qoyyad* 'judge', *tažer* pl. *toẓẓar* 'merchant', *ḥayek* pl. *ḥoyyak,* a kind of woman's garment.

The plural pattern *FoƐƐaL* also occasionally corresponds to singular patterns other than that of Measure I active participles. Some examples:

Singular	Plural	
hbil	*hobbal*	'fool'
ṣaḷiḥ[54]	*ṣoḷḷaḥ*	'saint'
ḥažib[54]	*ḥožžab*	'chamberlain'
ḥmeq	*ḥommaq*	'crazy'

(h) The Plural Pattern *FiLan:* This plural pattern corresponds almost exclusively to the singular pattern *FaL,* although there are a few cases of it corresponding to a singular *FuL.* Some examples:

Singular	Plural	
bab	*biban*	'door'
faṛ	*firan*[55]	'rat, mouse'
kas	*kisan*	'(drinking) glass'
tuṛ	*tiran*[55]	'bull'
žaṛ	*žiran*[55]	'neighbor'
ġaṛ	*ġiran*[55]	'cave, lair'
Ɛud	*Ɛidan*	'lute'

(i) The Plural Pattern *FoƐLan, FeƐLan:* There are five singular patterns from strong roots: (1) *FƐaL,* (2) *FƐiL,* (3) *FƐiLa,* (4) *FƐuL,* and (5) *FaƐeL.* Some examples:

Singular	Plural	
blad	*boldan*	'country'

[54] *ṣaḷiḥ* and *ḥažib* are classicizations of the *FaƐeL* pattern, see p. 59.

[55] The non-emphatic *r* of the plural corresponding to the emphatic final *ṛ* of the singular is characteristic of this pattern.

šrik	*šorkan*	'partner'
xlifa	*xolfan*	'caliph'
xṛuf	*xerfan*	'lamb'
ḥažeb	*ḥožban*	'eyebrow'

Singulars with final-weak roots regularly show *y* as the third consonant of the plural pattern. Some examples:[56]

Singular	Plural	
hri	*heryan*	'granary'
ṛaƐi	*ṛoƐyan*	'shepherd'
saƐi	*soƐyan*	'beggar'
ždi	*žedyan*	'kid goat'
Ɛdu	*Ɛedyan*	'enemy'

(j) The Plural Pattern *FuƐeL*: This plural pattern corresponds exclusively to the adjectives of color and defect[57], for which the singular pattern is *FƐeL*. Some examples:

Singular	Plural	
byeḍ	*buyeḍ*	'white'
kḥel	*kuḥel*	'black'
qṛeƐ	*quṛeƐ*	afflicted with scalp disease
ṭṛeš	*ṭuṛeš*	'deaf'
xḍeṛ	*xuḍeṛ*	'green'

The items *ḥwel* pl. *hiwel* 'squint-eyed' and *Ɛweṛ* pl. *Ɛiweṛ* 'one-eyed' also logically belong in this category. The *i* instead of *u* in the plural is correlated with the medial *w*. The word *Ɛma* pl. *Ɛumi* 'blind' shows the form to be expected from a final-weak root of this general category.

---

[56] *dwa* pl. *duyan* 'medicine' logically belongs in this category, although an expected *ew* is replaced by *u* in the plural pattern.

[57] For the adjectives of color and defect, see p. 87.

(k) The Plural Pattern *FƐeL*:

Singular	Plural	
buṭa	*bweṭ*	'cask, barrel'
gaƐa	*gyeƐ*	'threshing-floor'
qolla	*qlel*	'jug'
tekka	*tkek*	'draw-string' (of trousers)
xima	*xyem*	'tent'
xoṛṣa	*xṛeṣ*	'metal ring'[58]
Ɛmud	*Ɛmed*	'(wooden) column'

(l) The Plural Pattern *CaCaCiC*: This pattern is a classicization of the common plural pattern *CCaCeC* (see p. 113ff.). Some examples:

Singular	Plural	
beṛnamež	*baṛamiž*	'program'
mesʔala, msala	*masaʔil*	'matter, affair'
meskin	*masakin*	'poor'
qenbula	*qanabil*	'bomb'
šiṭan	*šayaṭin*	'devil'

(m) The Plural Pattern *CuCaCa*:

Singular	Plural	
ḍaƐif, ḍƐif	*ḍuƐafa*	'poor, miserable'
qṛib	*quṛaba*	'relative'
ṛayes	*ṛuʔasa*	'chief, president'
saƐid	*suƐada*	'happy'

---

[58] Of any sort except a finger ring.

xalifa	*xulafa*	'caliph'
xṭib	*xuṭaba*	'preacher'

(n) The Plural Pattern *FeƐLa, FoƐLa*:

Singular	Plural	
bṣiṛ	*beṣṛa*	'blind'
fqi	*feqya*	'teacher'
ṭbib	*ṭobba*	'physician, doctor'

(o) The Plural Pattern *CCaCCa*:

Singular	Plural	
bužadi	*bwaždi*	'novice'
kudši	*kwadša*	'carriage'
malak	*mlayka*	'angel'
mġeṛbi	*mġaṛba*	'Moroccan'
tunsi	*twansa*	'Tunisian'

(p) The Plural Pattern *ʔaCCiya*:

Singular	Plural	
dwa	*ʔadwiya*	'medicine'
nbi	*ʔanbiya*	'prophet'
wali	*ʔawliya*	'saint'
waṣi	*ʔawṣiya*	'executor' (of a will)
ġani	*ʔaġniya*	'rich'

(q) The Plural Pattern *FuƐuL*:

Singular	Plural	
ḍeṛṣ	*ḍuṛuṣ*	'lesson'
feṛḍ	*fuṛuḍ*	'religious obligation'

hemm	*humum*	'care, worry'
ṭaṛiqa	*ṭuṛuq*	'religious fraternity'
ṛemẓ	*ṛumuẓ*	'sign, symbol'
sžen	*sužun*	'prison'
ɛelm	*ɛulum*	'science'

(r) The Plural Pattern ***Fɛi*:**

Singular	Plural	
kodya	*kdi*	'hill'
qfa	*qfi*	'nape' (of neck)
šelya	*šli*	'chair'
ɛṣa	*ɛṣi*	'stick, club'

(s) The Plural Pattern ***CaCaCi*:**

Singular	Plural	
mebda	*mabadi*	'principle'
mašiya	*mawaši*	'cattle'
naḥiya	*nawaḥi*	'region, environment'

(t) The Plural Pattern ***FɛiL*:**

Singular	Plural	
meɛza	*mɛiz*	'goat'
ḥmaṛ	*ḥmir*	'donkey'
ɛebd	*ɛbid*	'slave'

(u) Some Miscellaneous Broken Plurals:

Singular	Plural	
ʔamṛ	*ʔumuṛ*	'matter, affair'
ʔustad	*ʔasatida*	'professor, teacher'
bulisi	*bwalis*	'policeman'

baġi	*buġat*	'wrong-doer'
demm	*dmayat*	'blood; splotches of blood'
žnaḥ	*ženḥin*	'wing'
miyyet	*muta*	'corpse, dead person'
mula	*mwalin*	'possessor, master'
mṛa	*ɛyalat*	'woman'
meṛḍ	*ʔamṛaḍ*	'illness, disease'
qaḍi	*quḍat*	'judge'
ṛami	*ṛma*	'marksman, archer'
ṛaṣ	*ṛuṣ*	'head'
siyyed	*sadat*	'gentleman, sir; saint'
sem	*asami, smawat*	'name'
ṣemṣaṛ	*ṣmaṣṛiya*	'broker'
ṭaḥuni	*ṭwaḥniya*	'miller'
waqiɛa	*waqayeɛ*	'event, fact'
wzir	*waẓaṛa*	'minister'
xu	*xut*	'brother'
oxt, xet	*xwatat*	'sister'
yum	*iyyam*	'day'
ẓṛeɛ	*ẓṛuɛat*	'(cereal) grain'
ġṛab	*ġṛobba*	'crow'
ɛaṣima	*ɛawaṣim*	'capitol'

V. The Combining Form

Only certain nouns and adjectives ending in *-a* have a special combining form. The combining form is used before the pronoun endings[59] and as the first term in

[59]For the pronoun endings, see p. 134ff.

the construct state.[60] The combining form is usually derived by the substitution of a *-t* for the final *-a* of the word involved, for example *ṛḍuma* 'bottle' and *ṛḍumti* 'my bottle', less often by the substitution of *-et* for the final *-a*, as in *sebba* 'reason' and *sebbetha* 'her reason', or by the addition of a *-t* to the final *-a*, as in *mṛa* 'woman, wife' and *mṛati* 'my wife'.

Of nouns and adjectives ending in *-a*, almost all feminine singular nouns have a combining form, while masculine singular nouns, plural nouns, and adjectives are only rarely found with a combining form. Participles in *-a* never have a combining form, for example *hiya šaryahom* 'she has bought them'.

1. **Feminine Nouns Ending in *-a*:** If the consonant before the final *-a* is preceded by a vowel, *-t* is substituted for *-a* without any change in the stem. For example:

ẓeṛbiya	'rug'	*xala*	'(maternal) aunt'
ẓeṛbiyti	'my rug'	*xalti*	'my aunt'
ẓeṛbiytna	'our rug'	*xaltna*	'our aunt'

etc.

If the *-a* is preceded by a double consonant, it is replaced by *-t* before a pronoun suffix beginning with a vowel and by *-et* before a pronoun suffix beginning with a consonant or in the construct state. For example:

sebba	'reason'
sebbti	'my reason'
sebbetha	'her reason'

etc.

If the final *-a* is preceded by any two consonants other than a double consonant or by three consonants, an *e* is usually inserted before the last consonant with the change of final *-a* to *-t* in the combining form. An expected *ey* is replaced by *iy*. For example:

faṣma	'bandages'	*sensla*	'chain, zipper'
faṣemti	'my bandages'	*senselti*	'my chain'

[60]For the construct state, see pp. 191ff.

faṣemtha	'her bandages'	*senseltha*	'her chain'
etc.		etc.	

mfafya	'embarrassment'
mfafiyti	'my embarrassment'
mfafiytha	'her embarrassment'
etc.	

With the insertion of *e* in the stem, words on the pattern *FeƐLa, FoƐLa* lose the original *e* or *o* of the stem. If the original stem vowel is *o* the inserted vowel is often *o* instead of *e*. Nouns of the pattern *FeƐLa, FoƐLa* are quite numerous, and these stem changes are thus frequently met with. Some examples:

ṣenƐa	'profession'	*xedma*	'work'
ṣneƐti	'my profession'	*xdemti*	'my work'
ṣneƐtek	'your (sg.) profession'	*xdemtek*	'your (sg.) work'
ṣneƐtu	'his profession'	*xdemtu*	'his work'
ṣneƐtha	'her profession'	*xdemtha*	'her work'
ṣneƐtna	'our profession'	*xdemtna*	'our work'
ṣneƐtkom	'your (pl.) profession'	*xdemtkom*	'your (pl.) work'
ṣneƐthom	'their profession'	*xdemthom*	'their work'

soxṛa	'commission' (payment for work)
sxoṛti	'my commission'
sxoṛtek	'your (sg.) commission'
sxoṛtu	'his commission'
sxoṛtha	'her commission'
sxoṛtna	'our commission'
sxoṛtkom	'your (pl.) commission'
sxoṛthom	'their commission'

Nouns of this sort in which the final *-a* is preceded by *w* or *y* usually have *uw* instead of *ew* and *iy* instead of *ey* in the combining form. For example:

keswa	'suit' (of clothes)	*qelya*	act of frying, thing fried
ksuwti	'my suit'	*qliyti*	'my frying'
ksuwtha	'her suit'	*qliytha*	'her frying'

etc.

Next to *Ɛ* or *ḥ* the *e* is retained before *w* or *y* by some speakers. For example:

deƐwa	'lawsuit'
dƐewti	'my lawsuit'
dƐewtha	'her lawsuit'

etc.

There are a few nouns on the pattern of *tFeƐya,* the verbal nouns of Measure II of final-weak roots.[61] The combining form of these nouns shows an inversion in the stem. The usual substitution of *uw* for *ew* and *iy* for *ey* takes place. For example:

tġeṭya	'(act of) covering'	*twelya*	'investiture'
teġṭiyti	'my covering'	*tuwliyti*	'my investiture'
teġṭiytha	'her covering'	*tuwliytha*	'her investiture'

etc.

There are a few nouns which show the *FeƐLa, FoƐLa* pattern preceded by a consonant prefix, for example *mƐelqa* 'spoon'. These nouns fail to show inversion. The final *-a* is replaced by *-t* before suffixed pronouns which begin with vowels and by *-et* before suffixed pronouns which begin with consonants. For example:

mƐelqa	'spoon'
mƐelqti	'my spoon'
mƐelqetha	'her spoon'

etc.

[61] See p. 32.

Feminine nouns on the pattern of *FƐa* add *-t* without dropping their final *-a* in the combining form. Most nouns of this sort, however, also take the pronoun endings without the addition of *-t,* for example *ġṭa* 'cover' with *ġṭaya* or *ġṭati* 'my cover', *Ɛṣa* 'stick' with *Ɛṣaya* or *Ɛṣati* 'my stick', etc. A few words of this sort, however, always require the addition of *-t* before the pronoun endings. The most common are:

bṛa	'letter'	*bṛati*	'my letter', etc.
mṛa[62]	'woman, wife'	*mṛati*	'my wife', etc.
nta	'female' (animal)	*ntati*	'my female', etc.
ḥma[63]	'mother-in-law' (husband's mother)	*ḥmati*	'my mother-in-law', etc.

2. **Masculine Nouns Ending in *-a*:** There are very few masculine nouns ending in *-a*. Most of these are on the pattern of *FƐa,*[64] and masculine nouns of this pattern never take the *-t* of the combining form; e.g., *xṭa* 'error', *xṭana* 'our error', etc. Other masculine nouns ending in *-a* have a combining form derived in the same manner as feminine nouns ending in *-a;* e.g., *xlifa* 'caliph', *xliftna* 'our caliph'.

3. **Plural Nouns Ending in *-a*:** There are not many plural nouns ending in *-a*[65], and the occurrence of the combining form of such a noun is even more rare. Of the two circumstances calling for the use of a combining form, the construct state is of limited occurrence[66], and pronoun endings are rarely used with plural nouns, especially those ending in *-a*[67]. When such a combining form is used, however, it follows one of two patterns, depending on dialect variation. Either the pattern of feminine singular nouns ending in *-a* is followed, for example *qluma* '(fountain) pens' and *qlumti* 'my fountain pens', etc., or else the final *-a* is retained with the addition of *-t,* for example *muta* 'dead (ones)', *mutatna* 'our dead'.

---

[62] *mṛa* is unique among nouns of its type in also showing an inverted combining form *meṛt-* beside *mṛat-,* thus both *meṛti* and *mṛati* 'my wife', etc. occur. Both forms are in common use.

[63] *ḥma* also has the meaning 'protection', in which case it does not take the *-t;* e.g., *ḥmaya* 'my protection', etc.

[64] See pp. 99-100.

[65] Most such plurals are sound plurals denoting professional or habitual activity, see pp. 105-107. Broken plurals ending in *-a* are less common.

[66] For the construct state, see pp. 191ff.

[67] The use of *dyal,* for which see pp. 202-203, is preferred for indicating possession in such cases.

4. **Feminine Singular Adjectives:** Very occasionally a feminine singular adjective is found as the first element of a construct state,[68] in which case it has a combining form. The form is the same as that of the combining form of feminine nouns, for example *kḥel* 'black', feminine *keḥla,* combining form *kḥelt,* as in *kḥelt l-kemmara* 'black-faced', literally 'black of the face'.[69]

[68] For the use of an adjective as the first term of a construct state, see p. 193.

[69] This particular phrase implies an insult, both in the use of *kḥel* 'black' and *kemmara,* a derogatory term for face.

VI. PRONOUNS

I. The Personal Pronouns

The personal pronouns fall into two categories, independent forms and suffixed forms. Both the independent and the suffixed pronouns have separate forms for the first, second, and third persons, and for the singular and plural numbers. Both the independent and the suffixed pronouns distinguish between a masculine and feminine gender in the third person singular, and the independent pronouns have in addition separate masculine and feminine forms for the second person singular. The independent pronouns are simple in form and limited in number. The suffixed pronouns show a greater variety of form and greater complexity in relation to the stems to which they are attached. The forms are:

The Independent Pronouns

		Singular		Plural	
First Person		*ana*	'I'	*ḥna*	'we'
Second Person	**Msc.**	*nta*[1]	'you'	*ntuma*	'you'
	Fem.	*nti, ntiya*			
Third Person	**Msc.**	*huwa*	'he'	*huma*	'they'
	Fem.	*hiya*	'she'		

The Suffixed Pronouns

		Singular		Plural	
First Person		*-i, -ya, -y, -ni*	'me, my'	*-na*	'us, our'
Second Person		*-ek, -k*	'you, your'	*-kom*	'you, your'
Third Person	**Msc.**	*-u, -h, -eh*	'him, his'	*-hom*	'them, their'
	Fem.	*-ha*	'her'		

[1]The form *ntina* also occurs, used for both masculine and feminine singular.

There is no direct equivalent for English "it", which is translated by the masculine or feminine third person singular pronouns according to context; e.g., *šeftu* 'I saw him, it', *šeftha* 'I saw her, it'.

1. Stems to Which Suffixed Pronouns are Attached: These pronoun endings are suffixed to nouns, verbs, prepositions, and a few other particles.[2] When attached to nouns, they translate the English possessive adjectives; e.g., *ktab* 'book' and *ktabi* 'my book'. When attached to verbs or prepositions, they translate the English object pronouns; e.g., *šaf* 'he saw' and *šafni* 'he saw me', *mƐa* 'with' and *mƐahom* 'with them'.

The usual phenomena of elision and inversion are encountered in stems which take the vowel endings; e.g., *ktef* 'shoulder' and *ketfi* 'my shoulder', *qmeš* 'he scratched' and *qemšu* 'he scratched him', *wekkel* 'he fed' and *wekklek* 'he fed you' (sg.).

2. The Alternate Forms of the Pronoun Endings: In the first person singular, the form *-ni* occurs almost exclusively with verbs, including the active participle; e.g., *tƐeddani* 'he surpassed me', *huwa mkellefni (b-)* 'he has put me in charge (of)'. A few particles also take *-ni* e.g., *Ɛemmeṛni* 'I never'. The form *-y* occurs only with a few irregular nouns; e.g., *xay* 'my brother'.

The alternate forms *-i, -ya* in the first person singular, *-ek, -k* in the second person singular, and *-u, -h* in the third person singular masculine depend on whether or not the stem to which they are attached ends in a consonant or a vowel. The forms *-i, -ek,* and *-u* are attached to stems ending in consonants[3] while the forms *-ya, -k,* and *-h* are attached to stems ending in vowels.[4] Some examples:

Stem Ends in Vowel		**Stem Ends in Consonant**	
xṭaya	'my error'	*ktabi*	'my book'
mƐaya	'with me'	*menni*[5]	'from me'

---

[2]For these particles see pp. 153, 214.

[3]An exception is that verb forms ending in *-w* or *-y* take the ending *-eh* instead of *-u* 'him'. See below.

[4]Except that nouns having a special combining form take the endings *-i, -ek,* and *-u*. See pp. 128ff.

[5]For all speakers the preposition *men* 'from' doubles the final *n* before vowel endings, as in *menni* 'from me'. Some speakers also double the final *n* before all the pronoun endings, thus both *menha* and *mennha* 'from her', *menna* and *mennna* 'from us', etc. are heard.

xṭak	'your (sg.) error'	*ktabek*	'your (sg.) book'
mɛak	'with you' (sg.)	*mennek*	'from you' (sg.)
šafuk	'they saw you' (sg.)	*šafek*	'he saw you' (sg.)
xṭah	'his error'	*ktabu*	'his book'
mɛah	'with him'	*mennu*	'from him'
šafuh	'they saw him'	*šafu*	'he saw him'

The ending *-eh* 'him' is used only after verb forms ending in *w* or *y* and the plural ending *-in* of the active participle. After verb forms ending in *w*, *-eh* is the only form possible; e.g., *šeftiweh* 'you (pl.) saw him'. After verb forms ending in *y* and after the plural ending *-in* of the active participle, some speakers use *-u* and some speakers use *-eh;* e.g., *ddayeh* or *ddayu* 'having taken him', *karyineh* or *karyinu* 'having rented it'.

3. Special Details With Verb Stems: There are four important details of form and distribution observable in connection with the addition of the suffixed pronouns to verb forms.

(a) Limitations of Person: In a form consisting of a verb with one or two pronoun endings, only one occurrence of the first or second person is possible; e.g., the pronoun ending *-ni* 'me' is not suffixed to *šeft* 'I saw', and *-lek* 'to, for you' (sg.) is not suffixed to *šriti* 'you (sg.) bought'. To express such combinations of meaning, the reflexive *ṛaṣ* 'self' with appropriate pronoun endings is used. Compare the following examples:

šafni	'he saw me'
šeft ṛaṣi	'I saw myself'
darha-li	'he did it for me'
dertha l-ṛaṣi	'I did it for myself'
šrahom-lek	'he bought them for you (sg.)'
šritihom l-ṛaṣek	'you (sg.) bought them for yourself'

(b) The Third Person Singular Feminine of the Perfect Tense: The third person singular feminine *-et* 'she' of the perfect tense, as in *šafet* 'she saw', *ketb̲et* 'she wrote', etc., undergoes various changes with the addition of the endings *-ek* 'you (sg.)' and *-u* 'him'. For the details, see pp. 41-42. Some summary examples:

žabettek or *žabtek*	'she brought you (sg.)'
žabettu or *žabtu*	'she brought him'
refdettek or *refdatek*	'she carried you (sg.)'
refdettu or *refdatu*	'she carried him'

(c) **Ambiguities With the Ending** *-u*: The ending *-u* 'him' as in *šafu* 'he saw him' is identical in form with the third person plural ending *-u* in the perfect, as in *šafu* 'they saw', and with the plural ending *-u* of the first, second, and third person forms of the imperfect and imperative, as in *nketbu* 'we write', *tketbu* 'you (pl.) write', *iketbu* 'they write', and *ketbu!* 'write! (pl.)'.

In cases such as these context is the only indication as to whether the verb form in question is a plural or a singular plus the ending *-u* 'him'. Some examples:

kteb	'he wrote'
ketbu	'he wrote it' or 'they wrote'
ketbuh	'they wrote it'
nekteb	'I write'
nketbu	'I write it' or 'we write'
nketbuh	'we write it'
tekteb	'you (sg.) write'
tketbu	'you (sg.) write it' or 'you (pl.) write'
tketbuh	'you (pl.) write it'
kteb!	'write!' (sg. imperative)
ketbu!	'write (sg. imperative) it!' or 'write!' (pl. imperative)
ketbuh!	'write (pl. imperative) it!'
ikteb	'he writes'
iketbu	'he writes it' or 'they write'
iketbuh	'they write it'

šaf	**'he saw'**
šafu	**'he saw him' or 'they saw'**
šafuh	**'they saw him'**
nšuf	**'I see'**
nšufu	**'I see him' or 'we see'**
nšufuh	**'we see him'**
tšuf	**'you (sg.) see'**
tšufu	**'you (sg.) see him' or 'you (pl.) see'**
tšufuh	**'you (pl.) see him'**
šuf!	**'look!' (sg. imperative)**
šufu!	**'look (sg. imperative) at him!' or 'look!' (pl. imperative)**
šufuh!	**'look (pl. imperative) at him!'**
išuf	**'he sees'**
išufu	**'he sees him' or 'they see'**
išufuh	**'they see him'**

(d) The Suffixed Prepositional Form: The suffixed forms of the preposition *l–* 'to, for' are:

–li	'to me, for me'	*–lna*	'to us, for us'
–lek	'to you, for you (sg.)'	*–lkom*	'to you, for you (pl.)'
–lu	'to him, for him'	*–lhom*	'to them, for them'
–lha	'to her, for her'		

These forms are suffixed directly to the verb. For example:

qal–li	'he said to me, told me'
qal–lek	'he told you (sg.)'

qal-lu	'he told him'
qal-lha	'he told her'
qal-lna	'he told us'
qal-lkom	'he told you (pl.)'
qal-lhom	'he told them'
ktebt-lek	'I wrote to you (sg.)'
ktebt-lu	'I wrote to him'
ktebt-lha	'I wrote to her'
ktebt-lkom	'I wrote to you (pl.)'
ktebt-lhom	'I wrote to them'

These suffixed prepositional forms are also added to a verb form which already has a third person pronoun object. For example:

ṣifṭu-li	'he sent him to me'
ṣifeṭha-li	'he sent her to me'
ṣifeṭhom-li	'he sent them to me'
Ɛṭitu-lek	'I gave it (msc.) to you (sg.)'
Ɛṭitha-lek	'I gave it (fem.) to you (sg.)'
Ɛṭithom-lek	'I gave them to you (sg.)'
werritih-li	'you (sg.) showed it (msc.) to me'
werritih-lu	'you (sg.) showed it (msc.) to him'
werritih-lha	'you (sg.) showed it (msc.) to her'
werritih-lhom	'you (sg.) showed it (msc.) to them'

Verb forms which have a first or second person pronoun object do not take the suffixed prepositional forms. For example:[6]

[6] For a complete list of the preposition *l-* 'to, for' with its pronoun endings, see p. 143.

qeddemni lilek	'he introduced me to you (sg.)'
qeddmek lili	'he introduced you (sg.) to me'
qeddemtina lilhom	'you (sg.) introduced us to them'
qeddemtkom lilha	'I introduced you (pl.) to her'

If a verb form already has one suffixed form of *l-* 'to, for', further suffixed forms cannot be added, for example *žebtha-lek lilu* 'I brought it (fem.) to you (sg.) for (you to give to) him'.

4. Special Details With Noun Stems: Nouns which have a combining form add the pronoun endings to the combining form rather than to the simple stem form (see pp. 128ff); e.g., *ṛḍuma* 'bottle', *ṛḍumti* 'my bottle', *ṛḍumtek* 'your (sg.) bottle', etc.

There are six noun plurals in *-in* which drop the final *-n* before the suffixed pronouns. These are:

režlin	'feet, legs'
režliya	'my feet'
režlik	'your (sg.) feet'
režlih	'his feet'
režliha	'her feet'
režlina	'our feet'
režlikom	'your (pl.) feet'
režlihom	'their feet'
wednin	'ears'
wedniya	'my ears'
etc.	
yeddin	'hands'
yeddiya	'my hands'
etc.	

Ɛeynin	'eyes'
Ɛeyniya	'my eyes'
etc.	
mwalin	'lords, masters, possessors'
mwaliya	'my...'
etc.	
waldin	'parents'
waldiya	'my parents'
etc.	

There are a small number of nouns with base forms ending in *-a* which do not distinguish a separate form for 'my'. These are all kinship terms. They are "inherently possessed", in the sense that they never occur without a possessive ending. The six most common are:

baba	'my father'
babak	'your (sg.) father'
babah	'his father'
babaha	'her father'
etc.	
ḅḅa	'my father'
ḅḅak	'your (sg.) father'
etc.	
dada	'my nanny'
dadak	'your (sg.) nanny'
etc.	
lalla	'my grandmother'
lallak	'your (sg.) grandmother'
etc.	

yemma	'my mother'
yemmak	'your (sg.) mother'
etc.	

ḥanna	'my grandmother'
ḥannak	'your (sg.) grandmother'
etc.	

Very few nouns take the ending *-y* 'my'. The two most common are *xay* 'my brother' and *mulay* 'my Lord'. The latter is used mostly as a prefixed title in saints' names.

5. Special Details With Particles and Prepositions: The preposition *ɛla* 'on' changes the final *-a* to *-i* and the prepositions *f-* 'in' and *b-* 'with, by' add *-i* before the pronoun endings. The forms are:

ɛliya	'on me'	*fiya*	'in me'	*biya*	'with me'
ɛlik	'on you (sg.)'	*fik*	'in you (sg.)'	*bik*	'with you (sg.)'
ɛlih	'on him'	*fih*	'in him'	*bih*	'with him'
ɛliha	'on her'	*fiha*	'in her'	*biha*	'with her'
ɛlina	'on us'	*fina*	'in us'	*bina*	'with us'
ɛlikom	'on you (pl.)'	*fikom*	'in you (pl.)'	*bikom*	'with you (pl.)'
ɛlihom	'on them'	*fihom*	'in them'	*bihom*	'with them'

The preposition *men* 'from' doubles the final *-n* before the vowel endings for all speakers, and for some speakers the *-n* is doubled before all the pronoun endings. The forms:

menni	'from me'
mennek	'from you (sg.)'
mennu	'from him'
menha or *mennha*	'from her'
menna or *mennna*	'from us'

menkom or *mennkom*	'from you (pl.)'
menhom or *mennhom*	'from them'

The preposition *l-* 'to, for' has two sets of forms. Thus:

Dependent Forms		**Independent Forms**
-li	'to me'	*lili, liya*
-lek	'to you (sg.)'	*lilek, lik*
-lu	'to him'	*lilu, lih*
-lha	'to her'	*lilha, liha*
-lna	'to us'	*lilna, lina*
-lkom	'to you (pl.)'	*lilkom, likom*
-lhom	'to them'	*lilhom, lihom*

The alternate independent forms are used interchangeably with no difference of meaning; e.g., *lilhom* or *lihom* 'to, for them'. The dependent forms occur mostly with verbs (see pp. 138-140). They are found only rarely with other forms: e.g., *ḥsen-li* '(it's) better for me', *ma-lek?* 'what's the matter with you (sg.)?'

The ending *-ni* 'me' of the first person singular is almost exclusively found with verbs, but a few particles take it. The three most common are *ɛemmeṛ* 'never' (see p. 153) and the presentational particles *ha* and *ṛa* (see p. 214).

II. The Demonstrative Pronouns

The near and the far demonstrative forms are:

hada	(msc.)	'this'	*hadak*	(msc.)	'that'
hadi	(fem.)	'this'	*hadik*	(fem.)	'that'
hadu	(pl.)	'those'	*haduk*	(pl.)	'those'

These forms almost always have a specific noun antecedent and are often to be translated as 'this one', 'that one', 'these (ones)', or 'those (ones)'; e.g., *hadi mezyana* 'this one is good'. These forms are scarcely ever used in the sense of English "this" or "that" referring to a general situation. In the general sense without a specific noun antecedent the usual usage is *had š-ši* 'this (thing)' and *dak š-ši* 'that (thing)'. Compare:

aš hada?	'what is this (one)?'
aš had š-ši?	'what is this (situation, affair)?'
bġit hadak	'I want that one'
dak š-ši lli bġit	'that's what I want'

With a durative verb form, an active participle indicating current or present activity, or in an equational sentence, *hadi* is used in equivalents to the English present perfect tense. For example:

hadi saεtayn w ana ka-ntsennah	'I've been waiting for him for two hours'
hadi modda u huwa naεes	'he's been asleep for a (long) time'
hadi telt snin u ḥna fe-l-meġṛib	'we've been in Morocco for three years'

III. The Interrogative Pronouns

There are five interrogative pronouns, *škun?* 'who?', *(mεa) men?* '(with) whom?', *aš?* 'what?', *ma?* 'what?', and *ina?* 'which?'. The form *men* is used only after prepositions, for example *mεa men?* 'with whom?', *dyal men?* 'whose?'. and occasionally as the second term of a construct state (see p. 193), for example *bent men hadi?* 'whose daughter is this?'. After the prepositions *b-* 'with, by', *l-* 'to', *f-* 'in', and *d-* 'of', the initial *m* of *men* is doubled, for example:

be-mmen?	'with, by whom?'
le-mmen?	'to whom?'
fe-mmen?	'in whom?'
de-mmen?	'of whom, whose?'

The form *škun* is used elsewhere, for example *škun nta?* 'who are you (sg.)?' As the subject or object of a verb, *škun* is usually followed by the relative *lli* (see p. 164), for example:

škun lli šafek?	'who (is it that) saw you (sg.)?'
škun lli šefti?	'who did you see, who is it that you (sg.) saw?'

The interrogative *aš* is used in a variety of ways; e.g., independently in *aš derti?* 'what did you (sg.) do?', *aš hada?* 'what is this (one)?', *b-aš?* 'what with, by means of what?' When followed by *men* 'from, of' before a noun, *aš* is equivalent to the English interrogative adjectives 'which, what', for example *aš men ražel?* 'what, which man?' It is used in the same sense directly following certain expressions of time, for example *weqt-aš?* '(at) what time?', *nhaṛ-aš?* '(on) what day?'

An abbreviated form *š-* is quite common before a following consonant; e.g., *waš fhemti š-ka-nqul?* 'do you (sg.) understand what I'm saying?' For the linkage of *aš* to *huwa* 'he', *hiya* 'she', and *huma* 'they' by the particle *-en,* see p. 168.

As an interrogative, *ma* is almost completely limited to use with dependent forms of the preposition *l-* 'to, for' (see p. 143), either in the sense of 'what's wrong, the matter with...?' or, with a following verb, as equivalent to 'why'; e.g., *ma-lu?* 'what's the matter with him?', *ma-lek ka-tġuwwet?* 'what are you (sg.) screaming for?'

The interrogative *ina* is always used with a following noun; e.g., *f-ina saᶓa žiti?* '(at) what time (hour) did you (sg.) come?' It is usually interchangeable with *(a)š men;* e.g., *fe-š-men saᶓa žiti?* '(at) what time (hour) did you (sg.) come?'

IV. The Indefinite Pronouns

The principle forms are:

ši-waḥed, ši-ḥedd	'someone'
ši-ḥaža	'something'
(ḥetta-)waḥed, (ḥetta-)ḥedd	'no one'
flan	'so-and-so'
(ḥetta-) ḥaža, walu	'nothing'
koll-ši	'everything, everyone'
koll-waḥed	'everyone'
koll	'all, every, each'
beᶓḍna beᶓḍ, beᶓḍiyatna	'we...each other'
beᶓḍkom beᶓḍ, beᶓḍiyatkom	'you (pl.)...each other'
beᶓḍhom beᶓḍ, beᶓḍiyathom	'they...each other'
ṛaṣ	'self'
škun-emma, škun-ma	'whoever'
(mᶓa) men-ma	'(with) whoever'
aš-emma	'whatever'
ma	'what, that which'

VII. THE ARTICLES

1. The Definite Article: The definite article is prefixed to nouns and to adjectives. The form of the definite article is determined by the first sound of the word to which it is prefixed. If the word begins with *š* or *ž* or one of the consonants made with the tip of the tongue (*t, s, d, z, n, l,* and *r,* as well as the corresponding emphatics), the definite article is a single consonant identical with the first consonant of the word to which it is prefixed. Some examples:

t-tub	'the cloth'	*ẓ-ẓeṛwaṭa*	'the stick, the club'
t-tben	'the straw'	*n-neṣṣ*	'the half'
ṭ-ṭub	'the brick'	*l-lḥem*	'the meat'
ṭ-ṭbib	'the doctor'	*ḷ-ḷeṛḍ*	'the earth'
s-sokkan	'the inhabitants'	*r-rakeb*	'the passenger'
ṣ-ṣiniya	'the tray'	*ṛ-ṛažel*	'the man'
d-drari	'the children'	*š-šemš*	'the sun'
ḍ-ḍhuṛ	'the backs'	*ž-žmel*	'the camel'
z-zwaq	'the decoration'		

Before vowels or other consonants the definite article is usually *l-* if the following word begins with a vowel or a single consonant and *le-* if it begins with a consonant cluster; e.g.,

l-bab	'the door'	*l-ʔislam*	'(the) Islam'
l-mektub	'the pocket'	*le-flayki*	'the boatman'
l-weld	'the boy'	*le-kbir*	'the big (one)'
l-yedd	'the hand'	*le-xbaṛži*	'the informer, the spy'
l-qeṛƐa	'the bottle'	*le-ḥrira*	'the soup'
l-Ɛers	'the wedding'		

If the word to which the definite article is prefixed begins with *wC-*, some speakers have *lu-* instead of *le-* for the definite article; e.g., *le-wlad* or *lu-wlad* 'the boys'. In some cases the *w* is changed to *u* and *l-ulad* is heard. Before words beginning with *yC-*, the definite article is either *li-* or *l-* with *yC-* becoming *iC-*; e.g., *li-yhud* or *l-ihud* 'the Jews'.

With the special adjectives of color and defect (see p. 87), all of which begin with consonant clusters, and a few other miscellaneous nouns and adjectives beginning with consonant clusters, the definite article is *le-* regardless of whether the following consonant usually calls for a repetition of itself as the form of the definite article; e.g., *le-ṣfeṛ* 'the yellow', *le-rneb* 'the rabbit'.

Occasionally *l-* rather than *ž-* is heard as the form of the article before a following *ž*, especially in religious terminology; e.g., *l-žud* '(the) generosity, nobility of spirit'.

2. The Indefinite Articles: There are two indefinite articles. The potential indefinite article is an invariable prefix *ši-*. It indicates vagueness, uncertainty, or potentiality. It is prefixed to both singular and plural nouns. Some examples:

ši-ṛažel	'a man, some sort of man, some man or other'
ši-ktab	'a book, some sort of book, some book or other'
ši-nas	'some people'

The concretizing indefinite article is an invariable *waḥed* plus the definite article; e.g., *waḥed ṛ-ṛažel* 'a man', *waḥed l-bent* 'a girl', etc. In the case of nouns which exclude the definite article (see pp. 189-190), *waḥed* is prefixed directly to the noun; e.g., *waḥed ṣaḥbi* 'a friend of mine', *waḥed bellarež* 'a stork'.

3. The General Demonstrative Article: The invariable form *had* plus the definite article functions as a demonstrative article; e.g., *had le-ktab* 'this, that book', *had le-ɛyalat* 'these, those women'. In the case of nouns which exclude the definite article (see pp. 189-190), *had* is placed directly before the noun; e.g., *had weldek* 'this, that son of yours (sg.)', *had atay* 'this, that tea'.

The demonstrative article *had* has a generalized demonstrative meaning and is translatable as either 'this' or 'that'. It has none of the implications of distinguishing between near and far as do the English demonstratives "this" and "that".

4. The Far Demonstrative Article: The far demonstrative article is inflected for masculine, feminine, and plural. It is placed before nouns and adjectives in the same manner as the general demonstrative *had*. The form is identical with that of the far demonstrative pronouns (see p. 143) with an optional dropping of the initial *ha-*. For example:

hadak ṛ-ṛažel	'that man'
or *dak ṛ-ṛažel*	
hadik le-mṛa	'that woman'
or *dik le-mṛa*	
haduk n-nas	'those people'
or *duk n-nas*	

PART THREE
SYNTAX

NOTES

SECTION ONE – THE SENTENCE

I. SOME GENERAL PROCEDURES

I. Interrogation

Interrogation is signaled in one of three ways in Moroccan, by an interrogative adverb, as in *fayn n-nas?* 'where are the people?'; by an interrogative pronoun, as in *škun huwa?* 'who's he?'; or by a rising intonation, as in *mšat l-bareḥ?* 'she went yesterday?'

There are two fundamentally different kinds of question, a type which calls for a "yes" or "no" answer, for example *waš wṣel wella baqi?* 'has he arrived (yet) or not?', and a type which calls for substantive information, for example *aš derti?* 'what did you (sg.) do?' Moroccan grammar is essentially the same as English in this respect.

Questions which call for a "yes" or "no" answer are introduced either by the interrogative adverb *waš* or by a rise in intonation. The Moroccan use of a rising intonation to indicate a question rather than a statement is quite similar to English. The interrogative *waš* has no other meaning or function than to indicate that the sentence which it introduces is a question,[1] for example *waš qalu-lek mnin žaw?* 'did they, have they told you where they came from?' Moroccan questions with *waš* usually correspond to English questions with a verb-subject word order. Compare:

ɛad dxel l-l-meġrib	'he has just arrived in Morocco'
waš ɛad dxel l-l-meġrib?	'has he just arrived in Morocco?'

For the interrogative pronouns, see p. 144. For the interrogative adverbs other than *waš,* see p. 213.

[1] But note the translation of *waš* as 'whether' in subordinate clauses, see p. 167. The particle *waš* should not be confused with *w aš* 'and what', although the two are pronounced identically.

II. Negation

1. **Basic Procedure:** Normal verbal negation consists of prefixing *ma-* to a verb form and suffixing *-š*. Instead of *-š* some Moroccans say *-ši*. A slightly more emphatic negative is indicated by *-šay* instead of *-š*. Some examples:

ma-ža-š	'he didn't, hasn't come'
ma-ža-šay	'he certainly did not, has not come'
ma-ka-yakol-š	'he isn't eating, he doesn't eat'
ma-nemšiw-š	'we won't go, let's not go'

The procedure is the same with verb forms which have pronoun endings attached. For example:

ma-ktebhom-li-š	'he didn't write them for me, to me'
ma-ka-nšufhom-s koll nhaṛ	'I don't see them every day'
ma-iquluha-lna-š	'they won't, aren't going to tell (it to) us'

2. **The Negative Imperative:** The imperative forms are not negated. The corresponding second person imperfect forms are used instead. For example:

qul-lhom!	'tell (sg.) them!'
ma-tqul-lhom-š!	'don't (sg.) tell them!'
Eṭiweh-lu!	'give (pl.) it to him!'
ma-teEṭiweh-lu-š!	'don't (pl.) give it to him!'

The irregular imperatives *sir!* 'go!' and *aži!* 'come!' have the negative forms:

ma-temši-š!	'don't (sg.) go!'
ma-temšiw-š!	'don't (pl.) go!'
ma-dži-š!	'don't (sg.) come!'
ma-džiw-š!	'don't (pl.) come!'

Some speakers also have a special negative form for *aṛa!* 'hand over, give!':

ma–taṛa–š!	'don't (msc.) hand over!'
ma–taṛi–š!	'don't (fem.) hand over!'
ma–taṛaw–š!	'don't (pl.) hand over!'

The substitution of *la–* for *ma–* in the negative imperative has a more general advisory or morally admonishing implication. For example:

ma–temši–š!	'don't (sg.) go!'
la–temši–š!	'you (sg.) shouldn't go, I advise you not to go'
ma–tkedbu–š!	'don't (pl.) lie!'
la–tkedbu–š!	'you (pl.) shouldn't lie, you are not to lie'

3. Additional Negative Forms: The following negatives call for a verb form with *ma–* prefixed but without the final *–š*.

walu	'nothing'
(ḥetta–)ḥaža	'nothing'
(ḥetta–)ši	'nothing'
(ḥetta–)ḥedd	'no one'
(ḥetta–)waḥed	'no one'
la...wa–la	'neither...nor'
ɛemmeṛ[2] (plus pronoun endings)	'never'

Some examples of the use of these forms:

[2]Some speakers place the *ma–* before *ɛemmeṛ* rather than before the verb, e.g. *ma–ɛemmeṛni ka–nexdem* 'I never work'. Some speakers also use the ending *–i* instead of *–ni* in the first person, thus *ɛemmṛi* or *ɛemmeṛni* 'I never'.

ma-rbeḥt walu	'I didn't make (earn) anything, I earned nothing'
ma-iddiw ḥetta-ḥàža	'they aren't going to take anything'
ma-šefna ḥedd	'we didn't see anyone, we saw no one'
ma-ža mƐa ḥedd	'he didn't come with anyone, he came with no one'
ma-ka-itheḷḷa la fe-xtu wa-la fe-ṃṃu	'he dosen't take care of either his sister or his mother, he takes care neither of his sister nor his mother'
ma-klit la xobz wa-la lḥem	'I ate neither bread nor meat, I didn't eat either bread or meat'
ḥetta ma-bqa-š ka-ižbeṛ la ma yakol wa-la ma išṛob	'until he no longer could find either anything to eat or anything to drink'
ši ma-qḍa	'he accomplished nothing'
Ɛemmeṛni ka-nexdem	'I never work'
Ɛemmeṛhom ma-šafuh	'they've never seen him, they never saw him'

The preposition *ġir* is used with a negative verb in the sense of 'only, nothing but', and it too calls for the omission of *-š* with the verb form. For example *ma-rbeḥt ġir fṛenk* 'I only made (earned) one franc'.

4. The Categorical Negative: When the direct object or the complement of a negative verb refers to a whole category rather than to some specific item or member of a category, the verb is also negated by *ma-* alone without *-š* being suffixed. Some examples:

ma-žbeṛt flus	'I didn't find (any) money'
cf. *ma-žbeṛt-š le-flus*	'I didn't find the money'
ma-kla xobz	'he didn't eat bread'
cf. *ma-kla-š l-xobz*	'he didn't eat the bread'

Such expressions as *ma-kla ma-šṛeb* 'he neither ate nor drank', with a categorical denial of the action of the verb itself, also belong to this classification.

5. **Verb Phases:** In verb phrases,[3] the negative particles are attached to the auxiliary. Some examples:

ma-bġit-š nddiha	'I don't want to take it'
ma-konna ka-nheḍṛu mɛa ḥedd	'we weren't talking with anyone'
ma-bqaw-š ixedmu ɛendna	'they don't work at our place any more'
ɛemmeṛhom ma-ġadi idiruha	'they're never going to do it'

6. **Negation in Subordinate Clauses:** Negation in subordinate clauses is usually the same as elsewhere, e.g. *xefthom ma-ižiw-š* 'I was afraid they weren't going to come, might not come, wouldn't come'. Negative purpose in a subordinate clause is, however, usually expressed by *la-* without a final *-š*, e.g. *šeddu la-iṭiḥ* 'grab him so that he won't fall'. The optional use of *la-* in such constructions where fear or doubt rather than purpose is expressed does not indicate negation of the verb to which it is prefixed but rather the contrary desire of the subject of the main clause, e.g. *xefnah la-iṭiḥ* 'we were afraid that he might fall' (and we didn't want him to), *xafuna la-nemšiw* 'they were afraid that we might go' (and they hoped we wouldn't). It is possible to omit *la-* in constructions of this sort expressing fear or doubt.

7. **Non-Verbal Negation:** The most common non-verbal negation is with *ma-ši* 'not'. For example:

ma-ši mezyan	'not good'
huwa ma-ši hna	'he isn't here'
ṛ-ṛažel ma-ši kbir	'the man isn't big'

Nouns and adjectives are also sometimes prefixed with *ma-* and suffixed with *-ši* or *-šay*, e.g. *ma-kbir-ši* 'not big', *ma-kbir-šay* 'not big at all'.

Equational sentences with personal pronouns as subject are often negated by intercalating the pronoun between *ma-* and *-š*. For example:

ma-ḥna-š drari galsin mɛak	'we aren't children sitting with you (sg.)'
(a father's admonition to a child for misbehaving in the presence of adults)	

[3]For verb phrases, see pp. 179ff.

ma–huwa–š qbiḥ	'he's not bad (ill-willed)'

In addition to the full form *ma–huwa–š* 'not he' the contracted forms *ma–hu–š* and *mawši* are also heard, and beside the full form *ma–hiya–š* the contracted form *mayši* is heard.

The prepositions *f–* 'in' and *ɛend* 'with, at, at the place of' are usually negated with *ma–ši* 'not' in their literal meanings, e.g.

ma–ši fe–ḍ–ḍaṛ	'not in the house'
ma–ši ɛenda	'not with us, not at our place'

But *ɛend* plus a pronoun ending in the sense of 'to have' is negated by intercalation between *ma–* and *–š,* e.g. *ma–ɛendi–š* 'I don't have (it)'. Negation of *f–* plus a pronoun ending in the sense of 'to feel inclined to, to be able' is expressed by a prefixed *ma–* alone, e.g. *ma–fiya ma nemši mɛak*[4] 'I don't feel like going with you'.

The omission of suffixed *–š* in various non-verbal negations is parallel to its omission with verb forms, e.g.

ma–ɛendha walu	'she doesn't have anything'
ma–ɛendi flus	'I don't have (any) money'
cf. *ma–ɛendi–š le–flus*	'I don't have the money'
ma–fiha bas	'there's no harm in it, that's all right'

In use with non-verbals as well as in verbal negation is *la...wa–la* 'neither... nor', e.g. *la l–weld wa–la l–bent* 'neither the boy nor the girl'. In addition to its use in such expressions as *ḥetta–ḥedd* 'no one' and *ḥetta–ḥaža* 'nothing', *ḥetta* is used in various non-verbal negations in the sense of 'not even', e.g. *ḥetta ši–fṛiyyeq* 'not even a little bitty difference'.

III. Gender and Number

1. Regular Agreement: There is, in general, agreement in number and in gender between pronouns and the nouns they refer to, between adjectives and the nouns or pronouns they modify, and between verbs and their subjects. Some examples:

[4]The *ma* of *ma nemši* is not a negation but the pronominal particle, see p. 145.

fayn ṛažlek? ma-šeftu-š	'where is your husband? I haven't seen him'
fayn mṛatek? ma-šeftha-š	'where is your wife? I haven't seen her'
fayn n-nas? ma-šefthom-š	'where are the people? I haven't seen them'
huwa neǆǆaṛ	'he is a carpenter'
hiya bent žaṛi	'she is my neighbor's daughter'
huma žirani	'they are my neighbors'
waḥed l-bit kbir	'a big room'
waḥed ḍ-ḍaṛ kbira	'a big house'
byut kbaṛ	'big rooms'
huwa mṛiḍ	'he is sick'
hiya mṛiḍa	'she is sick'
huma mṛaḍ	'they are sick'
ṛ-ṛažel ža	'the man came'
le-mṛa žat	'the woman came'
n-nas žaw	'the people came'
huwa xrež	'he went out'
hiya xeržet	'she went out'
huma xeržu	'they went out'

Being invariable, the comparative form of the adjective (see pp. 85-86) does not conform to this pattern, e.g. *huwa (hiya, huma) kbeṛ menni* 'he is (she is, they are) bigger than me'. There is also usually only one plural adjective form, regardless of the gender of the noun it accompanies (see p. 107), e.g. *ṛžal kbaṛ* 'big men', *Ɛyalat kbaṛ* 'big women'. The feminine plural adjective, ending in *-at*, is almost never used except in conjunction with a feminine plural noun also ending in *-at*, and even in this case its use is optional, e.g. *si-ḥkayat meġribiyat* 'some Moroccan stories', *le-Ɛyalat l-meƐṛuḍat* 'the invited women'.

2. Agreement of the Dual: Nouns are the only part of speech which have duals (see p. 100). When they occur in a construction calling for agreement, the agreeing pronoun or adjective is in the plural, e.g. *šehṛayn mezyanin* 'two good months'. Verbs with dual noun subjects on the other hand are usually feminine singular, e.g. *mnin ka-tebqa saƐtayn l-le-fžer* 'when two hours are left until dawn'.

3. **Inanimate Plurals as Feminine Singulars:** There are a few rare cases of inanimate plural nouns taking feminine singular agreement with pronouns, adjectives, and verbs, e.g. *dazet ši-iyyamat* 'a few days passed'. Only isolated idioms and stereotyped phrases require this type of agreement. In those dialects of Moroccan where it occurs more widely it is always interchangeable with regular plural agreement.

4. **The Feminine as a Neuter:** When phrases function as nouns or when a generalized situation is referred to, the feminine singular is usually used, e.g.

temm mažini b-dik "s-salamu Ɛlikom" dyalu	'he came up to me with that "peace be upon you" of his'
qul-li layn ġadi temši — ma-nqulha-lek-š	'tell me where you're going to go — I won't tell (it to) you'

5. **Words Denoting Pairs:** Some grammatically singular words refer to paired objects, e.g. *belġa* 'a pair of slippers', pl. *blaġi* 'pairs of slippers'. Besides *belġa,* the most frequently occurring word of this sort is *ṣebbaṭ* 'a pair of shoes'. To indicate one object of such a pair, the term *ferda,* sometimes *ferdi,* is used, e.g. *ferda de-l-belġa* 'a (single) slipper'. This usage is also sometimes found with words which designate things that are made up of coordinate parts although they are not strictly pairs, e.g. *ṛḥa* '(hand) mill', *ferda de-ṛ-ṛḥa* 'a (single) millstone'.

6. **Numerals:** The cardinal numerals agree as plurals. Some examples:

koll žuž menna ġadi ittšerku f-weḥda	'each two of us are going to share in one'
škun ž-žuž lli ġadi iddiw hadi?	'who are the two who are going to take this one?'
žuž oxṛin	'two others'
settin kbaṛ	'sixty big ones'
mya mezyanin	'a hundred good ones'

II. THE SIMPLE SENTENCE

1. The Simple Equational Sentence: The simple equational sentence consists of a subject, which is either a noun or a pronoun, and a predicate, which consists of a noun, a pronoun, an adverb, or a prepositional phrase. In the equational sentence there is no verb linking the subject and the predicate, and a form of English "to be" must usually be inserted in the translation.

Usually the subject precedes the predicate, e.g.

had ṛ-ṛažel nežžaṛ	'this man is a carpenter'
huma fe-ḍ-ḍaṛ	'they are in the house'
ana hna	'I am here'
ḥna galsin	'we are sitting'
ɛemmi mṛiḍ	'my (paternal) uncle is sick'

The predicate precedes the subject when the subject is a demonstrative pronoun in an exclamation or when the predicate is an interrogative pronoun, e.g.

škun nta?	'who are you?'
škun had l-bent?	'who is this girl?'
aš dak š-ši?	'what is that?'
s-siba hadi!	'this is anarchy!'
s-smen hada!	'this is butter!'
weḥla hadi!	'this is a dilemma!'

The noun subject also usually follows the predicate when the predicate is a preposition with a pronoun ending, e.g.

ɛendi waḥed s-slugi mezyan	'I have a good greyhound'
mɛaya ṭ-ṭumubil dyali	'I have my car with me'

fik n-nuba	'it's your turn'
Ɛlik l-luma	'it's your fault'

2. The Simple Verbal Sentence: The simple verbal sentence consists of a noun or a pronoun as a subject and a verb as a predicate. The subject usually follows the predicate. For example:

ǰaw ḍ-ḍyaf	'the guests have come'
mša huwa	'**he** went'

The pronoun subject of verbal sentences is usually expressed only by the inflected forms of the verb. The use of an independent pronoun subject usually implies contrastive emphasis, e.g.

mšit	'I went'
mšit ana	'**I** went' (not **you**, for example)

3. The Expansion of the Simple Sentence: The most elementary kind of simple sentence consists of a single verb form with the subject pronoun signaled by the affix of the verb, e.g. *klina* 'we ate'. Equally fundamental is the simple sentence which consists of a single word as the subject and a single word as the predicate, e.g. *ḥwayǰu mwessxin* 'his clothes are dirty'. Simple sentences are not necessarily short, however, and the expansion of the subject and predicate brings about simple sentences of considerable length.

Instead of a simple noun subject or predicate, there may be a phrase consisting of a noun with various modifications, for example a noun with an article, with modifying adjectives, in an annexion, etc. Instead of a single verb in the predicate, a verb phrase may occur, and the verb or verb phrase may be accompanied by various adverbial modifiers or by a complement of some sort such as a noun object or a predicate noun or adjective. Various elements of simple sentences may also be compounded by the use of such linking conjunctions as *u* 'and' or *wella* 'or'. A pair of examples:

weldi le-kbir u Ɛemmu bubker kanu mraḍ bezzaf Ɛam luwwel	'my oldest son and his (paternal) uncle Bubker were very sick last year'
waḥed š-šwiya, dexlet waḥed l-xadem, rafda f-yeddiha waḥed ṣ-ṣiniya	'after a little, a maid came in, carrying a tray in her hands'

A common expansion of the elementary simple sentence which does not involve any of the processes mentioned above is the **prestated topic.** The prestated topic is a noun or pronoun which is placed at the beginning of a sentence and which refers to a pronoun, either independent, suffixed, or signaled by verb inflection, occurring later in the sentence. Some examples:

amma ana, ṭaḥu ktafi	'I've worn my arms off' (i.e., 'my shoulders have fallen')
žḥa mƐah l-ḥeqq	'Jha is right'
u dak ṛ-ṛažel z-zoğbi ma-nefƐu ğir...	'and that unlucky man had no choice ('nothing helped him') but to...'
had š-šežṛa, ṛaha fiha l-kenz	'there is a treasure in this tree'
u le-bṭayen, ka-iḥeyydu menhom ṣ-ṣuf w ibiƐuhom le-d-debbağa ḥetta huma	'and they take the wool off the sheep hides and sell them to the tanners too'

In many cases a noun which seems to be the subject of a following verb is separated from the verb by a slight pause and is to be interpreted as a prestated topic rather than directly as the subject, e.g.

le-mğaṛba, ka-yaklu tlata wella ṛebƐa de-l-meṛṛat fe-n-nhaṛ	'(as for) the Moroccans, they eat three or four times a day'

III. THE COMPLEX SENTENCE

Complex sentences are those in which two or more simple sentences are combined in some way to form one larger sentence. In complex sentences, one of the constituent simple sentences stands as an independent sentence while the other simple sentence or sentences function as a subordinate part of it, e.g. *xella l-axoṛ ka-itsenna fih* 'he left the other one waiting for him', where the simple sentence *xella* 'he left' has for an object the entire sentence *l-axoṛ ka-itsenna fih* 'the other one is waiting for him'.

The simple sentence which functions as a subordinate part of a complex sentence may be referred to as the **subordinate clause**, and the simple sentence to which it is subordinated may be referred to as the **main clause**. Simple sentences function as subordinate clauses in complex sentences in only three ways, as nouns, as adjectives, and as adverbs. Complex sentences differ as to whether the constituent clauses are joined by a linking conjunction or by a prestated topic.

1. Complex Sentences Without a Linking Conjunction: Complex sentences of this sort always involve a noun or a pronoun in the main clause serving as a prestated topic for the subordinate clause, e.g. *bġitha dži mƐaya* 'I want her to come with me', where the *-ha* 'her' serves both as the object of *bġit* 'I want' and as the subject of *dži* 'she comes, should come'.

There are two important structural differences between Moroccan and English in such complex sentences. In such sentences as *ka-nƐeṛfu(bin)ka-ifhem š-šelḥa* 'I know (that) he speaks Shilha', the Moroccan equivalent for 'that', *bin,* is rarely used. And in such sentences as *qolt-lu iži* 'I told him to come', the English infinitive, in this case 'to come', is equivalent to a specific Moroccan tense form, in this case *iži* 'he comes, should come'.

The noun or pronoun prestated topic which serves as the link between the main clause and the subordinate clause may have any noun or pronoun function (subject, predicate, object of verb, object of preposition, etc.) in either clause, and the exact semantic relation between the two clauses must be inferred from context. Some examples:

(1) *ṣifeṭ Ɛemmu ixṭeb-lu waḥed le-mṛa Ɛend si-nas* 'he sent his paternal uncle to some people to ask for a certain woman in marriage for him'. The noun *Ɛemmu* 'his paternal uncle' functions as the object of the verb *ṣifeṭ* 'he sent' in the main clause and as the subject of the verb *ixṭeb-lu* 'he asks in marriage for him' in the subordinate clause.

(2) *šafu ši-ġezlan ka-iṛεaw* 'they saw some gazelles grazing'. The noun *ġezlan* 'gazelles' functions as the object of the verb *šafu* 'they saw' in the main clause and as the subject of the verb *ka-iṛεaw* 'they are grazing' in the subordinate clause.

(3) *žbeṛ l-meεza meṛbuṭa f-waḥed s-sedra* 'he found the goat tied to a jubjub tree'. The noun *l-meεza* 'the goat' is the object of the verb *žbeṛ* 'he found' in the main clause and the subject of the equational sentence *l-meεza meṛbuṭa f-waḥed s-sedra* 'the goat is tied to a jubjub tree', which functions as the subordinate clause.

(4) *kan weṣṣani mulah ma-nḥell-š fommi ḥetta newṣeḷ le-ḍ-ḍaṛ* 'its owner had warned me not to open my mouth until I arrived at the house'. The *-ni* 'me' of *weṣṣani* 'he warned me' in the main clause functions as the subject of *ma-nḥell-š* 'I do not, should not open' in the subordinate clause.

(5) *šeftha ġadi iddiha waḥed axoṛ* 'I saw that someone else was going to take (marry) her'. The *-ha* 'her' of *šeftha* 'I saw her' in the main clause is the prestated topic repeated by the *-ha* 'her' of *iddiha* 'he takes, will take her (in marriage)' in the subordinate clause.

(6) *huwa xarež men le-mḥekma u huwa itlaqa waḥed žaybinu saṛeq mkoḥla* 'as he was going out of the court he met someone that they were bringing in for having stolen a rifle'. The prestated topic *waḥed* 'one' is the object of *itlaqa* 'he meets, should meet'[1] in the main clause and is repeated in the subordinate clause by the pronoun object *-u* 'him' of *žaybinu* 'they (are) bringing him'. The *-u* 'him' of *žaybinu* further serves as a prestated topic which is the subject of the following *saṛeq mkoḥla* 'he has stolen a rifle'.

(7) *aṛa dik š-škaṛa nqesmu dak š-ši lli fiha* 'hand over that satchel so that we can divide what's in it'. The prestated topic *š-škaṛa* 'the satchel' is the object of *aṛa* 'hand over!' in the main clause and is repeated in the subordinate clause by the pronoun object *-ha* of *fiha* 'in it'.

(8) *εyit mεahom yeεṭiwha-lek* 'I tried hard to get them (i.e. 'I tired myself out with them') to give her to you (in marriage)'. The *-hom* of *mεahom* 'with them' in the main clause serves as the subject of *yeεṭiwha-lek* 'they give her to you' in the subordinate clause.

(9) *ka-iεawdu εla waḥed ṛ-ṛažel kan ġadi le-s-suq be-εṣatu f-yeddu u škaṛtu εamṛa b-le-flus* 'they recount of a certain man that he was on his way to the market with his stick in his hand and his satchel full of money'. The prestated topic *waḥed ṛ-ṛažel* 'a (certain) man' is the object of the preposition *εla* 'on, about' in the main clause and the subject of *kan ġadi* 'was going' in the subordinate clause.

(10) *ddaweh l-l-baša yeḥkem εlih* 'they took him to the pasha to judge him'. The prestated topic *l-baša* 'the pasha' is the object of the preposition *l-* 'to' in the main clause and the subject of *yeḥkem* 'he judges' in the subordinate clause'.

(11) *ana qolt-lek εṭini l-ḥellab u ntina εṭitini l-keskas* 'I told you to give me the milk-pot and you gave me the couscous-pot'. The *-ek* of *lek* 'to you' in the main clause is the subject of *εṭini* 'give me!' in the subordinate clause.

---

[1] In this context, 'he met'. For the use of the imperfect with a past meaning, see pp. 166, 175.

2. **The Relatives *lli* and *aš*:** The most common use of *lli* is to indicate that a preceding noun or pronoun is a prestated topic for a following subordinate clause. It is usually translatable as 'that', 'which', or 'who'. For example, *žbeṛt l-magana lli nsiti fe-ḍ-ḍaṛ* 'I found the watch that you forgot at home'.

As the object of a preposition or as the possessor of a noun in the subordinate clause, the prestated topic is repeated as a pronoun ending, e.g.

ha le-mkoḥla lli qtelt biha s-sbeƐ	'here's the rifle that I killed the lion with'
waš šefti ṛ-ṛazel lli šrit mennu ḍ-ḍaṛ?	'did you see the man that I bought the house from?'
ha l-bent lli xutha ka-iqṛaw f-bariz	'here's the girl whose brothers are studying in Paris'
ka-nḍuwweṛ Ɛel l-bent lli ḅḅaha mṛiḍ	'I'm looking for the girl whose father is sick'

As an alternative to *lli* and a preposition with a pronoun object, *aš* can be used after the preposition in those cases where a human being is not referred to, e.g. *le-mkoḥla b-aš qtelt s-sbeƐ* 'the rifle that I killed the lion with', *s-sfina f-aš kanu rakbin* the ship that they're riding in'. After *b-* 'with, by means of', the relative *aš* enters into a construction which translates English "ago", e.g. *hadi Ɛešrin Ɛam b-aš mat* 'he died twenty years ago, it's twenty years since he died'.

In other constructions, the pronominal repetition of the prestated topic referred to by *lli* is possible but less common, e.g.

žbeṛt l-magana lli nsiti (less commonly *nsitiha*) *fe-ḍ-ḍaṛ*	'I found the watch that you forgot at home'
ddi had le-ktab l-dak s-siyyed lli Ɛendkom (less commonly *lli huwa Ɛendkom*) *feḍ-ḍaṛ*	'take this book to the gentleman that you have with you at home'

In the case of complex sentences without any linking conjunction, the relation between the two clauses is indicated by the general context. The use of *lli* indicates specifically that the subordinate clause is a restrictive[2] adjectival modifier of the prestated topic. E.g.

waš šefti xutha lli ka-iqṛaw f-bariz?	'did you see her brothers who are studying in Paris?'

[2] 'restrictive', i.e. there are additional members of the class referred to by the prestated topic which do not share the adjectival qualifications of the subordinate clause, thus *xutha lli ka-iqṛaw f-bariz* 'her brothers who are studying in Paris' implies that she has other brothers who are not studying in Paris.

waš šefti xutha ka-iqṛaw f-bariz?	'did you see her brothers studying in Paris?'
bġit dik ṭ-ṭumubil lli ka-temši mezyan	'I want the car that runs good'
bġit ṭ-ṭumubil lli temši mezyan	'I want the car (out of several which are, perhaps, to be tested) that turns out to run good'
bġit dik ṭ-ṭumubil temši mezyan	'I want that car to run good' (perhaps you are instructing someone to repair it)
bġit ši-ṭumubil lli temši mezyan	'I want a car that will run good'

In the case of nouns with the indefinite article *ši*, the definite article, or one of the demonstrative articles (cf. the various examples cited above), the use of *lli* is mandatory if the subordinate clause is to be interpreted as a restrictive adjectival modifier of the prestated topic. The use of *lli* to refer to a prefixless noun or a noun with the indefinite article *waḥed* is, on the other hand, quite rare.

In the sense of 'the one who', 'those who', 'that which', etc., *lli* occurs without a prestated topic. Some examples:

lli bġiti, bġitu	'what you want, I want (it)'
daba ƐṛEft bin ma-iqedd Ɛlikom ġir lli xleqkom	'now I realize that no one has any power over you except the one who created you' (context: a man speaking to a woman)
ġir ila xeḷḷeṣtini fe-lli xṣeṛt	'only if you pay me for what I've spent'
šḥal ka-ddfeƐ de-ž-žebha qoddam lli iḥekku-lek xnafrek fe-l-ʔeṛḍ	'you're showing a lot of nerve in front of people that might rub your nose in the dirt for you'
šeftu ma-ka-yeƐmel ġir lli qal-lu xalu	'I've seen that he only does what his maternal uncle tells him'
lli ṭaṛ-lu fina, nqetluh	'the one among us that gets mad, we'll kill him'
ma-ṣabu, ma-ṣab ḥetta lli yeƐṭih xbaṛu	'he didn't find him, he didn't even find anyone who could give him news of him'
temm dayez Ɛla ḥanut lli Ɛṭaha-lu	'he passed by the shop of the one that had given it to him'
škun lli qal-lek ttṣaref mƐa dak ṛ-ṛažel?	'who is it that told you to do business with that man?'
nta lli sṛeqti	'you're the one who stole'

ma-ka-nsuwwel-š fe-lli ḥṛetha daba	'I'm not asking about the one who cultivated it now'

There are also occasional occurrences of *lli* as a simple subordinate conjunction, e.g.

l-ḥemdu l-llah lli žiti	'thank God you've come'
ana mbaṛek lli ma-dxelt-š l-ši-util	'I'm lucky that I didn't go into some hotel' (context: because it would have been too expensive)

3. Circumstancial *u* 'and': When two clauses are joined by *u* 'and', the second clause often indicates a modifying circumstance with respect to the first. The exact semantic relationship must be inferred from context.

One of the most common cases of this construction involves *u* introducing a personal pronoun (which may be either the subject or the prestated topic for the following verb) followed by an imperfect tense. In this context, *u* has approximately the meaning of 'thereupon', and the imperfect tense has the meaning of the perfect tense. The regular use of *u* in this sense is to be noted when the preceding clause is introduced by *ġir* 'as soon as, no sooner than'. Some examples:

ƐawdetduwwzetƐendu Ɛam, u hiya tewled-lu bnita	'she spent another year with him, and then she bore him a little girl'
ġir semƐuh l-ġezlan u huma iheṛbu	'as soon as the gazelles heard him, they ran away'
waḥed n-nhaṛ kan waḥed ṣ-ṣeḷṭan ġadi iṣiyyeḍ, u huwa itlaqa mƐa waḥed le-Ɛweṛ	'one day a sultan was going hunting and he met a one-eyed man'
bda ka-ixemmem kif-aš ittfokk mennu, u huwa iḍuṛ fih u qal-lu...	'he began thinking about how to get away from him, and he turned to him and said...'
ġir huwa xrež u hiya tƐemmeṛ l-ḥellab b-seksu	'as soon as he went out, she filled the milk-pot with couscous'

A wide variety of other attendant circumstances are indicated by clauses of this type, e.g.

Ɛlaš ka-tnuḍ u nta mṛiḍ?	'why are you getting up, seeing as how you're sick?'

Ɛlaš ka-iḍeṛbuh u huwa ṣġeṛ menhom? — 'why are they hitting him, seeing as how he's smaller than they are?'

had š-ši kollu, u mul l-Ɛeṛṣa ka-išuf fihom men t-tisaƐ — 'all this (was going on) with the owner of the garden watching them from a distance'

The English present perfect with respect to extent of time is rendered by *hadi* 'this' plus an expression of time followed by an equational sentence or a durative tense in a *u* circumstantial clause, e.g.

hadi telt snin w ana ka-nexdem hna — 'I've been working here for three years'

hadi xems šhuṛ u ḥna fe-l-meġṛib — 'we've been in Morocco for five months'

hadi Ɛešrin dqiqa u huwa ka-iƐayenni — 'he's been waiting for me for twenty minutes'

4. The Interrogatives: Interrogative sentences with the interrogative pronouns and adverbs,[3] e.g. *škun?* 'who?', *aš?* 'what?', *fayn?* 'where?', etc., function as subordinate clauses with little change. In subordinate clauses the interrogative *waš* translates as 'whether'. Some examples:

ma-ka-nsuwwel ġir fe-dyal men hiya u fe-škun fikom lli Ɛendu Ɛliha l-molkiya — 'I'm only asking about whose it is and about which one of you has legal title to it'

šuf waš huwa baqi fe-ḍ-ḍaṛ — 'see whether he's still at home'

baqi ma-Ɛṛeft-š l-aš iṣḷaḥ — 'I still haven't figured out what it might be good for'

ma-Ɛendna mn-aš nxafu — 'we don't have anything to be afraid of'

qul-li fayn ka-iskon — 'tell me where he lives'

werrini kif-aš neƐmelha — 'show me how to do it'

When a simple interrogative sentence enters into a complex sentence as a subordinate clause, a noun predicate in the interrogative clause is usually shifted to the main clause and replaced by a pronoun in the subordinate clause, e.g.

škun had ṛ-ṛažel? — 'who is this man?'

---

[3]For the interrogative pronouns, see p. 144. For the interrogative adverbs, see p. 213.

qelleb Ɛla had ṛ-ṛažel škun huwa	'investigate who this man is'
fayn mṛatek?	'where is your wife?'
qul-li mṛatek fayn hiya	'tell me where your wife is'

With *aš?* 'what?', the suffix *-en* is added before *huwa* 'he', *hiya* 'she', and *huma* 'they'. In addition to *aš-en huwa, aš-en hiya,* and *aš-en huma,* the contractions *šnuwa* or *šnu, šniya* or *šni,* and *šnuma* are heard. For example:

fesser-li had l-xedma aš-en hiya (šniya, šni)	'explain to me what this work is'
waš ka-teƐṛef le-xliƐ aš-en huwa (šnuwa, šnu)?	'do you know what *xliƐ* is?'

The interrogatives *ina?* and *aš men? (š-men?)* 'which, what?', e.g. *ina ḍaṛ?* or *aš men (š-men) ḍaṛ?* 'which, what house?', are usually replaced by simple relatives in subordinate clauses, e.g.

f-ina ḍaṛ ka-teskon?	'what house do you live in?'
werrini ḍ-ḍaṛ lli ka-teskon fiha	'show me the house (that) you live in'

5. **Conditional Sentences:** There are two basic types of conditional sentences in Moroccan, depending on whether the if-clause represents a possible or an impossible condition. The two types are distinguished from one another by the particle which introduces the if-clause.

(a) **Impossible Conditions:** Impossible conditions are introduced by the particle *kun* 'if'. Unlike English, Moroccan makes no distinction between past unfulfilled (as in 'If I had been...', implying 'I was not') conditions and present contrary to fact conditions (as in 'If I were...', implying 'I'm not'), e.g. *kun konti,* which is translated into English either as 'if you (sg.) were' or 'if you had been', depending on context.

The verb of if-clauses introduced by *kun* is regularly in the perfect tense. If the result clause is also in the perfect tense, it too is usually introduced by *kun*. Some examples:

kun ma-faqu-š biha, kun ṛaha qaḍat-lhom dak š-ši kollu	'if they hadn't caught her, she would have finished off the whole thing for them'
kun sket, kun flet	'if he had kept quiet, he would have gotten away'

kun tqebbḍet bik waḥed xti kbeṛ menni, kun xerržatek men le-blad bla ʕwin	'if one of my bigger sisters had gotten hold of you, she would have run you out of the town empty-handed'
kun konti ḥmeq, hiya kun šeftek ka-tenqoṣ men dyalek u dzid fe-dyal n-nas	'if you were crazy, the fact is I would have seen you taking away from your own and adding to other people's'
kun ʕmel-li hadi weld ši-axoṛ, kun ʕmelt-lu ši axoṛ kteṛ men had š-ši	'if someone else's son had done this to me, I would have done something more than this to him'
kun kan f-ṛaṣi ši-moxx, men hna la-ṛžeʕt	'if I had any brains in my head, I wouldn't have come back this way'

Various other kinds of result clauses also occur. If the subject of the result clause is a personal pronoun, the pronoun is usually suffixed to the particle *ṛa-* (see p. 214). Some examples:

kun qolt-lhom lilek nta, ma-ʕṛefthom waš ibġiw wella la	'if I had told them it was for you, I don't know whether they would have been willing or not'
kun ma-kanet-š režli mṛiḍa, neʕmelha	'if my foot weren't sore, I'd do it'
kun kont ṣġiṛa bḥalek, hadi hiya ṣ-ṣġiwṛa fe-fʕayli	'if I were young like you, this would be the smallest of my tricks'
a meṣṣab kun kont qedd had t-tuṛ u kanu ʕendi duk le-ktaf dyalu, kun ṛ-ana ma-baqi-š nxaf men bellarež u la men le-ḥnuša	'if only I were as big as this bull and had those shoulders of his, I wouldn't be afraid of either storks or snakes anymore'

Special mention must be accorded to the hortatory use of *kun*, usually without a result clause. Some examples:

kun ġir qoltiha men qbayla u hennitina	'you should have just said it a while ago and left us in peace'
kun žbeṛt ḥett(a)-ana kif nehbeṭ ma-nekṛeh-š	'I wish I could find out how to come down too, I'd like to'
ha-nta ṛak b-ʕeynik, kun qellebtiha	'you've got eyes, you should have inspected her'
kun šefti aš duwwez ʕliya dak ben l-kafer dyal l-xemmas	'you should have seen what that son of an infidel of a sharecropper did to me'
kun ṛak žmeʕti ma takol, bḥal n-nas, u kun ṛak daba la-bas ʕlik	'you should have collected something to eat like (other) people, and you'd be all right now'

(b) Possible Conditions: Possible conditions are introduced by *ila* 'if'. The usual case is for *ila* to be followed by the perfect tense. Result clauses are of various kinds and show little difference from ordinary sentences.

Unlike English, Moroccan makes no distinction among possible conditions between simple future conditions and conditions viewed as unlikely or improbable, e.g. English 'if he comes' and 'if he came' are both rendered by Moroccan *ila ža*. Another point for the English speaker to observe is the occasional occurrence of the perfect tense in result clauses where English usage and meaning call for the present or future, e.g. *ila kan hakda, xellit-lek koll-ši* 'if that's the way it is, I'll leave you everything'. Some general examples:

ila qebḍu ši-ḥedd ka-iritel, ka-iqe.tluh	'if they catch someone looting, they kill him'
ila kanet iyyam ṣ-ṣif, ka-inuḍ ṛ-ṛažel bekri	'if it's summertime, the man gets up early'
ila ṭaḷ fe-l-xabya, ka-itteẓmeɛ fe-l-qaɛ dyalha d-derd	'if it stays in the jar a long time, the lees collect in the bottom'
ila šaṭ ši, ka-yeɛṭiweh l-l-masakin	'if anything is left over, they give it to the poor'
ila šekkiti fiya, neɛṭik ḥeqq ḷḷah	'if you doubt me, I'll swear you an oath'
ila ɛežbuni, nɛeyyeṭ-lkom	'if I like them, I'll call you'
ila ma-ġenna-š, a sidi, itteqṭeɛ ṛaṣi	'if he doesn't sing, sir, let my head be cut off'
ila bġitiha, neɛṭiha-lek	'if you want her, I'll give her to you'
ila ma-žebti-š le-flus, ma-neɛṭik ma takol	'if you don't bring the money, I won't give you anything to eat'
ila neḍti, l-ḥiṭ ṛah iṭiḥ ɛlik	'if you get up, the wall will fall on you'
ila konti maši ttsuwweq, ya-ḷḷah!	'if you're going to market, let's go!'
ila kan ɛendek ši-klam axoṛ, qulu-li	'if you have something else to say, tell it to me'
ila žeɛti, ġir aži takol	'if you're hungry, just come and eat'
sameḥni ila faḷeṭt	'excuse me if I've made an error'

A common phrasing which is equivalent to English 'unless, not until' is to negate the verb of the result clause with *ma-* 'not' and place *ġir* 'only' before *ila* 'if'. Some examples:

ana ma-nesmeḥ ġir ila qbeḍt flusi	'I won't drop charges until I get my money'
kanu muṛaḍhom ma-iṛeḍḍuha-lu ġir ila Ɛmel-lhom n-nzaha	'their aim was, they wouldn't give it back to him unless he gave them a picnic'
r-ṛžal ma-ka-ibniw l-xima b-yeddhom ġir ila ḥažethom Ɛliha l-qoḍṛa	'the men don't put up the tent themselves unless they have to'
ṛakom ma-temšiw ġir ila ṭeḥtu f-l-amana	'you shouldn't go until you've found the treasure'
ma-neƐṭik ġir ila qolti liya aš kayen	'I won't give you (anything) unless you tell me what the matter is'

The sequence of *ila* plus the perfect tense of *mša* 'to go', plus *ḥetta* 'until, so that', plus the perfect tense of another verb, implies 'if it so happens that'. Some examples:

u le-Ɛyadu be-llah ila mša ḥetta Ɛeḍḍ ši-waḥed	'and God help us if he happens to bite somebody'
ila mšiti ḥetta qbeḍtini, ġir qṭeƐhom b-žuž gaƐ	'if you succeed in catching me, just cut them both off'
ila mša bnadem ḥetta kal menha neṣṣ mƐelqa wella mƐelqa gaƐ, ka-ibqa nhaṛ wella yumayn mžebbed f-le-fṛaš, ġayeb Ɛla Ɛeqlu	'if a person happens to eat half a spoonful of it, or a whole spoonful, he stays stretched out in bed out of his senses for a day or two'
ka-išeṛṭu Ɛlih ila mša ḥetta herres ši-ḥaža iġṛemha	'they impose the condition on him that if he happens to break something, he has to pay for it'

There are various exclamatory and hortatory uses of *ila*. For example, the use of *ma* between *ila* and a following verb to indicate a polite request:

ana mzaweg fik, ila ma šuf fiya l-llah u sellef-li ši-ẓṛiƐa	'I implore you, have pity on me and lend me a little grain'
ḷḷah ibarek fik ila ma teƐṭini dak le-ḥmaṛ dyalek, bġit nžib Ɛlih ši-ṭḥin men ṭ-ṭaḥuna	'God bless you, please give me your donkey, I want to bring some flour from the mill on him'
ḷḷah ibarek fik, a sidi, ila ma Ɛzelhom-lna	'God bless you, sir, please sort them out for us'

Another exclamatory pattern is with *ġir ila,* e.g.

ġir ila fditha f-had ṭ-ṭiyyaba!	'all I want to do is get revenge on that masseuse'
we-ḷḷah, ġir ila šeft Ɛemmi l-qenfud waš baqi hna fe-l-bir wella mat	'I think I'll just have a look at my friend the hedgehog and see whether he's still in the well or whether he's died'
tlaqa mƐa ṣaḥbu u ḥlef-lu ġir ila ža itġedda Ɛendu f-dik s-saƐa	'he met his friend and insisted that he come home and have lunch with him right then and there'

Occasionally *ila* is used in the sense of 'when', with no specific idea of condition implied, e.g. *ila ža ṛažlek fe-l-lil, xellih ḥetta inƐes* 'when your husband comes home tonight, leave him alone until he goes to sleep'.

SECTION TWO—THE PARTS OF SPEECH

I. THE VERB

1. **The Simple Verb:** There are four simple verb types. The perfect tense, the imperfect tense, and the imperative mood are defined by separate forms.[1] The fourth simple verb type, the **durative**, is characterized by prefixing *ka–*[2] to the imperfect. To these four types must be added the active participle, which functions as a verb in the sense that it takes objects and indicates various degrees of time and manner of verbal action.

(a) **The Perfect Tense:** With the verb *kan* 'to be', the perfect tense indicates a durative state in the past, e.g. *konna* 'we were'. Otherwise the perfect tense in independent clauses usually indicates simple past action, e.g. *šeftha* 'I saw her'.

For English verbs which inherently refer to actions, e.g. 'to see', 'to hit', 'to eat', etc., as opposed to durative states, e.g. 'to believe', 'to know', 'to be able', etc., the English past tense and the Moroccan perfect tense are directly equivalent to one another, e.g. *ḍṛebni* 'he hit me', *klinahom* 'we ate them', etc.

If the English equivalent of a Moroccan verb refers to a durative state rather than to an action, the Moroccan perfect tense is not directly equivalent to the English past tense. In such cases, some sort of paraphrase in the English translation is necessary to render accurately the meaning of the Moroccan, e.g. *waš Ɛṛeftihom?* 'did you get to know them, did you make their acquaintance?' Similarly the past tense of English durative verbs has to be rendered by some sort of paraphrase in Moroccan, usually by a verb phrase (see below, pp. 179-180), e.g. 'I knew him' is translatable as *kont ka-nƐeṛfu*.

The if-clauses of conditional sentences (see pp. 168ff) and dependent clauses introduced by indefinite relative pronouns or adverbs regularly require the perfect tense of the verb. In such cases the perfect tense itself has no time implications at all, and the time of the entire sentence is indicated either by the result clause or by general context, e.g.

ila žitiw fe-t-tesƐud, džebṛuni hna	'if you come (came) at nine o'clock, you will (would) find me here'

[1]For the inflectional forms of the verb, see pp. 40ff.

[2]Many Moroccans use the prefix *ta–* instead of *ka–*.

fayn-emma mšiti, nemši mɛak	'wherever you go, I'll go with you'
lli šafuh rfedhom, ɛeṛfuh hadak huwa š-šeffaṛ u qebṭuh	'whoever they see pick them up, (you'll) know that he is the thief and arrest him'

The Moroccan perfect tense in the result clause of a conditional sentence (see pp. 168ff) is usually equivalent to an English present or future, e.g. *ila kanet hakda, xellit-lek koll-ši* 'if that's the way it is, I'll give (leave, abandon claim to) everything to you', *ila huwa smeḥ, ḥett(a)-ana smeḥt* 'if he doesn't press charges (a specific legal sense of *smeḥ* 'to permit, to forgive'), neither will I'.

There are occasional cases, mostly in idiomatic expressions, where the perfect tense has a future meaning other than in the result clause of conditional sentences, e.g. *we-ḷḷah la-ɛṭit fih ġir ṛebɛa wa la-zedt ɛlihom ši-fels* 'by God, I'll only give four for it, and I won't add a cent more'.

The English present tense sometimes refers to a current perception, state of mind, or act of will which is logically the result of some preceding act of decision, for example 'Do you accept? — I accept!', in which the English present refers to a present state brought about by a decision of some sort. The perfect tense is usually used in corresponding Moroccan expressions. Some examples:

waš qbelti? — qbelt!	'do you accept? — I accept!'
bġithom	'I want them'
daba fehmetkom	'now she understands, has understood you (pl.)'
šeftu ma-ka-yeɛmel ġir lli qal-lu xalu	'I see that he doesn't do anything except what his (maternal) uncle tells him'

The use of the imperfect in such cases would refer to a future possibility or contingency, e.g. *neqbel* 'I would, I might accept' or *nebġihom* 'I would, I might want them'. The use of the durative instead of the perfect in the last example would indicate a current or habitual action rather than a conclusion based on previous observation.

(b) The Imperfect Tense: The imperfect tense occurs almost exclusively in verb phrases (see pp. 179ff) or in the dependent clauses of complex sentences (see pp. 162ff). Used independently, the imperfect refers to potential action with various shades of specific meaning, such as immediate future action, demands, exhortations, or proposals. Some examples:

nemšiw?	'shall we go?'
daba ixeḷḷeṣni!	'let him pay me now! he should pay me now!'

ġedda iži[3]	'he's supposed to come tomorrow'
daba nƐeyyeṭ-lek	'I'll (put in the) call for you right now'

The independent use of the imperfect is usually limited to the first and third persons of the verb. In contexts where the imperfect tense is used with a first or third person subject, the imperative rather than the imperfect is usual when the subject is in the second person (see p. 173, ex. 11), e.g. *mnin iži, ana nḍeṛbu u nta ṛbeṭ yeddih* 'when he comes I'll hit him and you tie his hands'.

In dependent circumstantial clauses introduced by *u* 'and' (see p. 166), the imperfect is equivalent to a perfect in meaning. The construction has the further peculiarity that the imperfect verb is always immediately preceded by an independent personal pronoun which serves as the prestated topic for the verb. In addition to being past in meaning, the construction also carries the implication of 'thereupon' or 'forthwith, suddenly'. This usage is quite common. Some examples:

ana qolt-lu nsit ma-žebt-š le-flus u huwa iṭṛešni	'I told him I forgot to bring the money, and he (hauled off and) slapped me'
temm ġadi qabeḍ le-ġzal men qeṛnu, u huwa itlaqa waḥed ṣaḥbu men d-dšeṛ u qal-lu...	'he went along holding the gazelle by the horn, and a friend of his from the village met him and said to him...'
huwa ġadi u huwa iban-lu waḥed d-dib ka-iḥuwwem-lu Ɛel n-neƐža	'as he was going along he noticed a wolf on the prowl for his sheep'
ġir semƐuh l-ġezlan u huma iheṛbu	'no sooner than the gazelles heard him than they ran away'
huwa kif xrež men l-bab u huwa itlaqa mul ḍ-ḍaṛ daxel	'he had just gone out the door when he met the master of the house coming in'

(c) **The Imperative:** The imperative is morphologically defined only for the second person (see p. 53ff.) and is of limited distribution in sentences. It occurs only rarely in subordinate clauses (see p. 173, ex. 11) and in verb phrases. The imperative has the further peculiarity that it is not used in the negative (see p. 152). Beyond these limitations, the imperative differs little either in meaning or in use from the English imperative. Some examples:

ddiweh l-l-ḥebs!	'take him to jail!'
aṛa dik š-škaṛa nqesmu dak š-ši lli fiha!	'hand over that satchel and let's divide what's in it!'
ġedda nuwweḍni bekri baš nemši ntsuwweq!	'tomorrow wake me up early so I can go to market!'

[3]Compare *ġadi iži ġedda* 'he'll come tomorrow'.

nuḍ, n-nhaṛ ṭḷeƐ!	'get up, it's daytime!'
ġir qṭeƐhom b-žuž gaƐ!	'just cut them both off!'
aṛaweh-li!	'hand it over to me!'
ya-ḷḷah, ya xuya, qul had l-heḍṛa l-l-qaḍi!	'let's go, brother, tell it to the judge!'
werrih-li!	'show it to me!'
Ɛemlu-li t-tižal!	'grant me a delay!'
neƐlu š-šiṭan!	'curse Satan!' (i.e., 'reconcile your quarrel and come to an agreement!')
ġir sektu!	'just be quiet!'

(d) **The Durative:** For most transitive verbs, the durative indicates either an enduring state or a habitual or progressive action, e.g. *ka-nekteb* 'I write, I am writing'. General context is the only indication as to the appropriate English translation. Some further examples:

ka-yaklu tlata wella ṛebƐa de-l-meṛṛat fe-n-nhaṛ	'they eat three or four times a day'
aš ka-ddir hna?	'what are you doing here?'
ka-idiru n-nuba mƐa beƐḍiyathom	'they take turns with one another'
waš ka-teƐṛef ši f-le-ḥsab?	'do you know anything about arithmetic?'
had l-lḥem ka-ixeṣṣu ši-šwiya d-le-mleḥ	'this meat needs a little salt'
ḷ-ḷeṛḍ ka-ḍḍuṛ Ɛel š-šemš	'the earth turns around the sun'

In a series of verbs, it often happens that the *ka-* is prefixed only to the first one but refers to the entire series, e.g. *koll nhaṛ ka-ixrož l-beṛṛa w iddi mƐah s-slugi* 'every day he goes out and takes the greyhound with him'.

With intransitive verbs referring to motions or states, the durative refers only to states or to habitual or repetitive actions, never to progressive action, e.g.

ka-ikun fe-l-biru dyalu[4] *koll nhaṛ*	'he's in his office every day'
ka-imši le-s-sekwila	'he goes to school'

[4] Cf. *huwa fe-l-biru dyalu daba* 'he's in his office now', where there is no equivalent for English 'is' in the Moroccan equational sentence (see p. 159). Such a sentence as *huwa ka-ikun fe-l-biru dyalu daba* means 'he is (regularly) in his office now(adays)'.

ka-nži fe-t-tesƐud	'I come at nine o'clock'
ka-ixeržu men ḍ-ḍaṛ koll nhaṛ	'they go out of the house every day'
ka-ddxol	'she goes in'
ka-inzel	'he descends, gets down'
ka-yehbeṭ	'he descends, gets down'
ka-iṭḷeƐ	'he ascends, goes up'
ka-yewqef	'he stands, stops'
ka-inƐes	'he sleeps'
ka-iskot	'he becomes, remains silent'
ka-yeƐṛef	'he knows'
ka-ifhem	'he understands'

Certain transitive verbs of motion are also limited to habitual or repetitive meanings in the durative, e.g. *ka-ižibhom* 'he brings them'. Certain verbs refer indifferently either to an immediate activity or a necessary resultant of that activity, e.g. *rkeb* 'to mount' or 'to ride' (mounting being a necessary prerequisite to riding), *lbes* 'to put on' (clothing) or 'to wear' (putting something on being a necessary prerequisite to wearing it). In reference to the immediate activity, the durative of such verbs is either habitual or progressive in meaning but in reference to the resultant of the immediate activity the durative is only habitual, never progressive, in meaning. The durative form of such verbs thus has three possible translations, e.g.

ka-irkeb	'he mounts'
	'he is mounting'
	'he rides' (but not 'he is riding')
ka-ilbesha	'he puts it on'
	'he is putting it on'
	'he wears it' (but not 'he is wearing it')

As is illustrated in all the examples above, the usual translation of the Moroccan durative is with the English present or present progressive verb forms, e.g. 'they write' or 'they are writing', etc. The Moroccan verb forms do not, however, inherently refer to present time. In a general context or in verb phrases referring to past time, the durative forms refer to past habitual action (i.e., 'used to') or past progressive action (i.e., 'was doing'), e.g. *kan ka-ikteb* 'he used to write, he was writing' (see pp. 166-167, 179ff.).

The use of the durative as a circumstantial adjective translating the English present participle is also common, e.g. *glesna mƐahom ka-naklu ši-tlata de-s-saƐat* 'we sat eating with them for some three hours'.

(e) **The Active Participle:** For those verbs of which the durative form indicates only habitual or repetitive action but not progressive action (see pp. 176-177, above), the active participle has a progressive meaning. Its place in the sentence is that of a predicate adjective in an equational sentence (see p. 159). Some examples:

huwa maši	'he is going'
huwa maži	'he is coming'
huwa xarež	'he is going out'
huwa daxel	'he is entering'
huwa gales	'he is seated'
huwa naƐes	'he is asleep'
huwa saket	'he is quiet'

The active participles of *Ɛṛef* 'to know' and *fhem* 'to understand', verbs which in English do not normally have a progressive form, are translated as the English present tense, just as is the durative. There are, however, different shades of meaning. Compare:

ka-yeƐṛef	'he knows' (in general, or not only now but also previously)
huwa Ɛaṛef	'(now) he knows' (but possibly he did not know previously)
ka-ifhem	'he understands' (in general, or not only now but also previously)
huwa fahem	'(now) he understands' (although possibly previously he did not)

The active participle of *kan* 'to be' is specialized in the meaning of 'there is, there are'. In terms of agreement, it is a predicate adjective, and it regularly precedes the subject in sentences, e.g.

kayen waḥed s-slugi l-l-biƐ temma	'there's a greyhound for sale there'
kayna z-zebda fe-l-qelluša	'there's some (fresh) butter in the pot'
kaynin ši-šeffaṛa fe-ṭ-ṭṛiq	'there are some robbers on the road'

The active participle of most transitive verbs signals an unchanged current state brought about by previous action. In this respect it contrasts with the perfect tense, which indicates only a previous action with no reference as to current relevance. Compare:

hiya ġeṭṭatha	'she covered it' (it may or may not be still covered)
hiya mġeṭṭyaha	'she has covered it' (it is still covered)
ana ktebt Ɛlih "felfel"	'I wrote "pepper" on it' (e.g. a label on a drawer, perhaps the label is no longer there)
ana kateb Ɛlih "felfel"	'I've written "pepper" on it' (and the label is still there)

This particular use of active participles, for the current relevance of previous actions, is used almost exclusively in contexts where a direct contrast exists between an action which is contemporary with a state brought about by some previous action. The examples of the active participle immediately above would scarcely occur in isolation as cited. In isolation the English present perfect is rendered by the Moroccan perfect, e.g. *ktebt* 'I have written', *ġeṭṭatha* 'she has covered it'. A proper contextual use of the examples cited in isolation above is illustrated by the following:

dexlet waḥed l-xadem, rafda f-yeddiha waḥed ṣ-ṣiniya..., mġeṭṭyaha b-waḥed z-zif meṭṛuẓ	'a maid came in, carrying in her hands a tray which she had covered ('she having covered it') with an embroidered napkin'
Ɛṛeftek bin bġiti s-sokkaṛ u huwa nnit lli f-had le-mžeṛ, belḥeqq ana kateb Ɛlih "felfel" baš ila žah n-nmel u qṛa le-ktaba iṛžeƐ f-ḥalu	'I know that you want sugar, and that's exactly what's in this drawer, but I've written "pepper" on it so that if the ants come they'll read the writing and go away'

2. **The Verb Phrase:** A verb phrase is a sequence of two or more verb forms, all of which have the same subject and in which each preceding verb form is a subordinate modifier of each following verb form, e.g. *bda ka-iġenni* 'he began singing, to sing'. Typically, a verb phrase consists of two verb forms, the first of which is an auxiliary which modifies the following verb form as to time (past, present, etc.) or manner (habitual, repetitive, progressive, etc.) of action. Phrases of three or more verb forms are relatively rare and consist entirely of a compounding of auxiliaries. The most common auxiliaries and types of verb phrases are listed below.

(a) **The Auxiliary** ***kan*:** Forms of *kan* 'to be' are used before the perfect, the imperfect, the durative, and the active participle of verbs. The most common use of *kan* as an auxiliary is in the perfect tense in combination with a following durative or with active participles which are equivalent to English progressives (see pp. 176-178). The meaning is that of past habitual, repetitive, durative, or progressive action. The distinction between progressive as opposed to habitual, repetitive, or durative (see pp. 176-178) with verbs of motion is maintained in the past. Some examples:

kont ka-nexdem	'I used to work, I was working'
konna ka-nfettšu Ɛlihom	'we used to look for them, we were looking for them'
ma-kont-š ka-neƐṛefhom	'I didn't know them'
kan ka-irkeb had l-Ɛewd	'he used to ride, he used to mount, he was mounting this horse'
kanu ka-ixeṛžu fe-t-tesƐud	'they used to go out at nine o'clock'
kanu xaṛžin fe-t-tesƐud	'they were going out (once, at a specific moment) at nine o'clock'
waš konti ka-temši l-had s-sekwila?	'did you use to go, were you going (regularly, habitually) to this school?'
waš konti maši l-had s-sekwila?	'were you going (on your way at a given moment) to this school?'[5]
kan wažed-lhom	'he was waiting for them'

The use of *kan* in the perfect tense as an auxiliary before a verb in the perfect or before the active participle of an ordinary transitive verb is rather uncommon. The time indicated is that of a past perfect, and such phrases are mostly limited to where the time of the verb phrase is emphatically prior to the time indicated by the perfect tense of some other verb in a broader context. The active participle of ordinary transitive verbs in such phrases usually indicates that the result of the past perfect action was still in force at the time of the other perfect tense in the broader context. The perfect indicates only the anteriority of the action with no implication as to subsequent state, e.g.

herrest l-xabya f-aš kanu Ɛamlin le-xliƐ	'I broke the jar that they had put the preserved meat in (and the meat was still in the jar at the time of breaking)'

---

[5]English 'going' is ambiguous in a way which its Moroccan translations are not. Note the three possible different meanings of 'he was going there', i.e. (1) regularly, habitually some time in the past, (2) he was progressively on his way at some one given moment in the past, (3) future intention, as 'he was going (to go) there, but he changed his mind'.

herrest l-xabya f-aš kanu Ɛemlu le-xliƐ — 'I broke the jar that they had put the preserved meat in (whether the meat was still in the jar at the time of breaking is not stated)'

mšat xebbatha fe-ḥwayež waḥed le-mṛa kanet žat tƐum — 'she went and hid it in the clothes of a woman that had come to bathe'

Auxiliary use of forms of *kan* other than the perfect occur rarely only because the meanings signaled by them are of relatively rare occurrence, e.g.

mnin dži ġedda, ġadi ikun feḍḍa l-xedma dyalu — 'when you come tomorrow, he will have finished his work'

koll nhaṛ ka-tkun režƐet fe-t-tesƐud — 'by nine o'clock every day, she has returned'

koll nhaṛ ka-tkun ṛažƐa fe-t-tesƐud — 'everyday at nine o'clock she's on her way back'

Such a phrase as *ka-tkun ṛažƐa* 'she is (regularly, repetitively, habitually) on the way back, returning' may be contrasted with *hiya ṛažƐa* 'she is (once, at one given moment) on her way back, returning'.

(b) The Auxiliary *bda* 'to begin': Forms of *bda* 'to begin' are followed by the durative.[6] Some examples:

bda ka-iƐum — 'he began, has already begun to swim'

bdaw ka-iḍḍaṛbu — 'they began to hit each other'

bdaw n-nas ka-iqulu... — 'the people began saying...'

bda ṛ-ṛẓuẓi ka-iƐeḍḍ fih — 'the wasps began biting him'

men temma l-qoddam, bda ka-ižib-li ḥeqqi — 'from then on he began to bring me my share'

(c) The Auxiliary *bqa* 'to remain': This auxiliary is followed by the durative or by the active participle when it corresponds to an English progressive (see pp. 176-178). Some examples:

bqat ka-tƐayenhom — 'she kept waiting for them'

---

[6] In some dialects of Moroccan, e.g. Fez, the imperfect is used.

bqa ka-ifetteš fe-l-bir ḥetta ɛya	'he kept on searching in the well for a long time ('until he got tired')'
bqa ka-yakol	'he kept on eating, he continued eating'
bqa ka-imši	'he kept going (habitually)'
bqa maši	'he kept going, continued on his way (once, on a given occasion)'

When negated, *bqa* in verb phrases is equivalent to 'no longer, not any more', with either past or present reference, e.g. *ma-bqa-š ka-iḍḥek ɛlihom* 'he didn't (doesn't) laugh at them any more'.

The active participle *baqi* preceding the durative is equivalent to English 'still'. In such cases it is invariable in gender and number for some speakers and agrees regularly for other speakers, e.g.

huwa baqi ka-ixdem mɛana	'he's still working with us'
hiya baqi (baqya, baqa) ka-texdem mɛana	'she's still working with us'
huma baqi (baqyin) ka-ixedmu mɛana	'they're still working with us'

(d) The Auxiliary ***bġa*** **'to want':** Verbs following *bġa* 'to want' are invariably in the imperfect, e.g. *bġit nemši* 'I want to go'. The perfect of *bġa* is usually equivalent to the English present tense, e.g. *bġina nšufukom* 'we want to see you all'.

In contexts where a perfect tense form of *bġa* refers to past time, English 'wanted' is usually not an appropriate translation, since the past tense of English 'to want' refers to a state rather than an action. Usual translations of *bġa* in such cases are 'to be about to', 'to decide to', or, in the negative, 'to refuse to'. Some examples:

ttawaw ɛlih xutu, bġaw iqetluh	'his brothers plotted against him and decided to kill him'
ḥefṛu waḥed l-ḥofṛa u bġaw isiyybuh fiha	'they dug a hole and were about to throw him into it'
ma-bġa-š išufni	'he refused to see me, he wouldn't see me'

The active participle of *bġa* preceded by the perfect of *kan* translates English 'wanted', e.g. *kont baġi nemši mɛahom, belḥeqq ma-xellawni-š* 'I wanted to go with them, but they didn't let me'. The imperfect of *bġa* is usually translatable as 'would like', e.g. *gaɛ ma-šefnak kif nebġiw* 'we haven't seen you at all as (much as) we would like to'.

(e) Auxiliary Verbs of Motion: The most common of these are *mša* 'to go' and *ža* 'to come'. When followed by the perfect, completed action is signaled, when followed by the imperfect, purpose without necessary completion is signaled, e.g. *mša šra l-lḥem* 'he went and bought some meat', *mša išri l-lḥem* 'he went to buy some meat' (perhaps he did not finally succeed in or get around to buying the meat). Some further examples:

mša xḷeṭ ɛla mul le-ḥlib	'he went and called on the milkman'
mša nzel fe-blad oxṛa	'he went and settled in another town'
mša žab-li ši-želd de-l-begri	'he went and brought me some old cowhide'
ažiw tšufu bnadem qedd-aš kan, zman, be-ṭ-ṭuḷ	'come look how tall human beings used to be in olden times'
ža waḥed ž-žebli l-fas itsuwweq	'a mountaineer came to Fez to shop'
mša ixṭeb le-mṛa l-weld xuh	'he went to ask for the woman's hand for his nephew'
mšaw l-l-wad iṣebbnu	'they went to the river to do their laundry'
mša waḥed fihom ibiɛu	'one of them went to sell it'
nemši nžib-lu waḥed l-berrada de-l-ma	'I'll go bring him a jug of water'
gles yakol	'he sat down to eat'
ɛad naḍ yehḍeṛ ḥetta huwa	'then he stood up to talk too'
tleffet išuf škun huwa hadak	'he turned around to see who it was'
wqef ž-ždi iṛɛa	'the kid stopped to graze'
xrež ṛaželha itqeḍḍa ḥaža fe-s-suq	'her husband went out to the market to shop'
zad l-axoṛ iḍuṛ muṛahom	'the other one set out to go around behind them'
ṛžeɛ ifetteš ɛla flusu	'he went back to look for his money'

(f) The Auxiliary *ġadi*: This auxiliary is invariably followed by the imperfect and indicates future time, e.g.

aš ġadi nelbes ana?	'what am I going to wear?'
u f-aš ġadi tɛemlu?	'and what are you going to put it in?'

ġadi nḍeṛbu l-Ɛud	'we're going to draw lots'
ġadi nnƐes	'I'm going to go to sleep'

Preceded by the perfect of *kan,* the auxiliary *ġadi* indicates a past future, e.g. *kan ġadi ixeḷḷeṣni* 'he was going to pay me'.

The use of *ġadi* as an auxiliary is to be distinguished from its use as a simple active participle meaning 'going', e.g. *kan ġadi le-s-suq be-Ɛṣatu f-yeddu* 'he was going, was on his way to the market with his stick in his hand'.

As an auxiliary *ġadi* is usually invariable in number and gender. As a participle, the feminine is *ġadya* or *ġada* and the plural is *ġadyin* or *ġadin.* Often at normal conversational speed, *ġadi* is shortened to *ġad* or even *ġa,* e.g. *ġa-nekteb-lek ġedda* 'I'm going to write to you tomorrow'.

(g) The Auxiliary *temm:* This auxiliary is used only before the active participle of verbs of motion or before *FeƐƐaL* forms with meanings equivalent to the active participle of verbs of motion (see p. 178). In this construction *temm* has no meaning of its own. The content is the meaning of the specific verb involved combined with the tense of *temm,* and such phrases are interchangeable with the simple tense of the specific verb in the construction. Some examples:

temm maši l-Ɛendhom	'he came up to them'
refdu le-Ɛwin dyalhom u temmu ġadyin	'they picked up their provisions and set off'
temm tabƐu	'he followed him'
temm maši l-Ɛend mṛatu u qal-lha...	'he came to his wife and said to her...'
temmina ġadyin l-Ɛend l-baša	'we went to the Pasha'
temm huwwad	'he went down'

(h) *Ɛawed* **'to return':** This auxiliary combines with a following verb in the sense of 'again'. The perfect of *Ɛawed* calls for the perfect of the following verb. Other forms of *Ɛawed* (imperfect, durative, imperative) call for the imperfect of the following verb. Some examples:

Ɛawdet duwwzet Ɛendu Ɛam	'she spent another year with him'
Ɛawed qal-lu	'he told him again'
Ɛawdet dexlet	'she went in again'
ma-tƐawed-š tšufu	'don't see him any more, again'

fuq-emma ka-iži le-s-suq, ka-iži isellem ɛliya w imši itqeḍḍa ḥaža w iɛawed iži išufni	'every time he comes to the market, he comes to greet me and (then) goes shopping and (then) comes to see me again'
ila mšiti ḥetta ɛawedti šeftiha...	'if you happen to see her again...'

(i) *xeṣṣ* **'must, to have to'**: This auxiliary is quite common. The pattern is for it to take object pronoun endings which serve as the subject of a following imperfect verb form. Some examples:

xeṣṣni nexdem l-yum	'I have to work today'
xeṣṣek ḍḍṛeb-li tilifun	'you (sg.) must (i.e. 'please do') give me a phone call'
xeṣṣha temši le-s-suq	'she has to go to the market'

To indicate a habitual or repetitive situation, the durative *ka-ixeṣṣ* is sometimes used, cf. *ka-ixeṣṣha temši le-s-suq koll nhaṛ* 'she has to go to the market every day' as opposed to *xeṣṣha temši le-s-suq l-yum* 'she has to go to the market today'. This distinction is not made absolutely consistently by all speakers, and the perfect *xeṣṣ* is also used to indicate habitual or repetitive action.

With a preceding *kan* the usual translation is 'should have', *kan xeṣṣkom teɛṭiwhom-li* 'you all should have given them to me'.

II. THE NOUN

I. General Functions

The general functions of the noun in Moroccan are similar to those of the English noun. Seven main functions are distinguishable: (1) As the subject of a sentence, e.g. *dexlet waḥed l-xadem* 'a maid came in'. (2) As the object of a verb, e.g. *šeft ṛ-ṛažel* 'I saw the man', *šra l-xobz* 'he bought some bread'. (3) As a predicate complement, e.g. *ana nežžaṛ* 'I am a carpenter'. (4) As an objective complement, e.g. *mesxu ṛebbi bellarež* 'God transformed him into a stork', *semmit weldi Ɛli* 'I named my son Ali'. (5) As the object of a preposition, e.g. *mƐa ṣaḥbi* 'with my friend', *fe-ḍ-ḍaṛ* 'in the house'. (6) As an adverb of time, e.g. *bqa yumayn* 'he stayed for two days'. (7) As a vocative, *a Ɛli, fayn konti?* 'Ali, where have you been?'

II. Modifications

There are five basic modifications of the noun. These are definition, annexion, pronominal possession, adjectival modification, and enumeration. Definition, annexion, and pronominal possession are discussed immediately below. Adjectival modification and enumeration of nouns are treated under the discussion of adjectives, see p. 204f., and numerals, see p. 206f., respectively.

1. Definition: There are four degrees of definition of the noun. Nouns occur **prefixless**, prefixed with an **indefinite article**, prefixed with the **definite article**, or prefixed with a **demonstrative article.**

Certain nouns never take the definite article, regardless of grammatical construction, and certain grammatical constructions exclude the occurrence of the definite article with a noun, regardless of whether the noun is found to occur with the definite article elsewhere. Otherwise, any noun may occur with any one of the four degrees of definition.

(a) The Prefixless Noun: Except for those nouns which never take the definite article (see below under **(c)**), prefixless nouns are of relatively restricted occurrence. Other than their use in the strict numerical sense of 'one', Moroccan prefixless nouns are approximately the same in meaning as nouns with an indefinite article (see below) and are usually translated into English as a noun with 'a', 'an', or 'some', or as a noun without article.

The most common use of the prefixless noun is as the predicate complement of some noun or pronoun. Some examples:

huwa qaḍi	'he is a judge'
Ɛžuba hadi!	'this is a miracle!'
weḥla hadi!	'this is a predicament!'
msexni ṛebbi ḥmaṛ	'God transformed me into a donkey'
kont Ɛezri Ɛend yemma, u ḥkayti ḥkaya	'I was a bachelor (living) with my mother, and my story is a (real) story'
ṣ-ṣemṭ ḥekma	'silence is wisdom'
melli Ɛeṛfu le-fqi ytim...	'as soon as the teacher knew him (to be; knew that he was) an orphan...'
huma kollhom nšaywiya	'they are all addicts'
babak ihudi	'your father is a Jew'
had le-mkoḥla Ɛendi melli kanet ferdi ḥetta kebret	'I've had this rifle from the time it was a pistol until it grew up'
hadi kedba mbeṛṛqa	'that's a plain lie'
kan waḥed ṛ-ṛažel ḥšayši u mžuwwež bentu l-waḥed le-ḥšayši bḥalu	'there was a man who was a marihuana addict, and he married his daughter to a marihuana addict like himself'

The last example provides a good illustration of the difference in usage between the prefixless noun and the noun with the indefinite article. The prefixless *ḥšayši* 'a marihuana addict' is used as a predicate equivalent of *waḥed ṛ-ṛažel* 'a man', whereas *waḥed le-ḥšayši* shows *ḥšayši* prefixed with the indefinite article and functioning as a simple indefinite noun.

The only other common uses of the prefixless noun are in categorical negative expressions (see p. 154), certain limited expressions of time, with the specific numerical meaning of 'one' (either with or without *waḥed* 'one'), and in miscellaneous idiomatic expressions.

Some examples of prefixless nouns in negative expressions:

ma fiha šekk	'there's no doubt about it'
bla šekk	'without doubt'

xellit l-luḥa bla ktaba	'I left the writing-board without any writing (on it)'
εemmṛek ma-εṭitini ḥetta ždi baš nefṛeḥ mεa ṣḥabi	'you've never given me even a single kid (i.e., for eating) so that I could have a party with my friends'
ma-fih fayda	'there's no good in him, he's not worth anything'
waš ma-seqti xbaṛ?	'haven't you heard the news?'
u ma-kayen-š lli iqḍeṛ iqul-lha ḥetta kelma	'and there's no one who can say even a single word to her'

Some examples with expressions of time:

duwwzet εendu εam	'she spent a year with him'
bġit neḥki-lek waḥed le-ḥkaya dyal nhaṛ bġat yemma ttqob-li wedniya	'I want to tell you a story about the day my mother wanted to pierce my ears for me'
ġab εliya εamayn	'he was away from me for two years'
bqa modda ṭwiḷa	'he stayed for a long time'

Some examples with the specific numerical meaning of 'one':

qolt-lek ma-teεṭini ma-εada telt awaq,...derhem bġit nekri bih waḥed l-fas..., u derhem bġit neεṭih l-le-εdul,...u derhem bġit nešri bih xobza	'I told you to give me only three dirhams, one dirham to rent an axe with, one dirham to give to the notaries, and one dirham to buy a loaf of bread with'
lqina waḥed le-mkuwwṛa ma-kayen-š ma kbeṛ menha, ġir weṛqa menha ḍḍeḷḷeḷna teḥt menha	'we found a cabbage, nothing could be bigger than it, just one leaf of it could give us shade under it'
ana u buh, konna gaε f-kanun waḥed	'his father and I were in the same affair'

Some idiomatic expressions:

ṭaṛet mennu xelεa	'he got scared' ('fear flew from him')
xrežna εla xir	'we came out all right, we got away safely'

bin fṭa u hwa	'between heaven and earth, up in the air'
daru ɛers men ɛerstayn	'they had a magnificent wedding' ('they made one wedding from two')
xrež ṛaželha itqeḍḍa ḥaža fe-s-suq	'her husband went out to shop in the market'

(b) The Indefinite Articles: The potential indefinite article *ši* is prefixed both to singular and plural nouns, e.g. *ši-ktab* 'a book, some book or other' and *ši-ktub* 'some books'. The concretizing indefinite article *waḥed*[1] is prefixed only to singular nouns.[2] A noun following *waḥed* regularly has the definite article unless it is of a type which categorically excludes the definite article or is in a grammatical construction which excludes the definite article (see (c) below), e.g. *waḥed ṛ-ṛažel* 'a man', *waḥed bellarež* 'a stork', *waḥed weld ɛemmi* 'a cousin (son of my paternal uncle) of mine', *waḥed ṣaḥbi* 'a friend of mine'. In these examples, *bellarež* 'stork' is a word which never takes the definite article, *weld* 'son, boy' is the first term of a construct state, which is a grammatical construction which excludes the definite article, and *ṣaḥbi* 'my friend' has a pronoun ending, the occurrence of which with a noun excludes the definite article.

The potential indefinite article *ši* is most usually translatable into English as 'some', e.g. *ši-ḍaṛ* 'some house (or other)', *ši-ḥaža* 'something'. The concretizing indefinite article always refers to something clearly specific and is usually translated with the English indefinite article, e.g. *waḥed le-ktab* 'a book'.

The difference between the two indefinite articles has various implications for usage and translation. For example, the two sentences *waḥed n-nhaṛ ana šeftu fe-s-suq* and *ši-nhaṛ ana šeftu fe-s-suq* are approximately the same in meaning and translate as 'I saw him in the market one day'. The same sentence structure applied to the future admits only *ši-nhaṛ* 'some day', since the time referred to is potential rather than actual, thus *ši-nhaṛ ana ġadi nšufu fe-s-suq* 'some day I'm going to see him in the market'.

(c) The Definite Article: There are two principal grammatical constructions that exclude the use of the definite article. These are nouns with pronoun endings (see pp. 134ff.) and nouns other than numerals which are the first term of a construct state (see pp. 191ff.) e.g. *benti* 'my daughter', *weld l-qaḍi* 'the son of the judge'.

In addition there are three groups of words which never take the definite article: (1) The abstract nouns of profession and personal characteristic (see pp. 88-89), e.g. *tanežžaṛet* 'carpentry', *tawekkalet* 'gluttony', *tamwagniyet* 'clock-, watch-making'. (2) Proper names, e.g. *fas* 'Fez', *fṛanṣa* 'France', *mḥemmed* 'Mohamed'. The only exception is that there are certain proper names which have

---

[1] The indefinite article *waḥed,* which is invariable for gender and which precedes its noun, is not to be confused with the numeral adjective msc. *waḥed,* fem. *weḥda* 'one', which follows its noun.

[2] In some dialects of Moroccan (e.g. Fez), *waḥed* is also used with plural nouns.

the definite article as an integral part of the name, e.g. *ṛ-ṛbaṭ* 'Rabat', *ḍ-daṛ l-biḍa* 'Casablanca'. (3) A number of words which must be memorized as individual lexical items, e.g. *bellarež* 'stork', which is translatable into English as 'a stork', 'the stork', or simply 'stork', depending on context. The most frequent of these words are:

atay	'tea'
bibi	'turkey' (the bird)
bellarež	'stork'
bnadem	'human being'
maṭiša	'tomatoes; (child's) swing'
muka	'owl'
seksu	'couscous'
tamara	'trouble, pain'
ṭaba	'tobacco'
xizzu	'carrots'
žahennam	'hell'

The definite article is prefixed to the noun and is often translatable as English 'the', e.g. *l-bab* 'the door'. However, the Moroccan definite article has a much wider range of use than the English definite article and is often used in situations where English uses no article at all.

The Moroccan definite article is regularly used in referring to abstractions, e.g. *s-siba hadi!* 'this is anarchy!', and to materials, e.g. *waḥed s-selham de-ṣ-ṣuf* 'a wool cloak, a cloak of wool'. The Moroccan definite article in such cases differs from English usage and does not appear in the English translation. For the use of the article in vocatives, see p. 215.

The Moroccan definite article is also widely used in referring to categories as a whole, in which case it is often omitted in English translation or rendered by 'some' or by the indefinite article, e.g. *l-ful* '(the) beans' in such a sentence as *sir le-s-suq u šri l-ful* 'go to the market and buy some beans'. Or *s-selham* '(the) cloak' in *l-yum huwa labes s-selham* 'today he's wearing a cloak'.

(d) The Demonstrative Articles: There are two demonstrative articles, the general demonstrative *had,* which is invariable for number and gender, and the far demonstrative *(ha)dak,* which agrees in number and gender with the noun it accompanies. For the forms see p. 143.

The demonstrative articles precede the noun they modify, and, as with the indefinite article *waḥed* (see above), the nouns they precede take the definite article unless they happen to be of a noun type or in a grammatical construction which excludes it. Some examples:

had l-weld	'this boy'
(ha)dak l-weld	'that boy'
had l-bent	'this girl'
(ha)dik l-bent	'that girl'
had d-drari	'these children'
(ha)duk d-drari	'those children'
had atay	'this tea'
(ha)dak atay	'that tea'
had ṣaḥbi	'this friend of mine'
(ha)dak ṣaḥbi	'that friend of mine'
had weld Ɛemmi	'this cousin of mine'
(ha)dak weld Ɛemmi	'that cousin of mine'

2. **Annexion:** There are two types of annexion, the **construct state** and **analytic annexion**. The construct state is relatively little used in expressing annexion, whereas analytic annexion is one of the most widespread and fundamental syntactic patterns of the language. There is no single English grammatical category corresponding to annexion in Moroccan, and translations assume a variety of forms.

(a) **The Construct State:** The construct state is characterized by a noun or an adjective followed directly by a noun or a pronoun, e.g. *ḥanut babaha* 'her father's shop'. These are referred to respectively as the **first term of the construct** and the **second term of the construct**. The first term of the construct never takes a pronoun ending or, except for numerals, the definite article. Nothing comes between the two terms of the construct except an article (indefinite, definite, demonstrative; see above pp. 146ff) modifying the second term, e.g. *Ɛyalat le-xwayež* 'the wives of the rich', *režlin had l-weld* 'this boy's feet'.

(1) **Constructs in Which Both the First and Second Terms are Nouns:** The typical and most common case is for both the first and second terms of the construct to be nouns. The semantic implication is that the second term is a subordinate modifier of the first, and the exact shade of meaning depends on the meaning of the specific nouns involved. There are three typical translations into English:

(1) The two terms are joined by 'of':

bab ḍ-ḍaṛ	'the door of the house'
(bḥal) fṣaḷt ši-hri kbir	'(like) the shape of some big granary'
hel fas	'the people of Fez'
qaƐ l-bir	'the bottom of the well'
ṣṭuḥ ḍyuṛkom	'the roofs of your houses'
taman feṛṛuž	'the price of a rooster'

(2) The second term is translated by an English possessive:

atay ṣ-ṣeḷṭan	'the sultan's tea'
ḍaṛ ṛ-ṛažel	'the man's house'
fḍayeḥ nsibu	'his son-in-law's rascalities'
klam baba	'my father's words'
bent t-tažer	'the merchant's daughter'
ḍhuṛ n-nas	'people's backs'

(3) The order of the terms is reversed and the subordinate noun functions as an adjectival modifier of the other:

bab le-mdina	'the city gate'
doxxan ṭaba	'tobacco smoke'
ḥanut nežžaṛ	'a carpenter shop'
mefṛeq ṭ-ṭoṛqan	'a road junction, a cross-roads'
ṣḷat le-Ɛša	'the evening prayer'
sġol ḍ-ḍaṛ	'the house work'

(2) **Constructs in Which the Second Term is a Pronoun:** The cases where the second term of a construct is a pronoun are relatively rare but are the same structurally and semantically as constructs in which both terms are nouns. Some examples:

ana Ɛemm dak lli žab-lek le-rneb	'I'm the (paternal) uncle of the one that brought you the rabbit'

ržel hada	'this one's (man's, person's) foot'
bu lli žitu ṭṭeḷḷu ʕlih	'the father of the one (whom, him whom, the one whom) you came to visit'
weld men nta?	'whose son are you?'
bent men hadi?	'whose daughter is this?'
sabab had š-ši kollu	'the reason for (of) this whole thing'

(3). **Constructs in Which the First Term is an Adjective:** Constructs with an adjective as the first term are rare and are usually descriptive clichés. The second term is always a noun. The entire construct functions adjectivally, and within it the second term specifies the area of reference of the adjective first term. Some examples:

byeḍ le-wžeh	'white-faced'[3]
kbir l-kerš	'big-bellied, greedy'
ṭwiḷ l-qama	'tall in stature'
ʕṛiḍ le-ktaf	'broad-shouldered'

(4) **Complex Constructs:** There are two kinds of complex constructs. In one type, the second term is two or more nouns coordinately joined by *u* 'and', e.g.

ʕyalat ṛ-ṛbaṭ u fas	'the women of Rabat and Fez'
zerriʕt l-qeṣbuṛ u l-kamun	'seed(s) of coriander and cumin'
ḍfaṛ yeddihom u režlihom	'the nails of their hands and feet'
le-ḍyaṛ l-wazaṛa u l-qoyyad u l-baša u l-metḥesseb	'to the houses of the ministers, the chiefs, the pasha, and the market inspector'

In the other type, a series of nouns are in construct to one another, and a noun which serves as a second term with reference to a preceding noun serves as a first term to a following noun. The occurrence of this type of complex construct is rare and is almost never made up of more than three terms, e.g.

[3]In the sense of having light colored skin, not in the sense of being pale with anger, fear, etc.

bab ḍaṛ ṣ-ṣeḷṭan	'the door of the Sultan's palace'
nhaṛ lilt ṣ-ṣafaṛ	'(the day of) the eve of the journey'
nhaṛ xluq sidna žebril	'the day of the birth of our Lord Gabriel'
riḥt bul bnadem	'the smell of human urine'
weld biyyaƐt le-ḥsuwa[4]	'son of a (female) soup seller'
ana ben Ɛemm mul le-rneb[5]	'I am the son of the paternal uncle of the rabbit man'

(5) **The Limitations of the Construct:** Theoretically any two nouns may occur together in construct. In actual practice, however, annexion between two nouns is usually expressed analytically (see below, p. 202, for analytic annexion), and only a limited number of nouns and noun types occur together in construct. Except for a set of clichés with *ḷḷah* 'God' as the second term of the construct, the limitation of occurrence is a matter of which nouns are found as the first term of a construct while any semantically appropriate noun occurs as the second term.

The chief nouns and noun types occurring in the construct state are as follows:[6]

(1) Body parts, either animal or human, whether used literally or metaphorically. Some examples:

demm wežhi	'retribution' (for an affront), literally 'the blood of my face'
ḍfaṛ yeddihom	'their fingernails' ('the nails of their hands')

[4] Pejorative.

[5] This construct is four terms long, and it is exceptional in many ways. Grammatically, the use of *mul* in construct with a following noun is such a common cliché that the function of the phrase is almost that of a single noun, and both *ben* 'son' and *Ɛemm* 'paternal uncle' are kinship terms. For the special status of kinship terms and the cliché noun *mul*, see below, pp. 196-197. Semantically, this example occurred with a deliberately humorous effect in an anecdotal context where the equivalent colloquial English translation would be something on the order of 'I'm the cousin of the guy that brought you the rabbit'. The interested reader can find the complete anecdote in G. S. Colin, *Chrestomathie marocaine* (2nd. ed. Paris: Librairie d'Amerique et d'Orient, 1955), story XLIV, pp. 106-107.

[6] For numerals see pp. 206-207.

ḍfaṛ s-slugi	'the greyhound's claws'
ḍheṛ yeddu	'the back of his hand'
ḍheṛ le-ḥmaṛ	'the donkey's back'
ḍeṛṣt le-ɛqel	'(the) wisdom tooth'
fomm l-bir	'the mouth of the well'
fsex l-ḥenš	'the snake's skin'
keff yeddik	'the palm of your hands'
lḥem ṛ-ṛaṣ	'the meat of the head'
f-qelb ḍ-ḍaṛ[7]	'in(side) the house', literally 'in the heart of the house'
men qelb t-tellis[7]	'from inside the sack', literally 'from the heart of the sack'
qṛun ž-žbal	'(the) mountain tops (horns)'
qezzibt s-slugi	'the greyhound's tail'
ṛaṣ d-dib	'the wolf's head'
ṛaṣ l-kodya	'the top (head) of the hill'
ṛaṣ ṣ-ṣemɛa	'the top (head) of the minaret'
ṛaṣ š-šheṛ	'the first (head) of the month'
režlin l-ḥewli	'the legs of the sheep'
ṣut ṭ-ṭaweṣ	'the voice of the peacock'
wežh l-ma	'the face of the water'
f-yedd l-mexzen	'in the hand(s) of the government'
yedd ṛ-ṛḥa	'the handle (hand) of the mill'
yedd d-derri	'the child's hand'
ɛḍam ṛ-ṛaṣ	'the bones of the head'
ɛonq ṛ-ṛažel	'the man's neck'
ɛeṛqub d-dib	'the Achilles' tendon of the wolf'

[7] This cliché use of *qelb* 'heart' is quite common.

ɛeyn l-feṛṛuž	'the rooster's eye'
ɛeyn š-šemš	'(the eye of) the sun'

(2) Verbal nouns occur freely as the first term of constructs. Some examples:

hbuṭ le-ɛlam	'the coming down of the flag'
kmalt ḍ-ḍaṛ	'the completion of the house'
qtil ṛ-ṛuḥ	'murder, (the) killing (of life)'
qoṭɛan ṭ-ṭṛiq	'brigandage', literally 'road cutting'
ṣriq le-ḥwayež	'clothes stealing, the theft of clothes'
šṛib atay	'tea drinking'
šṛib le-xmeṛ	'liquor drinking'
tehris le-mwaɛen	'dish breaking, the breaking of dishes'
teṣbin le-ḥwayež	'clothes washing, the washing of clothes'
teṭyib l-makla	'the cooking of food'
xluq sidna žebril	'the birth of our Lord Gabriel'
ġsil l-yeddin	'the washing of hands'
ɛžin l-xobz	'the kneading of bread'

(3) The annexion of kinship terms, except for those inherently possessed, is regularly expressed by means of the construct state rather than analytically. Some examples:

a ben l-kafer (l-axoṛ)![8]	'(vile) son of an unbeliever!'
bni hlal[9]	'Bani Hilal' (tribal name)
bent t-tažer	'the merchant's daughter'
a bent le-ḥmaṛ l-axoṛ![10]	'(miserable) daughter of a donkey!'

[8] *ben* is rarely used except in pejorative vocatives. *axoṛ* 'other', modifying the second term of the construct, is used as a pejorative intensifier.

[9] *bni* 'sons' is rarely used except in tribal names.

[10] *axoṛ* 'other' as a pejorative intensifier.

bent le-ḥšayši	'the daughter of the marihuana addict'
omm žḥa	'Jha's mother'
mṛat ḅḅa	'my father's wife, my stepmother'
waldin d-drari	'the children's parents'
wlad l-meqtul	'the murdered man's children'
wlad n-nas	'people's children'
weld xti	'my sister's son'
xa le-mṛa	'the woman's brother'

(4) The particle *mul,* fem. *mula* with combining form *mulat-,* pl. *mwalin,* is regularly annexed by means of the construct state rather than analytically. This particle has a wide variety of idiomatic meanings. The core meaning is anyone in charge of something. Some examples:

mul l-beẓṭam	'the owner of the wallet'
mul le-bḥiṛa	'the vegetable gardener'
mul d-džaž	'the chicken-seller'
mul ḍ-ḍaṛ	'the head of the house'
mul l-feṛṛan	'the furnace-tender'
mul l-gaṛṛu	'the man with the cigaret'
mul l-kif	'the man with the marihuana'
mul l-kommiya	'the owner of the dagger'
mul le-ktir	'he who has much, many'
mul le-qlil	'he who has little, few'
mul l-kudši	'the coachman'
(ddi) mul le-qṛun	'(take) the one with the horns'
mul š-ši	'the one in charge of the affair'
mul l-ḥanut	'the shopkeeper'
mul l-ḥemman	'the tender of the bath(s)'
mul l-ɛewd	'the man with the horse'

mwalin atay	'tea merchants'
mwalin ḍ-ḍaṛ	'the family, the folks at home'
mwalin l-musiqa	'the musicians'
mwalin zman	'(the) people of former times'
mulat l-mešṭa	'the woman with the comb'

(5) A limited number of time-words used in stereotyped expressions. The following examples illustrate those most commonly used:

iyyam l-berd	'the days of cold (weather)'
iyyam ṛ-ṛbiɛ	'the days of spring'
ḷḷah izid f-iyyam sidi!	'may God add to the days of my Lord!', i.e., 'God grant you a long life!'
iyyam ṣ-ṣif	'the days of summer'
iyyam š-šta	'the days of winter'
iyyam ž-žemɛa	'the days of the week'
lilt ṛemḍan	'the eve of Ramadan'
lilt sebɛa u ɛešrin	'the eve of the twenty-seventh'
lilt ṣ-ṣafaṛ	'the eve of the journey'
nhaṛ l-miɛad	'the day of the rendez-vous'
nhaṛ s-suq	'market day'
ṛaṣ š-šheṛ	'the first of the month'
ṛaṣ l-ɛam	'the first of the year, new year's'
weqt d-dras	'threshing time'
weqt ṣ-ṣḷa	'prayer time'
weqt le-ġda	'noon-meal time'
weqt le-ḥṣaḍ	'harvest time'
fe-xxer le-xrif	'at the end of autumn'
ḥetta le-xxer yennayer	'until the end of January'
mn-uwwel š-šheṛ	'from the beginning of the month'

(6) A small group of words which may be referred to as quantifiers. Often these quantifiers have no particular meaning of their own and serve merely as an intensification or an attenuation of an expression. The following examples illustrate the use of the principle ones:

beƐḍ l-meṛṛat	'some times'
ktirt le-Ɛyalat	'most women'
fṛeḥ bih, be-ktert l-feṛḥ	'he was extremely happy with him', i.e., 'he rejoiced with him with an abundance of joy'
men ketret le-Ɛfen u le-wsex	'on account of the excessive amount of dirtiness'
neṣṣ mƐelqa	'half a spoonful'
qedd l-mešmaša	'the size of an apricot'
qedd l-feṛṛuž	'as big as, the size of a rooster'
hadi hiya qellt le-ḥya!	'this is a lack of modesty, decency!'
men quwwt le-fyaq	'on account of so much staying awake'
men quwwt ṣ-ṣḷa u s-sužud	'on account of so much prayer and prosternation'
fiha quwwt le-škal	'(there are) all sorts of different kinds in it'
ġir žehd ma iġli	'just enough for it to boil'
žehd mitṛu de-z-zeft	'(the amount of) a meter of tar'
žehd ši-ṛṭeḷ wella ṛeṭḷayn	'(the amount of) a pound or two'
žehd ši-saƐa wella kteṛ	'(the amount of) an hour or more'
žehd ši-Ɛam u neṣṣ	'a year and a half or so'
men žmelt l-quwwa u r-režla lli fiya	'by virtue of ('from the totality of') my strength and manliness'
men zmelt le-mġanna dyalu	'he's so contrary that...', i.e., 'from the totality of his contrariness'
men žmelt š-šṭaṛa dyal žḥa	'by virtue of Jha's great amount of cleverness'

(7) There are a limited number of ~~cliché~~ construct states with *ḷḷah* 'God' as the second term. In addition to the fixed expressions, there is a wide range of freedom of occurrence of common nouns in the construct state with *ḷḷah* 'God' as the second term. The regular meaning in such cases is 'brought by chance, by God's good grace, by accident or fortune or fate'. Some typical examples:

ḍif ḷḷah	'the guest of God', a fixed expression used in requesting hospitality
waḥed l-yum men iyyamat ḷḷah	'one day, a certain day'
sebḥan ḷḷah!	'the praise of God', a stereotyped expression of surprise, also various idiomatic uses
lqina ṭuṛ ḷḷah u dbeḥnah	'we found a bull of God and slaughtered it (for eating)'
ɛṭini yedd ḷḷah	'give me a helping hand'
ɛibad ḷḷah	'the servants of God', i.e., believers in Islam, Moslems

(8) The two terms *ben* 'son' and *ɛebd* 'slave' occur as the first term of construct states in a large number of personal names. Names with *ɛebd* always have a reference to God as the second term, e.g., *ɛebd ṛ-ṛeḥman,* literally 'slave of the Merciful One', and names with *ben* always occur with some other personal name as the second term, e.g. *mḥemmed ben ɛisa* 'Mohamed, the son of Isa'.

(9) A number of other words which are not readily classifiable occur as the first term of construct states. Many of them must be learned as lexical items since they are fixed clichés which have meanings not immediately deducible from the meaning of the individual constituents, e.g. *ḍeṛṛab ṭ-ṭeṛf* 'pickpocket', *flus le-ḥram* 'money gained illegitimately'. In almost all cases, these constructs indicate either an unusually close semantic or else frequently occurring relation, as opposed to the more general or incidental relation implied by analytic annexion (see below, p. 202). Some typical examples:

bab ḍ-ḍaṛ	'the (main) door of the house'
bit l-ma	'water closet, toilet room'
bit n-naṛ	'forge'
blad l-hend	'India'
ḍaṛ l-feṛḥ	'the house where the party is taking place'
ḍaṛ l-ɛers	'the house where the wedding is taking place'

fḍayeḥ nsibu	'his nephew's tricks'
bḥal fṣaḷt ši-hṛi kbir	'like the shape of some big granary'
gdem bleġtu	'the heel of his slippers'
hel dik le-mdina	'the people of that city'
klam n-nas	'people's talk, what people say'
nas bekri	'the people of former times'
qaɛ l-bir	'the bottom of the well'
qaɛ l-ġaṛ	'the back of the cave'
ṣḷat ž-žemɛa	'the Friday prayer'
ṣḷat le-ɛša	'the evening prayer'
ṣyam ṛemḍan	'the fast of Ramadan'
ṭeṛf l-wad	'the edge of the river, the river bank'
ṭṛiq s-suq	'the road to the market'
f-weṣṭ ḍ-ḍaṛ	'in the (internal) patio, in the middle of the house'
f-weṣṭ n-nas	'among the people'
f-weṣṭ n-nhaṛ	'in the middle of the day'
men weṣṭ s-suq	'from the middle of the market'
l-weṣṭ s-suq	'to the middle of the market'
aš xbaṛ mṛati?	'how's my wife, what's the news of my wife?'
xeṭṭ yeddu	'his signature'
men žiht l-ḥiṭ	'from the direction of the wall', i.e., on the side next to the wall'
ḥṛub n-nsa	'women's tricks'
ḥwayež n-nas	'people's clothes'
ɛud le-qmari	'sandalwood' (used for incense)
ɛyalat le-xwayež	'the wives of the rich'

(b) Analytic Annexion: In addition to the construct state, annexion between two terms is expressed by joining them with the particle *d-* or, more rarely, the particle *dyal*[11], e.g. *z-znaqi d-le-mdina* 'the streets of the city', *ž-žmel dyal had ṛ-ṛažel* 'this man's camels'. There is no difference of meaning between *d-* and *dyal* in analytic annexion except a stylistic one.

Analytic annexion is equivalent both in general meaning and structure with the construct state. Except for idiomatic expressions, any two items which occur together in a construct state can also be put together in analytic annexion, e.g. *weld t-tažer, l-weld de-t-tažer, l-weld dyal t-tažer* 'the merchant's son'. The reverse, however, is not true, since the use of the construct state is limited (see p. 191ff.), and many words which occur together in analytic annexion do not normally occur together in a construct state.

Analytic annexion differs in several details from the construct state. These mostly have to do with analytic annexion being less restricted in what occurs as the first and second term of the annexion. The chief differences are:

(1) Unlike the construct state, the first term of an analytic annexion does not categorically exclude the definite article, e.g. *l-ḥilat de-n-nsa* 'women's tricks'.

(2) Unlike the construct state, there are cases of analytic annexion where the first term is a descriptive equivalent of the second term. This is always so when the first term of an analytic annexion is an adjective. Some examples:

dik le-mfellsa d-le-mṛa	'that idiot of a woman'
dak n-nems d-weldu	'that fox of a son of his'
waḥed l-ɛaḍama d-waḥed bu-sekka	'a giant of a cobra'
had le-ḥmeq dyal weldi	'this fool of a son of mine'
dak ben l-kafer dyal l-xemmas	'that son of an infidel of a sharecropper'
ši-ḥommaq dyal ši-qoyyad	'some idiot judges'

(3) Analytic annexion in general agrees with the construct state in excluding a noun with a pronoun ending as the first term, but the inherently possessed kinship terms (see pp. 141-142) are found as the first term of an analytic annexion, e.g. *babah de-ṛ-ṛažel* 'the man's father'.

(4) Demonstrative pronouns (see p. 143) occur as the first term of analytic annexions, although not as the first term of construct states, e.g. *hadik de-d-dheb* 'the gold one, that one of gold'.

---

[11]There is a variation in form between *d-* and *de-*, the latter occurring before consonant clusters. Some speakers use the particle *mtaɛ* instead of *dyal*, with no difference of meaning. For the use of *dyal* other than in analytic annexion, see p. 203.

(5) The second term of a construct state is either a noun or a pronoun. A wider range is found in the second term of analytic annexions, e.g. *l-faṛ d-le-mdina u l-faṛ dyal beṛṛa* 'the city mouse and the mouse from outside'.

3. Pronominal Possession: Pronominal possession is expressed either directly by the attachment of suffixed pronoun forms to nouns (see pp. 00-00) or by the attachment of suffixed pronoun forms to the particle *dyal*, which is placed after the noun, e.g. *ḍaṛi* or *ḍ-ḍaṛ dyali* 'my house', *ṛaželha* or *ṛ-ṛažel dyalha* 'her husband'.

The usual pattern is for the noun preceding *dyal* in such cases to have the definite article, e.g. *le-mlakat dyalhom* 'their possessions'. Cases of prefixless nouns followed by possessive *dyal* also occur, however, e.g. *atay dyalu* 'his tea', where *atay* 'tea' is a noun which never takes the definite article, and *ana xadem memluka dyalek* 'I am (will be) a slave ('owned') servant of yours' (taken from a context in which it was a metaphorical expression of gratitude in anticipation of a favor), where the absence of the definite article signals a meaning different from that which would be indicated by the presence of the definite article. Compare the two English expressions 'a servant of yours' and 'your servant'.

Nouns prefixed with an indefinite article rarely occur with possessive *dyal*, but nouns with demonstrative prefixes occur freely, e.g.

had l-meƐza dyalek	'this goat of yours'
had l-weld dyali	'this son of mine'
dak l-biḍ dyali	'those eggs of mine'
duk le-ktaf dyalu	'those shoulders of his'

Only a limited number of nouns take the pronoun endings directly, and pronominal possession is usually indicated by *dyal*. The relationship is approximately the same as that between the construct state and analytic annexion (see pp. 191ff). Nouns which commonly occur as the first term of construct states also commonly occur with pronoun endings, and nouns which typically occur as the first term in analytic annexion also typically occur with *dyal* in expressions of pronominal possession, e.g. construct state *bent t-tažer* 'the merchant's daughter' and *bentu* 'his daughter', in comparison with *ž-žnanat de-n-nas* 'people's gardens' and *ž-žnanat dyalhom* 'their gardens'.

III. THE ADJECTIVE

I. The Adjective as a Noun

Adjectives are used freely as nouns, and as such they have all the general sentence functions of nouns, e.g. as the object or a preposition in *mɛa le-kbir* 'with the big one'. Adjectives used as nouns, however, have several characteristics which distinguish them from actual nouns. They regularly have either the definite article or a demonstrative article, e.g. *l-buyeḍ* 'the white ones', *hadak ṣ-ṣġiṛ* 'that little one'. There are no adjectives which never take the definite article (see pp. 189-190), and the pronominal possession of adjectives is always expressed by *dyal* plus a pronoun ending, e.g. *le-kbaṛ dyalhom* 'their big ones'. Adjectives furthermore usually do not take an indefinite article, compare *le-kbir* 'the big one' and *le-kbaṛ* 'the big ones' with *ši-waḥed kbir* 'a big one' and *ši-weḥdin kbaṛ* 'some big ones'.

Some words which are used freely either as nouns or adjectives in the singular make a distinction between noun and adjective in the plural, e.g. singular *miyyet* 'dead', adjectival plural *miyytin*, nominal plural *muta*. In such cases the adjective plural does not have the sentence functions of a noun. Geographical nisbas (see p. 73) are especially common in having such twin plurals, e.g. singular *tunsi* 'Tunisian', adjectival plural *tunsiyin*, nominal plural *twansa* 'Tunisians'. Such geographical nisbas are among the rare adjectives which occur with an indefinite article, compare *waḥed t-tunsi* 'a Tunisian' with *waḥed tunsi* 'a Tunisian one'.

For the occurrence of the adjective as the first term of a construct state, see p. 193.

II. The Adjective as a Noun Modifier

1. The Attributive Adjective: The usual place of the attributive adjective is directly after the noun it modifies, e.g. *ši-nas mezyanin* some good people', *modda ṭwila* 'a long time', *ši-ḥwayež ždidin* 'some new clothes'. The only exception is that an attributive adjective modifying the first term of a construct state is placed after the entire construct rather than immediately after the noun it modifies. Examples of this sort are rare and almost exclusively limited to the adjectives *kamel* and *mežmuɛ* 'all', e.g. *hel le-mdina kamlin* 'all the people of the city', *xdemt ḍ-ḍaṛ mežmuɛa* 'all the house work'.

The presence or absence of the definite article with the attributive adjective is largely a function of the noun it modifies. The chief patterns are:

(a) The attributive adjective regularly takes the definitie article if the noun it modifies is preceded by a demonstrative, e.g. *duk s-skayriya le-mxezzzin* 'those incorrigible drunkards'.[12]

(b) The attributive adjective never takes the definite article if the noun it modifies is preceded by an indefinite article, e.g. *ši-m̃m̃iha barda* 'some cold water', *waḥed ṛ-ṛažel mezyan* 'a good man'.

(c) An attributive adjective modifying a prefixless noun takes the definite article only if the noun has a pronoun ending, e.g. *modda ṭwila* 'a long time', *wladha l-oxṛin* 'her other children'.

(d) If the noun it modifies has the definite article, there is considerable variation as to whether the attributive adjective does or does not take the definite article. In general, the definite article with the adjective in such a case implies a superlative meaning, e.g. *le-ḥwayež l-mezyanin* 'the best clothes', or else specific reference to something previously identified, e.g. *l-yum huwa labes s-selham le-byeḍ* 'today he's wearing the (known by previous reference) white cloak'. In cases where the Moroccan definite article with the noun does not indicate specific previous reference, the attributive adjective usually does not take the definite article, e.g. *žab-li l-ma sxun* 'he brought me some hot water', *l-yum huwa labes s-selham byeḍ* 'he's wearing a white cloak today'.

2. **The Predicate Adjective:** The predicate adjective occurs either as a predicate complement or as an objective complement, e.g. as a predicate complement *konna feṛḥanin* 'we were happy', *xeržet ɛewža* 'it came out crooked', as an objective complement *ṣbeġhom xuḍeṛ* 'he painted them green'. The position of predicate adjectives in the sentence is similar to English.

3. **Comparison:** The comparative form of the adjective (see p. 85) is used almost exclusively as a predicate, e.g. *ana kbeṛ mennu* 'I'm bigger than he is'. There is a limited use of the comparative form as a superlative. As such it occurs in a construct state with a following noun and both it and the noun are prefixless, e.g. *kbeṛ žameɛ f-fas* 'the biggest mosque in Fez'.

The comparison of superiority is also expressed by *kteṛ* 'more', which is placed after the adjective it accompanies, e.g. *ana ɛeyyan kteṛ mennu* 'I'm tireder (sicker) than he is'.

There is no separate form for the superlative. The superlative is usually expressed by the simple adjective with the definite article, e.g. *hiya l-mezyana fe-ṛ-ṛbaṭ* 'it's the best (one) in Rabat', *huwa ṣ-ṣġiṛ fihom* 'he's the smallest (one) of them'.

Comparisons of equality are usually expressed with *bḥal* 'like, as', e.g. *ana kbir bḥalek* 'I'm as big as you are'.

---

[12]Cf. the equational sentence *duk s-skayriya mxezzzin* 'those drunkards are incorrigible'.

IV. NUMERALS

The ordinals and the fractions function as ordinary nouns and adjectives. The cardinals *waḥed* (msc.) and *weḥda* (fem.) 'one' function as adjectives, e.g. *ṛažel waḥed* 'one man', *mṛa wehda* 'one woman'. The other cardinals function independently as plural nouns, e.g. *ɛešrin kbaṛ* 'twenty big ones', *ši-xemsa u tlatin žaw* 'some thirty-five came', or else occur as the first term of an annexion.

The number *žuž* 'two' occurs alternately as the first term of a construct state before a prefixless plural noun or as the first term of an analytic annexion before a plural noun prefixed with the definite article, e.g. *žuž ktub* or *žuž d-le-ktub* 'two books'. From three through ten, the full forms of the numerals occur as the first term of an analytic annexion before a plural noun prefixed with the definite article, and the short forms occur as the first term of a construct state before a prefixless plural noun.[1] The short form of the numeral is used only with a limited number of nouns which must be memorized as lexical items.[2] Other nouns are counted with the full form of the numeral. Some examples:

tlata de-n-nas	'three people'
ṛebɛa de-n-nas	'four people'
xemsa de-n-nas	'five people'
etc.	
telt šhuṛ	'three months'
xems šhuṛ	'five months'
etc.	

Numerals from eleven through one hundred are used with singular prefixless nouns. The numerals from eleven through nineteen take the ending *-eṛ* or *-el* when annexed to a following noun, and *mya* 'hundred' has a combining form *myat,* as is usual with feminine nouns used as the first term of a construct. In complex numbers, the units precede the decades and are joined to them by *u* 'and'. Some examples:

---

[1]A few nouns, mostly units of currency or measurement, sometimes occur in the singular, e.g. *tlata de-r-ryal* 'three ryals'.

[2]On the whole, these nouns are the same as those which take the dual ending, see p. 100.

ṭnašeṛ, -el bent	'twelve girls'
sbeƐtašeṛ, -el bent	'seventeen girls'
Ɛešrin yum	'twenty days'
xemsa u Ɛešrin xeṭwa	'twenty-five steps'
tesƐud u tesƐin meṛṛa	'ninety-nine times'
myat neƐla	'a hundred curses'

The multiples of one hundred combine with nouns either in analytic annexion or in a construct state, e.g. *xems-emya de-r-ryal* 'five hundred ryals', *telt-emyat metqal* 'three hundred metqals'.

In complex numerals, the units and decades come last, they are preceded by the hundreds, which are in turn preceded by the thousands, etc. Each of these larger units is joined to the next by *u* 'and', e.g. *ḥḍašeṛ ʔalef u xems-emya u xemsa u settin* 'eleven thousand, five hundred and sixty-five'.

In addition to being prefixless, numerals in annexion with nouns occur prefixed with an indefinite article, the definite article, or a demonstrative article. The indefinite article with a numeral other than *žuž* 'two' has the meaning 'some' or 'approximately'. With *žuž* 'two', an indefinite article is translated as 'a pair of, a couple of'. Some examples:

waḥed t-telt snin	'some three years or so'
waḥed le-myat meṛṛa	'a hundred times or so'
waḥed le-myatayn de-l-xil	'some two hundred horses'
ši-xemsa wella setta de-n-nas	'some five or six people'
fe-t-telt iyyam l-luwwla	'in the first three days'
le-ḥḍašeṛ ryal	'the eleven ryals'
l-xemsa u ṛebƐin metqal	'the forty-five metqals'
duk l-xemsa de-r-ryal	'those five ryals'
dik t-telt mya d-le-Ɛṣa	'those three hundred blows (with a stick)'
ṣebt ṛaṣi mġeṛṛeqha mƐah f-ši-tmenya u sebƐin ryal	'I found that I had let him run up a bill of some seventy-eight ryals with me'

A common idiomatic expression involves the use of the preposition *b-* 'with, by' before a numeral, e.g. *huma b-žuž* 'the two of them, both of them', *huma b-xemsa* 'the five of them, all five of them'.

V. PARTICLES

Particles play an important role in Moroccan grammatical structure. Most Moroccan particles are comparable to such familiar English categories as prepositions, conjunctions, adverbs, and pronouns. Some, however, fit none of these categories. As a group particles share certain general characteristics. Formally they are for the most part short and invariable, e.g. *bla* 'without'. Syntactically, they always function as subordinate modifiers of verbs, nouns, pronouns, and adjectives.

1. **Prepositions:** No Moroccan preposition is exactly equivalent to any given English preposition. Each one has its own range of meaning, and the translation of a given Moroccan preposition into English often differs widely from context to context. The principal prepositions are:

amma — 'as for, with respect to'; does not take the suffixed pronoun endings, e.g. *amma huwa* 'as for him'

b-, bi- — 'with, by means of'; the form *bi-* is used only before suffixed pronouns, e.g. *bihom* 'with them, by means of them'; the meaning of *b-* is to be contrasted with *mƐa* 'with, in the company of'

bin, binat — 'between'; the form *binat* is used before plural pronoun endings, e.g. *binatkom* 'between you (pl.)'; with singular pronoun endings or with nouns, *bin* is repeated before each of its objects, e.g. *bini u binek* 'between you (sg.) and me', *binek u bin weldek* 'between you (sg.) and your son', *bin l-qaḍi u bin ḅḅa* 'between the judge and my father'; contrary to English, a first person object pronoun precedes a second person object pronoun, as in *bini u binek* 'between you (sg.) and me'.

bla — 'without'; contrary to English usage, the indefinite article is not usually used after *bla*, e.g. *bla žellaba* 'without a jellaba', *bla flus* 'without (any) money'; *bla* does not take pronoun endings, but is followed by *b-* plus pronoun endings, e.g. *bla biya* 'without me', *bla bik* 'without you', etc.

bḥal — 'like, as'; often occurs in pairs, e.g. *bḥalha bḥal l-fila* 'she's like an elephant', compare the common idiom *bḥal bḥal* '(they're) just alike'

beƐd — 'after'; usually used with *men* 'from' preceding, e.g. *men beƐd ši-šwiya* 'after a little', *men beƐd le-Ɛša* 'after supper'

d-, dyal The form *d-* never occurs with pronouns; for the use of *d-* and *dyal* in annexion, see p. 202; in equational sentences *dyal* is often translatable as 'to belong to', e.g. *ma-hiya-š dyali* 'it (fem.) isn't mine, it doesn't belong to me', *ma-ši dyal l-qaḍi* 'not the judge's, (it) doesn't belong to the judge'

f-, fi- The form *fi-* is used only before the pronoun endings, e.g. *fihom* 'among them'; the basic literal meaning of this preposition is 'in', e.g. *fe-ḍ-ḍaṛ* 'in the house'; it has, however, a wide variety of different uses and translations, e.g. *fina* 'among us'; it is often bound up with specific verbs, e.g. *theḷḷa f-* 'to take care of', *ka-itheḷḷa fe-mmu* 'he's taking care of his mother'; this preposition is widely used to introduce the object of almost any transitive verb to indicate partialness, incompleteness, or duration of an action, e.g. *kla fe-l-xobz* 'he ate some (of the) bread' as opposed to *kla l-xobz* 'he ate the bread', or compare *kan ka-iherres l-luz* 'he was cracking the, some almonds' (probably a specific bunch of almonds, possibly with the intention of finishing the job and cracking them all) as opposed to *kan ka-iherres fe-l-luz* 'he was cracking (some) almonds'

fuq 'above, over', often followed by *men* 'from' before the object, e.g. *fuq had š-ši* or *fuq men had š-ši* 'above, on top of this'

l-, li- lil- 'to, for'; the forms *li-* and *lil-* are used before pronoun endings in independent forms, e.g. *liya* or *lili* 'to, for me', *lik* or *lilek* 'to , for you (sg.)', *lih* or *lilu* 'to, for him', etc.; the form *l-* is used before other parts of speech, e.g. *l-had le-mṛa* 'to, for this woman', and before pronoun endings when the resulting form is prefixed to a preceding word, usually a verb (see pp. 138-140, 143) but occasionally other forms as well, e.g. *ɛṭinahom-lha* 'we gave them to her', *ḥsen-li* '(it's) better for me, I prefer'

men, menn mn- 'from, of, than'; the form *menn* is used before endings beginning with a vowel, e.g. *menni* 'from me'; before the endings beginning with a consonant, some speakers use *men* and others use *menn*, e.g. *menna* or *mennna* 'from us', *menhom* or *mennhom* 'from them'; elsewhere *men* is usually used, e.g. *men l-ɛud* 'from the wood, (made) of wood', but *mn-* is often found in context before vowels, e.g. *mn-aš?* 'what from?'

mtaɛ, ntaɛ used by some speakers instead of *dyal*, in all functions

muṛ(a) 'behind, after'

mɛa 'with', indicates accompaniment, e.g. *mɛa mṛati* 'with my wife', as distinguished from *b-* 'with', which indicates instrument or means, e.g. *be-ṭ-ṭumubil* 'with the car, by car'

qbel 'before', with reference to time only, e.g. *(men) qbel had š-ši b-ɛam* 'a year before this, earlier than this by a year'

qoddam 'in front of, facing', e.g. *qoddamu* 'in front of him'

teḥt 'under, beneath, below', e.g. *teḥt š-šelya* 'under the chair'

wiya 'with, and'; serves only to join two pronouns, never takes the first person singular ending, e.g. *ana wiyah* 'he and I', *ana wiyak* 'I with you (sg.), you and I'

wṛa 'behind, after'

ġir 'except, other than, nothing but', e.g. *ġir t-tben* 'only, just straw, nothing but straw', frequently used with negative *ma-* in the sense of 'only, just', e.g. *ma-ɛendi ġir xemsa de-l-fṛenk* 'I've only got five francs'

ḥda 'beside, next to'

ḥetta 'until', often takes *l-* 'to' before a following object, e.g. *ḥetta l-ġedda* 'until tomorrow'

ɛla, ɛli-, ɛel 'on'; the form *ɛli-* is used only before pronoun endings, e.g. *ɛliya* 'on me', *ɛlihom* 'on them', etc.; the form *ɛel* is used before the definite article, e.g. *ɛel le-ḥmaṛ* 'on the donkey'; the form *ɛla* is used elsewhere, e.g. *ɛla had š-ši* 'on (account of) this'

ɛend 'at, with, by, at the place of'; with pronoun endings *ɛend* translates English 'to have', e.g. *ɛendi waḥed ḍ-ḍaṛ kbira* 'I have a big house', *kanet ɛendi waḥed ḍ-ḍaṛ kbira* 'I had, used to have a big house'; English 'to have' with a noun subject involves a prestated topic in Arabic, e.g. *ḅḅana ɛendu* 'our father has'; a pair of typical idiomatic differences between English and Moroccan is illustrated by *ɛend n-neššaṛ* 'at the carpenter's', *ɛendna ka-nheḍṛu l-ɛeṛbiya* 'at our house, at our place, in our country we speak Arabic'

The prepositions which basically consist of a single consonant, that is *b-, d-, f-,* and *l-* regularly add *e* if they are prefixed to a form which begins with two or more consonants, e.g. *be-flusek* 'with your money', *le-qšaweš de-r-ržal* 'the men's things', *fe-ž-žameɛ* 'in the mosque', *le-mṛati* 'for my wife'. An exception to this pattern occurs if the following consonant is the same as that of the preposition, e.g. *l-l-bab* 'to the door'.

As a group, the prepositions typically take nouns or pronouns as objects, as in the examples above. According to meaning, however, prepositions are also found with clauses or prepositional phrases as objects. For example in *ma-ka-nsuwwel ġir fe-dyal men hiya u fe-škun fikom lli ɛendu ɛliha l-molkiya* 'I'm only asking about who it belongs to and about which one of you has legal title to it', the preposition *f-* 'in, about' (*suwwel f-* 'to ask about') has successively for objects the clause *dyal men hiya?* 'who does it belong to?' and the clause *škun fikom lli ɛendu ɛliha l-molkiya?* 'which one of you (who among you) is it that has legal title to it?' Examples of a preposition taking an entire prepositional phrase as object are fairly common, e.g. *huma bḥalhom bḥal de-ṛ-ṛbaṭ* 'they are like (those) of Rabat, like Rabat's', *bḥal dyalna* 'like ours', *ža l-ɛendi* 'he came to my place, to my house', *men binathom* 'from between them'.

2. The Particles of Spatial Relation: These particles are essentially adverbs. Some of them also function as prepositions, however, and their use as invariable nouns is also common. The particles are:

beṛṛa	'outside'
daxel	'inside'
fuq	'above'
ḷ-ḷuṛ	'the rear'
muṛ(a)	'behind, after'
qoddam	'in front, up front, facing'
teḥt	'below'
wṛa	'behind, after'

The particles *ḷuṛ, muṛ,* and *wṛa* are originally one and the same. The *ḷ-* of *ḷuṛ* is originally the definite article, and *muṛ* represents a fusion of *men* 'from' with *wṛa*. The forms *daxel, fuq, ḷuṛ, qoddam,* and *teḥt* take the definite article, always with the form *l-,* e.g. *l-qefṭan ka-ikun meftuḥ men l-qoddam, men l-fuq ḥetta l-l-teḥt* 'the caftan is open in the front, from top to bottom'.

These particles are also typically combined with prepositions in various ways, e.g. *šeddu men teḥt* 'hold it from underneath', *huwa ɛla beṛṛa* 'he's outside', *šufu l-l-qoddam* 'look (pl.) up ahead'. Their use independently as pure adverbs is relatively rare.

3. Conjunctions: The most common primary conjunctions are as follows:

imma, amma... wella, wla, aw	'either...or', e.g. *imma aži mɛaya aw nṣifeṭha-lek* 'either come with me or I'll send it to you'
baš[1]	'so that, in order to', usually expresses purpose rather than result, e.g. *ṣuwwebt s-siyara baš ma-ibqa fiha ṣḍaɛ* 'I fixed the car so that it wouldn't rattle (noise would not remain in it) any more', *xeṣṣek dzreb baš teqbeḍ bḷaṣa mezyana* 'you'll have to hurry to get a good place'

[1]Although historically identical, the conjunction *baš* and *b-aš,* preposition plus pronoun object, 'what with?, by means of what?' are separate both in meaning and function.

belḥeqq — 'but'

ila — 'if', see the discussion of conditional sentences, pp. 168ff.

kun — 'if', see the discussion of conditional sentences, pp. 168ff.

lakin, lakenn, wa-lakenn — 'but'

melli — 'since', usually expresses a causal rather than a temporal relation, e.g. *melli ma-hiya-š dyali ma-bġit-š nddiha* 'since it's not mine, I don't want to take it'

mnin — 'when, since'; usually expresses a temporal rather than a causal relation, e.g. *mnin ka-ibda iġiyyeṭ ka-itšeddu Ɛeynih u ka-ittnefxu ḥnaku* 'when he begins to play the *ġiṭa* (a kind of Moroccan oboe) his eyes close and his cheeks puff up'

u, w — 'and'; the form *u* occurs before consonants, e.g. *u bda* 'and he began', and the form *w* occurs before vowels, e.g. *w ana* 'and I'

waxxa — 'although, even if', e.g. *waxxa teƐṭini kada u kada, ma-nbiƐha-lek-š* 'even if you give me such and such, I won't sell it to you (sg.)'

wella, wla, aw — 'or'

ġir — 'as soon as, no sooner than', e.g. *ġir smeƐt had š-ši žit nšufek* 'as soon as I heard this I came to see you (sg.)'

ḥit — 'since, when'; expresses both temporal and causal relations, *ḥit Ɛṛeftiw aš ġadi nqul-lkom, Ɛlaš nqul-lkom?* 'since you know what I'm going to tell you (pl.), why should I tell you?', *ḥit kan ḅḅa sidi wzir, kanu Ɛendna le-Ɛbid* 'when my grandfather was a (government) minister we had some slaves'

ḥetta — 'when, until, so that', e.g. in an expression of time, *ma-nṣafṛu-š ḥetta iduz ṛemḍan* 'we won't leave until Ramadan passes', *ḥetta iduz ṛemḍan Ɛad nṣafṛu* 'when Ramadan passes, then we'll leave'; *l-maƐida dyali meṛḍet ḥetta ma-qeddit nnuḍ* 'my stomach got so sick that I couldn't get up'

beƐd-ella — 'although, even if', cf. *waxxa* above

In addition to these primary conjunctions, a number of other conjunctions are formed by suffixing the indefinite pronoun *ma* (see p. 145), often in the form *-emma,* to various words, especially the prepositions and the interrogative pronouns and adverbs. The most common of these compound conjunctions are:

aš-emma	'whatever'
bid-ma	'while'
bla-ma	'without'[2]
beƐd-ma	'after'
fayn-emma	'wherever'
kif-ma, -emma	'however, as'
koll-ma	'whenever, as often as, every time that'
layn-emma	'to wherever'
mnin-emma	'from wherever, whenever'
qbel-ma	'before', requires the imperfect tense even when past time is referred to, e.g. *nebbehtu qbel-ma idirha* 'I warned him before he did it'
qedd-ma	'to the extent that, the...the', e.g. *qedd-ma iṭwaḷ qedd-ma iṛqaq* 'the taller it gets the thinner it gets'
škun-emma	'whoever'
šḥal-emma	'however much'
weqt-emma	'at whatever time, whenever'

The conjunction *ma-ḥedd...u* 'the more...the more' deviates from the above pattern by having *ma* as a prefix and by admitting pronoun endings attached to *ḥedd*. An example, *ma-ḥeddu ka-iqṛa u huwa ka-itfelles* 'the more he studies the worse he gets'. The various equivalents of English 'because' are all compounds of one sort or another. The three most common are *Ɛla wedd, Ɛla qibal,* and *Ɛla ḥeqq-aš.*

---

[2]Although 'without' does not function as a conjunction in standard educated English usage.

4. **Interrogative Adverbs:** The principal interrogative adverbs are:

fayn?	'where?'
kif?, kif-aš?	'how?'
layn?	'to where?'
mnin?	'from where?'
šḥal?	'how much? how many?'
yemta?	'when?'
ɛlaš?	'why?'
liyyah?	'why?'

Both *layn* and *fayn* also translate 'nowhere' and 'anywhere' in negative expressions, e.g. *ma-ġadi layn* or *ma-ġadi fayn* '(I'm) not going anywhere', *ma-žbeṛ-š fayn idirha* 'he didn't find anywhere to put it'. The form *ɛlaš?* 'why?' is a compound of *ɛla* 'on' and *aš?* 'what?', compare such an English expression as 'what for?' When governing a following noun, *šḥal* is joined to it by *d-* 'of' or *men* 'of, from'. The usage with *d-* requires a plural and the usage with *men* requires a singular, e.g. *šḥal d-le-ktub?* or *šḥal men ktab?* 'how many books?' In referring to prices, *šḥal* is almost always preceded by the preposition *b-* 'with, by means of', e.g. *be-šḥal had ṭ-ṭumubil?* '(for) how much is this car?', how much does this car cost?', *be-šḥal šritihom?* 'how much did you (sg.) buy them for?, how much did they cost you?'

Several secondary interrogatives are formed by the use of *-aš?* 'what?' as a suffix, e.g.

weqt-aš?	'when, at what time?'
fuq-aš?	'when, on what date?'
nhaṛ-aš?	'which day?'

These forms are usually used in preference to *yemta?* 'when?', which is of limited use among urban Moroccans. Some Moroccans are fairly consistent in differentiating *weqt-aš?* as 'at what time?' from *fuq-aš?* as 'on what date?', e.g. *weqt-aš mšiti le-s-suq?* 'what time did you (sg.) go to the market?' and *fuq-aš xlaqiti?* 'when were you born?' Other Moroccans use *weqt-aš* and *fuq-aš* interchangeably. Greater specificity is possible by means of such expressions as *fe-šḥal men saɛa?* or *f-ina saɛa?* 'at what time (o'clock)?'

5. The Presentational Particles: The two particles *ha* and *ṛa* have approximately the meaning 'here is, here are', e.g. *ha-huwa qoddamek* or *ṛa-huwa qoddamek* 'here it is in front of you'. These particles take either the independent pronouns or the suffixed pronouns, e.g. *h-ana* or *hani* and *ṛ-ana* or *ṛani* 'here I am', *ha-nta* or *hak* and *ṛa-nta* or *ṛak* 'here you (sg.) are', etc. The *a* of *ha* and *ṛa* fuses with the initial *a* of *ana* 'I' and thus gives rise to the possibility of ambiguity with the suffixed pronoun ending *-na* 'us, our'. Thus *h-ana* 'here I am' and *hana* 'here we are' are pronounced identically, likewise *ṛ-ana* 'here I am' and *ṛana* 'here we are'.

The particles are sometimes used merely as a reinforcement for the subject of a sentence, e.g. *ha-huwa maži* 'here he comes'. The use of *ṛa* in this way is especially common when some sort of logical connection or consequent result is implied, e.g. *xud ṭaksi u ṛah iweṣṣḷek* 'take a taxi and he'll get you (sg.) there', *ḍṛeb l-xadiža tilifun, ṛaha fe-ḍ-ḍaṛ* 'give Khadija a telephone call, she's at home'. For the use of *ṛa* in conditional sentences see p. 169.

6. The Vocative: The vocative particle is usually *a,* less commonly *ya.* It is usually not translatable into English, although certain colloquial uses of 'hey' for hailing purposes are sometimes roughly equivalent, e.g. *a d-drari, ma-ddiru-š ṣ-ṣdaƐ* 'hey, kids, don't make a racket'.

The vocative particle has no other meaning than to indicate that a person or persons are being spoken to. The vocative particle requires the definite article when used with a common noun, e.g. *a le-bnat, fiqu u siru le-s-sekwila* 'girls, get up and go to school'.

NOTES

APPENDIX

TEXTS IN URBAN MOROCCAN ARABIC

Collected and annotated by

LOUIS BRUNOT

Edited by

RICHARD S. HARRELL

NOTES

PREFACE

In the spring and summer of 1961 I had the pleasure of becoming personally acquainted with Professor Louis Brunot of Rabat, Morocco, whom I had known previously only through the medium of his many fine publications in the field of Moroccan Arabic studies. Before I left Morocco in August, 1961, Professor Brunot gave me — commenting that 'you might be able to amuse yourself with these' — two of his unpublished manuscripts on Moroccan Arabic. One of them, an outline of comparative French and Moroccan syntax, is scarcely translatable into English in view of the subject matter. The other, an annotated collection of texts in urban Moroccan Arabic, is presented herewith.

In editing these texts I have attempted to be as faithful to the author's manuscript as possible. Only two major changes have been made. The texts have been retranscribed to fit the orthographic conventions to which Americans working with Moroccan Arabic have become accustomed, and the notes have been translated from French into English. In addition to these fundamental changes, occasional inconsistencies and errors of the type which are always to be found in an author's rough draft have been corrected, and a few of the notes have had to be substantially revised in order to make them fit an English rather than a French frame of reference. Throughout the work I have attempted to play as purely editorial a role as possible and serve as a faithful reflector of the thought and work of the author. Professor Brunot is, of course, in no way responsible for errors of my making or those reproduced mechanically from a draft manuscript which he had not finally revised with his own hand. Problems of time, distance, and communication unfortunately made consultation impossible.

It has been a rich source of pleasure to me to be able to contribute to the appearance of this latest work of Professor Brunot, who is in his eighty-first year at the time of this writing. I offer my editorial efforts as a small token of my respect and esteem for him.

Richard S. Harrell
Washington, D. C.
July 16, 1962

(1)

mšit l-fas f-ʔaxir yolyuz nduwwez ṭeṛf m-el-ɛwašer wo-nɛăyyed l-ɛid el-kbir, ana u-uladi mɛa imma u-xay wo-nsari mṛati bḥal sidi ḥṛaẓem u-mulay yăɛqub u-ṣfṛu ɛla-ḥăqq hiyya beṛṛaniya, mn-eš-šam. mnin uṣelna f-fas ṣebnaha ṣăḥṛa, ṣ-ṣehḍ lil u-nhaṛ ma-kayen ġir ṛebɛin l-fuq. u-f-lilt el-ɛid uqăɛ š-šwaš u-sebɛin aw tmanin f-el-mya ma-ḍeḥḥaw-š, u-daz ɛid mkeffes.

u-men băɛd waḥd eṣ-ṣbaḥ xrežt ɛla ɛadti u-nfeqt u-šrit koll-emma ta-ixeṣṣ. ṛžăɛt l-eḍ-ḍaṛ. qolt-lhom iṭiybu-li l-ma l-atay. xrežt l-bab ḥanut xay. waḥd eš-šway kif glest u-mqeddem el-ḥăwma wo-l-xlifa ɛayṭu-li (ɛăyyeṭ + u = ɛăyyṭu = ɛayṭu) negles mɛahom nfeṛṛqu l-lġa. mšit u-glesna, hadi kanet hadi ma-kanet. ḥna hakdak u-hadi žmaɛa d-el-bulis mašya, telṭaš fṛanṣawiyin, rafdin miṭṛayuz u-sebɛa mġaṛba rafdin el-kḷayṭ. ana šefthom wo-l-xăwf tṣeḷḷeṭ ɛliya. žit nehṛeb, xeft iḍeṛbuni, bqit gales. ža l-kbir dyalhom qal l-le-mqeddem: "škun hada?" w-ana kanet l-bṛa d-et-tăɛrif d-le-mḍṛaṣa mwožžda. žbedtha u-medditha-lu. ġir šafha qal-li: "mezyan!" u-ḍaṛ f-el-mqeddem u-qal-lu: "kayen atay?" žit ana qolt-lu: "mužud!" u-mšit l-eḍ-ḍaṛ ɛămmeṛt žuž d-el-brared. u-kan ɛăndi ši-atay nimiru sfer, ɛăbbitu mɛay mn-eṛ-ṛbat; u-ɛămmeṛt s-siniya (only Fez has s instead of ṣ in this word) *b-el-kisan u-ġeṭṭitha b-mendil meṭṛuz u-ɛăbbitha-lhom. šeṛbuh u-ɛžebhom u-ɛawed le-mqeddem ɛămmeṛ el-brared. ɛad mšaw u-hakda duwwezt ṛebɛin yum kollha ṣehḍ u-xlayăɛ* (pl. of *xelɛa*) *u-dfiɛ l-flus bla ledda bla ṭiba.*

(2)

Alms

ṣ-ṣaḍaqa[1]

mešnuɛ[2] ɛăndna waḥd eṛ-ṛažel kan m-el-ɛulama l-kbaṛ u-ɛaṛef ma-binu u-bin eḷḷah[3] kteṛ men koll-waḥăd. u-kanet ɛăndu retba[4] ɛalya, u-kan ɛăndu usex ed-denya[5] bla qyas.[6] u-men ṭbiɛtu bxil, ma-ka-iɛteq,[7] ma-ka-iṛḥem,[8] ma-ka-iṣeḍḍeq, ma-ka-izekki[9] wa-la-iɛăššeṛ,[10] u-ma-ka-iɛṛef ġir "aṛa!" wa-amma "hak" ma-ka-itiḥ-lu-ši f-balu, băɛd-ella z-zka ɛăndna feṛd men fṛuḍ tamselmiyet.[11]

nhaṛ ɛašuṛa koll-waḥăd ka-ixerrež ez-zka ɛla qḍeṛ resmalu,[12] bḥal es-selɛa, u-d-dheb, u-l-flus lli daz ɛlihom ɛam ɛănd mulahom, u-l-ksiba[13] ḥetta hiyya.

u-had el-bxil el-mešḥaḥ el-kazz,[14] ila deqq ɛlih ši-waḥăd nhaṛ ɛašuṛa ma-ka-ismăɛ mennu ġir: "ḷḷah iftăḥ, sir ɛănd t-težžaṛ", fă-ḥṛa[15] ila žah ši-saɛi men ġir had n-nhaṛ lli n-huwwa mešhuṛ b-eṣ-ṣaḍaqa u-ṛ-ṛăḥma ɛl-eḍ-ḍuɛafa u-d-draweš.[16]

u-had en-nas lli ɛla had eš-škel ka-insaw muṛahom l-axra u-l-ḥsab[17] u-l-ɛqab[18] u-žohănnam.[19] balhom mešġul ġir išriw ḍ-ḍyuṛ, u-l-ɛăzban,[20] u-ṭ-ṭumubilat u-l-msaryat[21] ha-huma f-sbanya, a-huma f-fṛanṣa.

u-had eš-ši kollu ka-izemmemuh ɛlihom l-malayka: ġedda yum l-qiyama, ixrež dak eš-ši kollu men ḍhuṛhom.[22]

Notes

1. *ṣaḍaqa* = ‘alms’ in general. The alms distributed on the occasion of Achoura are called *zka.*
2. *măƐṛuf — măƐlum — mešhuṛ*
3. He knew his duties toward God.
4. A social position.
5. ‘The filth of this low world’, i.e. wealth, fortune.
6. Immense, without measure.
7. ‘To help’.
8. ‘To have compassion’.
9. To give the alms legally fixed on livestock and goods other than grain.
10. To give a tenth of the harvest of cereals.
11. Moslem behaviour, cf. *taneṣṛaniyet, tayhudiyet,* etc.
12. For *ṛaṣ-malu* ‘his capital’.
13. ‘Herds’.
14. Synonyms which reinforce each other’s meanings, *kazz* = ‘hard(-hearted)’.
15. ‘Even more so’, synonyms *Ɛăssak, ḥăsb-ellah.*
16. The poor and needy.
17. The accounting that will have to be rendered for one’s behaviour on the Day of Judgment.
18. Punishment.
19. English ‘gehenna’, from Hebrew *ghêhinnon,* name of a valley near Jerusalem where idolatrous Jews subjected their children to fire in honor of Moloch.
20. *Ɛzib,* pl. *Ɛăzban* ‘agricultural property’.
21. ‘Excursions, touristic travels’.
22. Koran Sura IX, v. 35, someday their gold, heated red-hot in the fire of gehenna, will be applied to their foreheads, their sides, and their backs.

(3)

The Mortmains of Fez

ḥbas[1] *fas*

koll-waḥăd ka-iḥăbbes mlaku b-šhuwtu u-Ɛla men ḥăbb. u-l-ktir fihom ka-iḥăbbsu Ɛla umuṛ ed-din bḥal l-qărwiyin[2] *u-ž-žwamăƐ eṣ-ṣġaṛ. u-l-medxul d-had le-ḥbus ka-yettṣṛef*[3] *Ɛăl l-xṭib u-l-imam u-l-mwodden, u-l-ma, u-l-ḥṣuṛ*[4] *u-l-muneḍḍifin*[5] *u-l-ḥezzaba,*[6] *u-l-iṣḷaḥat.*

u-kaynin elli ka-iḥăbbsu Ɛl-eš-šoṛfa lli ka-iƐăyyenuhom, u-l-ḥžažel, u-l-itama lli ḍuƐafa.[7] *u-kaynin elli ka-iḥăbbsu Ɛla uladom u-ḥfaḍhom baš ma-iḍiyƐu-ši*[8] *ma-xellaw-lhom, ḥit le-ḥbus ma-yettbaƐ ma-yettšra.*

u-le-ḥbus sidi fṛeš mḥăbbsa ٤ăl l-ḥumeq[9] *u-bellareš.*[10] *ila therres bellareš f-ši-ṣom٤a aw ši-žamă٤, ka-ižibuh l-temma u-i٤ămlu-lu ž-žbira*[11] *u-iṭelquh yakol w-išṛob ḥetta imut.*

u-ḥetta l-met٤ăllmin d-eṣ-ṣnay٤iya kanu zman ka-itsfadu[12] *men had le-ḥbus d-sidi fṛeš. ila therrsu-lhom l-brared au l-ğṛaṛef*[13] *yemšiw l-suq lă-ḥṛeš*[14] *yaxdu ma-therres-lhom bla flus baš m٤ăllminhom ma-iḍeṛbuhom-ši. ḥit dak s-suq hda s-siyyed u-n-naḍiṛ*[15] *d-sidi fṛeš huwwa lli mkellef l-had es-suq.*[16]

Notes

1. Both *ḥbas fas* and *le-ḥbus d-fas* are said. The two words are synonyms, the first is fancier than the second. Neither one has a singular.
2. Famous mosque-university of Fez.
3. Synonym *yetṣiyyeṛ* 'is spent'.
4. Also *ḥṣayeṛ,* pl. of *ḥṣiṛa* 'reed mat'.
5. A classical word, refers to the men charged with cleaning the latrines, *miḍat,* of the large mosques, public latrines outside the building. The cleanness of the interior of all the mosques and the interior latrines of the small ones is the responsibility of the muezzins.
6. They recite two *ḥzab* a day.
7. Sg. *ḍ٤if* 'impecunious, economically bad off', synonyms *derwiš* pl. *draweš, meskin* pl. *msaken, faqiṛ* pl. *fuqaṛa.*
8. *ḍa٤,* imperfect *iḍi٤* 'to perish, to be lost'; *ḍiyye٤* 'to waste, to squander', *iḍiyye٤* → *iḍiyy(e)٤u* → *iḍiy٤u.*
9. Formerly the insane lived in cells near the tomb of the saint. They are now in more satisfactory conditions elsewhere. The cells have become shops, the income from which serves for the support of the sick.
10. *bellareš* 'stork', of Greek origin, simultaneously both collective and and singular; *bellarša* refers to the female; does not take the definite article.
11. A device for setting fractures, 'splints' in this case.
12. 'To benefit', verb Measure X.
13. The singular *ğoṛṛaf* is anciently, via French, the source of English "carafe".
14. *ḥṛeš* 'rough'; the reference is to unglazed pottery, as opposed to *mzeddeš.*
15. *naḍiṛ* pl. *neḍḍaṛ,* manager or director of mortmain properties.
16. He collects the rental revenues from the shops in the market.

(4)

Commercial Tribunal

ž-žmaᶜa[1] *d-et-tožžaṛ*[2]

l-biᶜ u-š-šra[3] *dyal fas ᶜăndu qawanin*[4] *xaṣṣa*[5] *bih. l-mexzen ka-iᶜăyyen*[6] *žmaᶜa men kbaṛ et-tožžaṛ, xemsa aw setta, ka-iᶜăṛfu šuṛuṭ l-biᶜ u-š-šra, baš ila kanet ši-dăᶜwa tižariya mšekkla*[7] *ma-iḥkem fiha illa had et-tožžaṛ lli qolna. men băᶜd ka-itdaᶜaw*[8] *ši-biyyaᶜa-šerraya ᶜănd l-baša au ᶜănd l-mḥătteb,*[9] *ka-iṣifeṭhom l-ᶜănd t-tožžaṛ u-mᶜahom mxezni. dak es-saᶜa koll waḥăd men l-metdaᶜiyin ka-iṭleb žuž d-et-tožžaṛ lli ḥăbb iḥăkmu ᶜlih; u-ka-ittafqu fayn igelsu, imma f-el-qaṛawiyin, aw f-mulay idris,*[10] *aw ḍaṛ ši-waḥăd menhom. mnayn ka-ittžemᶜu, lli ᶜăndu ši-ḥožža*[11] *ka-ižbedha.*[12] *u-t-tožžaṛ ka-išufu d-dăᶜwa men koll žiha, u-ka-iḥăkmu b-fommhom bla teqṛiṛ*[13] *bla ktaba. u-l-mxezni ka-iṛeḍḍ l-xbaṛ ᶜăl l-mexzen.*[14] *f-dak el-woqt, ka-iḥkem b-et-tenfid*[15] *aw ṣ-ṣolḥ.*[16]

Notes

1. *žmaᶜa,* a more or less spontaneous assemblage or gathering of a small number of people; *žemᶜiya,* an organized assembly or association of a larger number of people; *šerka,* a 'corporation' of people with the aim of financial profit; *ṭayfa* (popular usage), *ṭaṛiqa* (formal usage), 'religious association'; *mežlis* 'administrative council'.
2. *tažer* pl. *tožžaṛ* 'very rich merchant', the pronunciation *ddžaṛ* is also heard for the plural; *biyyaᶜ-šerray* pl. *biyyaᶜa-šerraya* '(ordinary) merchant'; *sbaybi* pl. *sbaybiya* 'second-hand dealer'; *ḥwanti* pl. *ḥwantiya* 'shop-keeper'.
3. *l-biᶜ u-š-šra* 'business, commerce'; *tižaṛa* 'business, commerce' is a learned word.
4. *qanun* pl. *qawanin* 'regulation, (human) law' (cf. English "The canons of the church"); *šṛăᶜ* 'law' (of Koranic origin); *qaᶜida* pl. *qawaᶜid* 'customs, usages', implying moral obligation.
5. *xaṣṣ* 'special, particular', fem. sg. adjective modifying a plural noun.
6. 'Appoints'.
7. From *škel* 'shackle, fetter'; *dăᶜwa mšekkla* 'difficult, complicated affair'; synonym *waᶜṛa.*
8. *dᶜa* imperfect *idᶜi* 'to take (someone) to court'; *ana daᶜik l-ᶜănd l-qaḍi* 'I summon you (sg.) before the cadi'; *daᶜi* 'plaintiff', *medᶜi* 'defendant', *tdaᶜa* 'to be in litigation', *dăᶜwa* 'lawsuit'.
9. See Gaudefroy-Demombynes, p. 158. The official is called *mḥătteb* in Fez, *metḥăsseb* in Rabat and Marrekesh.
10. Under the gallery, near the sanctuary.
11. *ḥožža* pl. *ḥžaž* 'evidential document', such as a receipt, a title, etc.
12. *žbed* 'to pull (out), to take out'. One could also say *iḥăḍḍeṛha* 'he produces it'.
13. 'Written judgment, report'; *qaṛaṛ* 'governmental decree'.

14. *mexzen,* the court of the *baša* or the *metḥăsseb; šṛăε,* the court of the cadi.

15. 'Execution of the sentence': *l-baša ka-ineffed l-ḥkam d-et-tożžaṛ, d-el-qaḍi, d-el-mḥătteb...* 'the *baša* executes the judgments of the merchants, the cadi, the *mḥătteb...*'

16. He induces the parties to come to an amicable agreement.

(5)

How to Make the Husband Obey

kanet waḥd le-mṛa waxda[1] *ṛažel ṣεib*[2] *mεaha, smu l-măεṭi. waḥd en-nhaṛ žat εăndha immaha u-ṣabetha ka-txemmem.*[3] *qalet-lha: "ma-lek a bniyti? u-ma l-ožhek ṣfeṛ?"*[4] *qalet-lha: "ṛ-ṛažel ma-ka-ixălLini la-nexṛož wa-la-nedṛež.*[5] *dak en-nhaṛ kan el-făṛḥ*[6] *f-ḍaṛ xalti u-εăṛdu εliya, u-ṛ-ṛažel sženni f-eḍ-ḍaṛ. u-ka-nesmăε eṭ-ṭebbal u-l-ğeyyaṭ*[7] *ka-iḍeṛbu, u-qliybi*[8] *ya-mmwimti*[8] *ka-iεmel dekk-dekk. u-ḥlef-li, la-txeṭṭit*[9] *el-εătba d-bab ed-ḍaṛ."*

qalet-lha immaha: "ḥaža qṛiba hadi! nuḍi! aṛi-li ṭ-ṭḥin u-l-xmira u-l-melḥa u-l-geṣṛiya."[10] *u-bdat ka-tăεžžn ši-ṛğiyfat*[11] *u-xellathom ḥetta xemru. εad bdat ka-tgeṛṛeṣhom*[12] *fuq el-beṛdεa d-lă-ḥmaṛ u-hiyya ka-tqul: "ila qolt-lek, ya-l-măεṭi 'šša!', šša!*[13] *w-ila qolt-lek 'erra!', erra!"*[14] *zăεma, "lli qolt-lek, εămlu!" u-men băεd ṭiybet had el-ğṛayef u-εṭathom l-ṛažel bentha. klahom. u-men dak en-nhaṛ u-huwwa ṭayăε mṛatu f-koll-ma qalet-lu, u-ka-iεămlu bla tuxir.*[15]

waḥd en-nhaṛ axoṛ žat εăndha immaha tšuf waš qḍa-lha dak es-sḥur ši-ḥaža wella-la. qalet-lha bentha: "lăḥla ixeṭṭik εliya ya mmwimti! ṛah eṛ-ṛažel ṛžăε msegged mnegged mεaya. u-ḥăgga (fekkeṛtini) bğit nseqṣik aš ka-iqulu f-el-εăyn l-imna ila bdat ka-tferfer?" qalet-lha ommha: "ğadi tšufi l-ğayeb lli huwwa men žihtek. w-ila ferfrat l-iṣṛa, ğadi tšufi ši-ḥaža lli ma-tεăžbek-ši. w-ila kalek l-ḥažeb l-imen u-ḥăkkitih b-ši-ṣbăε men ṣbaεăk, εăqli εla dak eṣ-ṣbăε b-aš ḥăkkitih, baš ila kan ṭwil εăṛfi bin ṛah ši-waḥăd ṭwil ka-išekṛek. w-ila kan qṣiṛ εăṛfi bin dak elli išekṛek ḥetta huwwa qṣiṛ. w-ila kalek l-ḥažeb l-iṣeṛ u-ḥăkkitih b-ši-ṣbăε ṭwil, εăṛfi bin ši-waḥăd ṭwil ka-ištem fik. w-ila ḥăkkitih b-ṣbăε qṣiṛ εăṛfi bin dak eš-šettam ḥetta huwwa qṣiṛ. u-tani ila ḥăkkiti l-ḥažeb l-imni b-ṣbăε l-iṣṛa εăṛfi bin duk elli išekṛek ihudi, w-ila ḥăkkiti l-ḥažeb l-iṣṛi b-ṣbăε l-yedd l-imna, εăṛfi bin dak eš-šettam meslem. w-ila kalek eš-šareb l-fuqani u-ḥăkkiti ka-iqulu s-slam ka-yaklek, ğadi tsellmi εăl l-ğayeb.

ila kaltek qaε yeddek l-imna, εṛef bin ğadi teqbeḍ l-flus. w-ila kaltek qaε yeddek l-iṣṛa, ğadi tăεṭi l-flus.

ila smăεti ṭnin f-wodnik εṛef bin mat ši-ḥădd ka-tεăṛfu u-ğadi ižik xbaṛu. ta-iqulu ṭaḥet el-weṛqa dyalu u-qaset l-weṛqa dyalek u-tesmăε l-ḥăss dyalha f-wodnik enta.

ila ġuwtat muka fuq eṣ-ṣṭaḥ dyal ši-ḍaṛ ka-iqulu dik eḍ-ḍaṛ ġadi texrež menha ši-gnasa. ila dxel ši-waḥădd f-ši-maḥăll u-nessel l-belġa men režlu u-rekbat-lu ferda fuq ferda ka-iqulu mulaha bġa iṣafeṛ.

ila bġit nqul ši-klam u-ḥetta nta bġiti tqulu u-sbeqt qoltu ana l-luwwel, ka-tqul-li: "sebḥan eḷḷah! ṛah dak eš-ši lli kont bġit nqul nnit. wa-qila illa ġadi nšerku ši-ḥaža fiha r-rbaḥ."

ila konna ka-naklu u-bda l-mwodden ka-iwodden, ila kan dak t-tudan b-nhaṛ ka-nqulu: "ġdana ḥlal", w-ila kan f-el-lil ka-nqulu: "Ɛšana ḥlal".

Notes

1. *xḍa* 'to take in marriage', man or woman.
2. Synonyms *waƐăṛ* 'difficult', *qaṣăḥ* 'hard', *šrir* 'mean, cruel'.
3. *xemmem* 'to think hard', as when one has a vexing problem or worry; synonym *xeṛṛeṣ* 'to rack one's brains'.
4. *ṣfeṛ* 'yellow', here 'pale'.
5. *dṛež* takes here an archaic meaning which it no longer has except in its paired usage with *xrež*, i.e. to leave the house for the first time, in speaking of an adolescent or of a young woman. The meaning here is 'he doesn't even let me put my foot outside the door'.
6. *făṛḥ* 'family celebration' pl. *fṛaḥat; Ɛid* 'religious celebration' pl. *Ɛyad; nzaha* 'country outing, picnic' pl. *nzayeh; fišta* 'non-religious public celebration' pl. *fištat.*
7. A player of the *ġiṭa* pl. *ġiṭat,* a kind of rustic oboe.
8. Women make frequent use of the diminutive, 'my little heart', 'my little mother'.
9. 'I haven't crossed the threshold'; *xeṭwa* '(a) step', *txeṭṭa* 'to take a step', from this 'to cross, to step over'.
10. *geṣṛiya* or *qeṣṛiya,* an earthenware plate, rather wide and shallow, pl. *qṣaṛi; geṣƐa,* the same plate but made out of wood, pl. *gṣaƐi* or *gṣaƐ.*
11. Diminutive of *ṛġifa* pl. *ṛġayef* 'pancake'; if it is made with leavened dough it is called *mxemmṛa,* otherwise it is called *fṭiṛa.*
12. *geṛṛeṣ,* to knead dough into a flat round loaf.
13. *šša!,* interjection for halting an animal, 'whoa'; thus, 'when I tell you "whoa!", you stop!'
14. *rra!,* interjection for setting an animal on the march, 'giddy up!, get up!'
15. 'Without delay'.

(6)

The Muezzin

l-mwodden

koll žamăƐ ka-ikun fih mwodden, u-kayn ž-žamăƐ elli fih tlata, u-ž-žamăƐ l-kbir[1] *ka-ikunu fih sebƐa.*[2] *ka-idiru n-nuba, amma koll waḥădd ka-iqum*[3] *be-nhaṛ, wella koll waḥăd ka-iqum žemɛa kamla. u-nhaṛ ž-žemɛa f-woqt ṣ-ṣḷa ka-iwoddnu kollhom waḥăd tabăɛ l-axoṛ.*

ila mat waḥăd m-el-mwoddnin, ka-ixtaṛu hel l-ḥuma ši-waḥăd elli iṣlaḥ u-iɛămlu bih mužeb[4] *b-el-ɛdul w-iddiweh*[5] *l-en-naḍiṛ*[6] *d-l-ăḥbas, u-iɛămlu huwwa f-blaṣṭ elli mat, u-iqiyduh f-el-konnaš baš ibda yetxeḷḷeṣ f-el-menžṛa.*[7]

l-mwodden l-luwwel kan sidna blal f-iyyam n-nbi, kan ɛăndu waḥd eṣ-ṣuṭ mezyan.

ḥiṭ konna ṣġaṛ u-ka-nqṛaw f-le-msid,[8] *mnin ka-nsemɛu l-mwodden dyal ež-žemɛa,*[9] *ka-nrefdu-lu fatḥa meqluba,*[10] *u-ka-nebdaw nsebbuh u-nqulu: "ḷḷah izăɛlu iṭiḥ men eṣ-ṣemɛa ḷ-ḷeṛḍ u-ittebžeġ*[11] *w-imut!" u-ɛlaš dak eš-ši? ɛla ḥăqq ġir tduz ṣlat ž-žemɛa, u-nemšiw l-el-msid bezz menna, men băɛd dik eṛ-ṛaḥa dyal yumayn. ka-ixeṣṣkom tɛăṛfu bin sidna ɛumaṛ*[12] *huwwa lli ḥeṛṛeṛ d-drari m-el-qṛaya men l-ɛaṣeṛ dyal l-aṛbăɛ ḥetta tduz ṣlat ež-žemɛa.*

Notes

1. 'The great mosque', the one where the Friday sermon is given at noon.
2. The reference is to the *kutubiya* in Marrakesh.
3. *qam* imperfect *iqum* 'to assume a task', *iqum b-el-wažibat* 'he assumes the obligations'; *qam* imperfect *iqim* 'to prepare', *l-mwodden iqim ṣ-ṣla,* coming down from the minaret into the mosque, next to the imam, he announces that the prayer is about to begin.
4. 'Affidavit', a formal declaration done before a magistrate.
5. *dda* 'he took', imperfect *yeddi* 'he takes', *yeddiw* 'they take'; after *-w* the ending for 'him' is *-eh, yeddiweh* 'they take him'.
6. Pl. *neḍḍaṛ,* administrator of mortmain properties.
7. Literally 'carpentry shop'; formerly such a shop was attached to the office of the *naḍiṛ* for the maintenance and repair of furnishings and equipment of the mortmain properties. By metonymy the name of the shop designated the name of the office. When the shop was done away with, its name was retained with the unexpected meaning of 'office of mortmain properties'.
8. 'Koranic school', among country people *žamăɛ,* at Marrakesh *ḥḍaṛ.*
9. Announcing the Friday noon prayer.
10. The ritual of reciting the *fatiḥa* with hands raised and touching one another and with the palms up is a common way of petitioning God to grant an entreaty. The children, in their mock prayer, turned their palms toward the earth since their request was not of the sort acceptable to the Deity.
11. 'To be squashed to a pulp'.
12. The reference is to the second caliph.

(7)

Legends of the Prophet

f-dik el-ğezwa[1] *uqăƐ bin le-mselmin ăğnan*[2] *f-woqt f-aš kanu idzaḥmu*[3] *Ɛăl l-bir baš isgiw,*[4] *ḥetta Ɛlayn*[5] *itšabku*[6] *l-muhažirin*[7] *mƐa l-ʔănṣaṛ*[8] *b-l-iddin, u-kan Ɛăbd-eḷḷah, men žiht el-ʔănṣaṛ, ka-inuwweḍ el-Ɛafya bin en-nas Ɛl-en-nbi. u-men žmelt*[9] *ez-ziğa lli fih, zƐăm ḥetta xerrež el-klam el-qbiḥ f-en-nbi. u-zad f-ḍṣaṛtu u-bda ka-ithedded*[10] *Ɛl-en-nbi w-iqul ğadi ižri Ɛlih*[11] *m-el-madina.*[12] *u-siyyedna*[13] *muḥămmed saq-lu l-xbaṛ. u-kan ṣidna Ɛumaṛ ka-ineṣḥu iṭiyyeṛ ṛaṣ had ez-zayeğ. qal-lu siyyedna muḥămmed: "kun qtelt ṛefqani*[14] *aš ğadi iḍemnu*[15] *fiya n-nas?" u-kan wold Ɛăbd-eḷḷah islamu qwi. qal: "a n-nbi! bbwa sebbek; ameṛni, nžib-lek ṛaṣu!" qal-lu: "lawah! la-tăḥreq ed-demm, u-ḥăqq Ɛlik*[16] *tbiyyen-lu l-uqeṛ u-l-mḥăbba lli wažba Ɛlik." had ež-žud elli šafu hedden-lhom dmağathom,*[17] *u-ṣ-siyyed Ɛăbd-eḷḷah šhed f-ṛaṣu bayn zayeğ*[18] *u-xza ṛaṣu*[19] *Ɛla dak eš-ši lli kan ka-idir.*

Notes

1. 'War-expedition', of the time of the Prophet, pl. *ğzawat;* synonyms *mdagga* 'encounter, combat'; *mḍaṛba* 'fight'; *šeṛṛ* 'intertribal war'; *l-baṛuḍ* 'war', in general; *ḥăṛb* 'war' is a learned word; *girra,* European war.
2. *ăğnan,* a Berberized Arabic word, synonym *mğanna,* from the verb *ġanen,* to be stubbornly contrary.
3. 'To jostle one another'.
4. *sga* imperfect *isgi* 'to go for water'; *sqa* imperfect *isqi* 'to irrigate'.
5. *Ɛlayn,* 'to be about to, to be on the point of'; one could also say here *ḥetta bğaw itšabku.*
6. Here, 'to come to blows'. Some synonyms, all with *b-l-iddin,* are: *itqabṭu, itšabku, itšanqu, itṛamaw.* The following expressions, used with *băƐḍiyathom* after them, are also synonyms: *itdabzu, itḍaṛbu, itsarfu.*
7. *muhažir,* one who followed the Prophet when he left Mecca.
8. *ʔănṣaṛi* pl. *ʔănṣaṛ,* those of Medina who accepted and followed the Prophet.
9. *men žmelt,* followed by a noun, expresses intensity: 'he was in such a mood of revolt and arrogance that...'
10. 'To voice threats'.
11. 'To banish'; synonyms: *ṭṛeḍ, dḥa* imperfect *idḥi, xerrež, žla* imperfect *ižli, nfa* imperfect *infi.*
12. *l-madina,* proper name of the holy city of Medina; *le-mdina,* 'city, town', a common noun.
13. The great names of Islam are preceded by *siyyedna* 'our Lord', especially the name of Mohammed. The saints and the shereefs have their names preceded by *sidna.*

14. Pl. of *ṛfiq* 'travelling companion'; *ɛšir* pl. *ɛăšran,* someone who shares a dwelling or place of business.

15. Other possible phraseologies are: *aš ġadi iqulu fiya, iḥăsbu ɛliya, inwiw fiya.*

16. *ḥaqq,* here 'duty, obligation', construed with *ɛla.*

17. A shorter phraseology would be *theddnu* 'they became calm'.

18. He recognized that he had been carried away with anger.

19. Here, 'to disavow'.

(8)

š-šoṛfa l-beqqaliyin

kan f-waḥd et-tarix waḥd l-ihudi smu ben-mešɛal,[1] *ɛăndu l-mal u-l-quwwa u-le-ṣḥab men koll gens. lăɛbet ɛlih*[2] *nefsu u-kedbet ɛlih u-qalet-lu ma-kayn-ši ma ḥsen mennu f-ed-denya mežmuɛa, u-taq biha. u-bġa, qal-lek,*[3] *yeṛžăɛ ṣoḷṭan. u-ḥlef ḥetta yetrek*[5] *n-nsel*[6] *d-ed-drisiyin*[7] *baš iwolli huwwa ṣoḷṭan.*[8] *u-modda u-huwwa ka-iqtel fihom*[9] *ḥetta ma-bqaw ġir žuž mxebyin ɛănd waḥd el-beqqal.*[10] *u-kan dak el-beqqal ɛăndu žuž d-l-ulad ḥetta huwwa. waḥd en-nhar žaw sḥab ben-mešɛal ɛănd el-beqqal u-qal-lu: "aṛa-lna duk š-šoṛfa lli mxebyin ɛăndek!" dxel huwwa l-ḍaṛu u-xerrež-lhom uladu dyalu. ddawhom l-l-ihudi, qtelhom, u-bqaw ulad mulay idris ɛănd el-beqqal. u-kun ma-ɛmel-ši had el-ḥila, kun tteqṭăɛ nsel mulay idris b-el-kolliya. u-had el-beqqal lli sxa b-kbadu*[11] *baš ma-ittemḥaw š-šoṛfa d-drisiyin, hada huwwa l-muḥibb*[12] *f-ulad en-nbi. u-daba ṛah mebniya ɛlih*[13] *waḥd el-qobba, w-eḍ-ḍeṛbuz,*[14] *ka-iẓuṛuh en-nas u-ka-iqulu-lu sid el-beqqal.*[15] *u-biha baš*[16] *ka-iqulu n-nas ɛawed tani: "ulad sid el-beqqal huma d-drisiyin d-beṣṣăḥḥ".*[17]

Notes

1. The legend has it that this Jew, rich and powerful, lived in Taza, that he was killed by Moulay Rachid while the latter was not yet Sultan but still a student. See *Hespéris,* 1925, deuxième trimestre. The word *mešɛal* pl. *mšaɛel* designates an enormous candle of virgin wax; they are seen at certain votive festivals (*musem*), carried upright, with some difficulty, by four men.

2. *lɛăb mɛa* 'to play with'; *lɛăb ɛla* 'to play a trick on, to deceive'; here, 'to lead into temptation'; *ġwah eš-šiṭan* 'the devil led him astray'.

3. Serves to emphasize the man's presumptiousness.

4. *ṛžăɛ* 'to return, to come back to one's point of departure', also 'to become'; synonym, *iwolli ṣoḷṭan.*

5. Synonym *yeqṭăɛ.*

6. 'Posterity, descendants'.

7. Dynasty which reigned from 788 to 985, descendants of Moulay Idris, buried in the city which bears his name. The Idrissids are *šoṛfa,* sg. *šrif,* i.e. descendants of the Prophet.

8. Si Ben Mechal did actually exist at the time of Moulay Rachid, but the Idrissid Shorfa had no longer constituted an obstacle to his ambitions for a long time. This fact alone shows that we are here dealing with a legend.

9. The use of *f-* 'in' before the direct object of a transitive verb indicates continuity or incompleteness of action, e.g. *qtelhom* 'he killed them', *qtel fihom* 'he killed (some) among them', *kan ka-iqtel fihom* 'he went about killing them'.

10. *beqqal,* formerly 'merchant of fatty substances', invariably a full-blooded Berber from the Sous region.

11. *sxa b-,* 'to hold cheap, to abandon willingly'; politeness formula, *ma-sxina-ši bik* 'we can't, couldn't make up our minds to do without you, we missed you'. *kebda* pl. *kbad* 'liver', the liver is the seat of the emotions (in English, the heart); *kbadu,* 'that which he held most dear'.

12. A classical word, 'he who loves, serves well'; with *f-* 'in' governing the object, the beggars say *a-l-muḥibbin f-en-nbi,* 'Oh you who love the Prophet'.

13. *ṛah,* refers to the *beqqal.*

14. Ornate wooden catafalque erected on top of the tomb.

15. When the proper name is preceded by the definite article, *sidi* is abbreviated to *sid.*

16. *u-biha baš* 'and that is the reason why'; synonym, *εla had eš-ši.*

17. Synonyms: *l-ḥaqiqiyin, n-nit, bla šekk.*

(9)

Our Lady Kessaba of Rabat

lalla kessaba d-eṛ-ṛbaṭ

lalla kessaba[1] *ka-tkun nhaṛ ež-žemεa l-luwlaniya*[2] *f-ṛžeb.*[3] *l-lila lli qbel menha ka-iqulu-lha "lila kbira". bǎεḍ en-nas ka-iṣumu f-dak en-nhar.*[4] *ka-inefqu εla ulidathom nefqa mezyana, ka-išriw d-džaž u-ka-iεǎžnu l-xobz mzuwweq,*[5] *u-ka-išriw š-šebbakiya u-nwaε oxṛin d-el-ḥlawat. u-f-el-lil ka-iḥǎnniw*[6] *l-el-bnitat. u-nhaṛ lalla kessaba, ka-iziynu-lhom u-ka-ixerržuhom iẓuṛu ṣ-ṣaliḥin.*[7] *u-men temma ka-iṭellεu l-el-εlu,*[8] *itṛaḥmu mεa l-muta.*[9] *u-men bǎεd ka-igelsu fuq el-qbuṛ. d-drari ṣ-ṣġaṛ ka-iṭeḷεu l-el-εlu w-ibdaw itsaraw w-iqulu: "a lalla kessaba, εṭini mṛa daba daba!" u-l-bnitat ka-iqulu: "a lalla kessaba, εṭini ṛažel daba daba u-lḥitu qedd eš-šeṭṭaba".*

u-ktir m-l-ulad ka-ihǎbṭu iεumu f-le-bḥǎṛ qoddam sidi l-yaburi[10] *waxxa l-berd.*

u-ka-ikunu l-ḥlaywiya[11] *bezzaf mṣeṭṭṛin f-el-mḥǎžž*[12] *d-lǎ-εlu, u-l-ḥlaqi*[13] *mežmuεin hna u-hna, koll ḥǎlqa w-aš fiha. hak ulad sidi ḥmad u-musa*[14] *b-qrudhom, u-hak l-msiḥ*[15] *lli ka-iḍǎḥḥǎk en-nas, u-hak mwalin el-bendir u-l-εǎwwada,*[16] *u-ka-tkun waḥd el-fṛaža šǎhwa menha.*[17]

(Extracted from *L'arabe dialectal marocain,* by Brunot and Ben Daoud, p. 34.)

Notes

1. A local festival which a zealous *baša* has suppressed. There is no tomb of this *lalla,* who is in any event not a saint; a mythical person.
2. The adjective agrees with the last word of the complex.
3. Holy month, the seventh of the Moslem religious calendar.
4. The day is the first Thursday in the month of *ṛžeb*.
5. A decorated aromatic loaf of bread.
6. The hands and feet are colored with henna.
7. The tombs of the saints who are buried within the city itself.
8. 'The height', the name given to the high quarter of Rabat and the adjoining cemetary, along the ocean shore.
9. *itṛaḥmu mƐa l-muta,* 'they visit the dead'.
10. Patron saint of sailors, buried on the sea-shore.
11. Sellers of sweets.
12. Boulevard, broad avenue.
13. *ḥălqa* pl. *ḥlaqi* 'circle of spectators'.
14. Acrobats native to the Sous region.
15. Grotesque character with a wool beard, assumes a venerable air for rakish jokes.
16. A reed flute, long and without mouth-piece.
17. *šăhwa menha,* literally 'passion from it', i.e. 'thrilling, delightful'.

(10)

Jha Learns to Pray[1]

kan žḥa Ɛămmṛu ma-ṣeḷḷa. waḥd en-nhaṛ, mša iṣeḷḷi ṣ-ṣobḥ[2] *mƐa n-nas f-ež-žamăƐ. bqa l-imam ka-iṣeḷḷi b-en-nas*[3] *b-el-žhaṛ.*[4] *ḥit qṛa l-fatiḥa u-ṣ-ṣuṛa*[5] *f-eṛ-ṛekƐa t-tanya, bda ka-iqṛa l-qunut*[6] *b-es-serr.*[7] *mn-ayn salaw mn-eṣ-ṣḷa, seqṣa*[8] *žḥa waḥăd u-qal-lu: "dik es-saƐa lli qṛa l-fqi u-sket, aš kan huwwa u-n-nas ka-idiru?" qal-lu: "kanu ka-yaklu l-ḥemmeṣ!" lla-ġedda, žab žḥa l-ḥemmeṣ mƐah l-ež-žamăƐ u-ḥḍa l-imam. ġir huwwa sket u-huwwa ižbed el-ḥemmeṣ u-bda ka-iġeẓẓeẓ fih u-n-nas ka-isemƐu. neġzu waḥed, kan ḥdah, b-draƐu. qal-lu žḥa: "u-Ɛlaš? waš nta duwweqtini*[9] *l-barăḥ baš bġitini*[10] *nduwqek l-yum?"*

(G.-S. Colin, *Chrestomathie marocaine,* p. 90.)

Notes

1. See Gaudefroy-Demombynes, *Institutions,* p. 74 ff.
2. *Ibid.,* p. 74. This prayer is obligatory, *feṛḍ*. It is the first of the day.

3. One says *ǯḥa iṣeḷḷi mɛa n-nas,* using *mɛa,* because he is in among those who are praying; but *l-imam iṣeḷḷi b-en-nas,* using *b-,* because he is in front of the people leading the prayer.

4. 'Aloud'. The *l-* of the definite article does not assimilate to the following *ǯ* because the word is a classicism.

5. Notice the emphasis in this word. The classical is *sūrah,* with non-emphatics.

6. *l-qunut.* These are litanies, precise formulas of adoration which the imam recites for himself and for those present who don't know them and who therefore remain silent. Anyone who does his prayers outside the oratory, without an *imam,* must know them precisely.

7. Note the opposition between *b-el-ǯhaṛ* and *b-es-serr.*

8. Remnant of a classical Measure X *ʔistaqṣa,* 'to be curious to know something'.

9. When one is eating something, it is good usage to give a taste to the people present: One might arouse the envy of people who could be quite hungry. This is the reason why one is supposed never to eat in the street.

10. *bġitini nduwqek,* 'you want me to give you a taste'; note the Arabic usage of an object pronoun followed by the imperfect as opposed to the English pattern of an object pronoun followed by the infinitive.

(11)

The Request for Rain

ṭeḷbu l-ġit[1]

ṭ-ṭolba[2] *ka-iqulu-lha ṣaḷat l-istiqṣa.*[3] *ila ma-ṣebbet eš-šta u-ṭalet ḥetta l-dužanbir u-yennayr mɛa yebṛayeṛ,*[4] *ka-ittžemɛu n-nas f-ši-žamăɛ kbir. w-ittafqu ɛl-en-nhaṛ f-aš ġadi ixeržu iṭeḷbu l-ġit. u-l-ḥaḍṛin ka-ixebṛu l-ġaybin b-dak n-nhaṛ u-b-dik es-saɛa.*

u-m-eṣ-ṣbaḥ ka-ibdaw n-nas ka-ittžemɛu f-ež-žamăɛ mɛa t-tmenya, kbaṛ u-ṣġaṛ,[5] *men ġir lă-ɛyalat. f-el-ɛăšṛa ka-ižiw l-ɛulama w-iqṛaw ši-baṛaka*[6] *men l-qoṛʔan, ɛad ka-ixeržu w-itebɛuhom n-nas mežmuɛin, ka-iqulu: "ya ɛzizu! ya žebbaṛ! ġit ɛibadek*[7] *b-el-maṭaṛ."*[8] *u-ka-iɛawdu iqulu: "ṛa s-sbula ɛăṭšana, ġitha ya mulana!"*[9] *u-ḥit ka-ikunu ġadyen, ka-ixerržu lă-ɛyaḷat s-sṭuḷa d-el-ma u-ka-iṛeššu bihom dak bnadem lli dayz, u-hada b-niyt el-fal.*[10]

ḥit ka-iwoṣlu l-bab el-mdina, ka-iḥiydu l-blaġi w-iɛărriw ṛuṣhom, w-itemmu ġadyin hakdak ḥetta žbel sidi bu-mnina.[11] *ɛad ka-itqeddem l-imam w-iṣeḷḷi bihom ṣaḷat l-istiqṣa. mn-ayn kanet n-nas qlubhom ṣafya u-niythom ḥasana kanu ma-ka-ižiw ikemmlu ṣ-ṣla ḥetta iġithom ṛebbi b-eš-šta.*

u-zman, mn-ayn kan l-imam, lli ġadi iṣeḷḷi b-en-nas, xarež l-eṣ-ṣḷa, ka-ilbes l-ḥwayž kollhom meqlubin[12] *f-ḍhuṛhom.*[13] *u-kan men š-šuṛuṭ, iṣeḍḍeq koll-ma ka-yemlek; u-men băɛd ka-tenzel*[14] *š-šta, l-fellaḥa ka-ifdiw-lu dak eš-ši lli ṣeḍḍeq metni mtellet.*[15]

Notes

1. *ġit* 'help', in this context 'rain'.
2. *ṭolba* sg. *ṭaleb* 'scholar, cleric'; distinguish the plural *ṭolba* from *ṭelba* 'mania for begging'.
3. See Gaudefroy-Demombynes, p. 84.
4. Months of the agricultural calendar, see Buret, *Cours gradué*, p. 76. The description in the text is then that of a year of drought, *ɛam el-qăḥt (=kăḥt)*.
5. Even the (male) children are brought along, 'because their prayer is granted', *ḥit dɛuthom meqbula*.
6. Synonyms: *ši-šwiyya men, ši-naṣib, ši ma tayssara;* or else *ši-ṣuṛa* or *ši-tmon,* names for certain subdivisions of the Koran.
7. *ɛăbd* 'slave', pl. *ɛbid; ɛăbd* 'servant, worshipper of God', pl. *ɛibad.*
8. Synonym of *šta* 'rain', a learned word.
9. The *ṭolba* declaim these prayers in Classical Arabic, but the people say them in the colloquial. The children, before the exit of the procession, go about the streets asking for rain in their own way:

a-žṛada fuq eṣ-ṣuṛ	'Oh grasshopper on the wall.
ġitha ya-ben-mănṣuṛ	Help him, Oh Ben Mansour!
a-žṛada ɛăṭšana	Oh thirsty grasshopper,
ġitha ya-mulana	Help him, Oh our Lord!'

10. 'With the intention of a good omen'; i.e., a case of sympathetic magic.
11. Holy Man buried near Rabat, on a height. Prayers are customarily held, in so far as possible, on high ground.
12. Rite of sympathetic magic, aimed at making the disastrous situation reverse itself.
13. 'Turned over on their backs', i.e. worn backwards; *užeh* 'face, observe side' of something, *ḍheṛ* 'back, reverse side' of something.
14. Various verbs are used for 'fall' in connection with rain: *nezlet eš-šta, ṣebbet eš-šta, ṭaḥet eš-šta, hebṭet eš-šta,* 'rain has fallen'.
15. *metni mtellet* 'doubled tripled'.

(12)

Song of the Rain

l-ulad mn-ayn ka-ixeržu mn-el-msid u-tkun eš-šta xiṭ mn-es-sma,[1] *ka-ibdaw iġenniw:*

a š-šta ta-ta ta-ta,
a ulad el-ḥăṛṛata,
a le-mɛăllem bu-zekri,[2]
ṭiyyeṛ šelxa[3] *men ṛaṣu*
baš iṛeqqăɛ ṣebbaṭu.

ṣebbaṭu Ɛănd el-qaḍi,
w-el-qaḍi ma-saq xbaṛ,
w-el-xbaṛ Ɛănd en-nemla,
w-en-nemla b-qṭaṭiha,[4]
w-el-fekṛun b-tăhlilu,[5]
žat el-qemla tefli-lu,[6]
Ɛăḍḍatu men zenbilu.[7]

* * * * * * * *

Song of the rain at Tangier:[8]

a šta ta-ta ta-ta,
a ulad el-ḥăṛṛata,
Ɛayṭu-li[9] *Ɛla baba*
yešri ž-žellaba
baš nƐăyyed had el-Ɛid
b-eš-šwiya[10] *w-el-qeddid.*[11]

Notes

1. The rain falls like thread coming down from the sky.
2. Proper name of a man.
3. A piece of skin.
4. Sg. *qeṭṭaya,* lock of hair on the crown of the head.
5. A small square box of leather, containing a copy of the *dalil* (a pious work), which the child carries on a shoulder-strap as a protective talisman. Sometimes this box is made of silver.
6. A louse which delouses someone!
7. *zenbil,* usually 'tea box'; here, 'paunch, potbelly'.
8. In Marçais, *Tanger,* p. 120.
9. From *Ɛăyyeṭ* 'to call'.
10. Roasted meat.
11. A strip of meat, salted and dried.

(13)

To Make the Rain Stop

tetqaf[1] *eš-šta*

had tetqaf eš-šta b-es-sḥur[2] *ḥṛam.*[3] *qal ḷḷah tƐala*[4]*: "wa la-ifliḥu s-saḥiru ḥăytu ʔata."*[5] *ila ġeṛqet en-nas b-quwwet eš-šta, ka-iqṛaw l-laṭif*[6] *f-ež-žwamăƐ u-ka-tkeff*[7] *eš-šta. had eš-ši ḥlal.*[3]

b-el-ḥăqq kaynin ši-seḥḥarin[8] *ka-iqulu bin ka-iteqqfu š-šta b-es-sḥur. ka-iṣawbu ši-mḥiṛet ṣġiweṛ*[9] *w-iṛebṭuh f-el-qṭuṭ*[10] *iḥăṛtu bih l-melḥa fuq es-sṭăḥ. u-lă-Ɛqul el-mfellsa hiyya lli ka-tenwi had eš-ši ṣḥiḥ.*

u-kaynin ši-ṭolba šyaṭen,[11] *ka-iketbu zlafa*[12] *u-ka-yăƐṭiwha l-dak elli ma-bġa š-šta. ka-ikfiha (=iqlebha) fuq l-Ɛăṛṛam d-ez-zṛăƐ u-ma-ka-tṣebb-ši š-šta. u-had eš-ši ma-ka-iƐămluh ġir s-sbaybiya*[13] *d-ez-zṛăƐ qlalin ed-din. Ɛla ḥăqq ila ma-kanet š-šta, ka-iġla*[14] *w-ibiƐuh b-aš bġaw. w-elli bġa ifessed-lhom l-Ɛazima,*[15] *ka-iqleb dik ez-zlafa Ɛla užehha u-ka-tṭiḥ š-šta b-qdeṛt eḷḷah.*

n-nas d-el-yum ma-bqaw-ši itiqu b-had eš-ši, u-lli qal bih ka-iƐăṛfuh ma-zal mfelles, mšemmăƐ.

Notes

1. *tetqaf* 'action of enchanting, casting a spell'; *tqaf* 'enchantment, spell'; *dayrin-lha ši-tqaf* 'they have cast a spell on her'.
2. *sḥur* 'sorcery'; distinguish from *sḥuṛ* (sometimes *ṣḥuṛ*), last meal of the night during the fast of Ramadan.
3. *ḥṛam* 'illegitimate, illicit, unlawful'; opposed to *ḥlal* 'lawful, licit, proper'; *mekṛuh* 'hated, scorned', refers to things which it is preferable to avoid; *žayz* 'admissible', i.e. morally neutral.
4. Introduces a Koranic quotation, the Koran being the word of God.
5. Koran, XX, 72 'the sorcerer shall not prosper wherever he may go'; the pronunciation indicated in the text is colloquial.
6. Public supplication recited in the mosque when any calamity occurs; *l-laṭif* 'the good par excellence', i.e. 'God'.
7. Synonyms: *š-šta terfed, tesḥa.*
8. *seḥḥar* 'sorcerer'; *ṭellaƐa, šuwwafa* '(female) clairvoyant, fortune-teller'; *gezzan* 'sorcerer, magician'; *ždawli,* someone who tells fortunes by making magic squares called *žedwel* pl. *ždawl.*
9. Diminutive of *ṣġiṛ*. Adjectives with the pattern *FƐiL* usually have diminutives of the form *FƐiƐeL,* e.g. *kbir* 'big' dim. *kbibeṛ, ṭwil* 'long' dim. *ṭwiwel.* Exceptions are *qṣiṛ* 'short' dim. *qṣiweṛ* and *ṣġiṛ* 'little, small' dim. *ṣġiweṛ.*
10. *qeṭṭ* or *mešš* 'cat'. The cat, especially when black, is considered an animal of the devil.
11. *š-šiṭan* 'Satan', synonym *iblis,* subsequently used as a common noun, 'devil', and adjective 'devilish, fiendish'.
12. A common occurrence. The *ṭaleb* writes some cabalistic words or phrases, or even some verses from the Koran, without the diacritical marks. If the object is to cure a sick person, water, which partially dissolves the writing, is placed in the bowl and the sick person drinks it.
13. Synonyms: *musebbib, berġaz;* trader who buys any sort of merchandise with a view to as quick a resale as possible, 'second-hand dealer', generally has no shop or store; *tsebbeb,* to ply the trade of a second-hand dealer; *tažer,* '(rich) merchant'; *ḥwanti,* 'shop-keeper'; *Ɛăṭṭaṛ,* 'peddler'.
14. *ġla* imperfect *iġla,* 'to become expensive'; *ṛxeṣ* or *ṛxaṣ* 'to become cheap'; *Ɛam eṛ-ṛxa* 'year of plenty, of abundance'; *Ɛam el-ġla,* 'year of high prices'; *ġla* imperfect *iġli* 'to boil' (of liquids).

(14)

The Vampires

s-sġana[1]

ɛănd es-sudan[2] *kayen waḥd el-gens ka-iqulu-lu s-sġana, koll waḥăd menhom soġni, u-l-waḥda soġniya. u-ka-iɛawdu ɛlihom*[3] *n-nas le-mḍabăɛ*[4] *men qaɛidethom ka-inuḍu f-neṣṣ el-lil w-ifesxu*[5] *želdhom w-ixelliweh*[6] *f-dik eḍ-ḍaṛ f-aš-en huma w-iṭiṛu f-es-sma, w-imšiw idexlu ɛl-en-nas lli naɛsin b-uḥedhom, w-iweqfu ɛănd ṛuṣhom w-iseffu-lhom*[7] *demmhom, ɛad iṛežɛu l-ḍyuṛhom w-ilebsu žludhom. u-dak elli seffu-lu demmu ka-ibqa mṛiḍ ḥetta imut.*

had eš-ši ḥkah-lna waḥăd ɛămmaṛ es-swarež.[8] *kanet ɛăndna waḥd el-xadem*[9] *soġniya, u-ḥna ma-ɛṛefnaha-ši soġniya. waḥd el-lila fettešna ɛliha u-ma-ṣebnaha-ši. w-el-lila l-oxṛa ɛăssina ɛliha ḥetta ṛežɛet u-šefnaha ḥetta ḥăllet waḥd eṣ-ṣenḍuq u-žebdet želdha u-lebsatu.*[10] *l-lila t-talta ḥit fettešna ɛliha u-ma-ṣebnaha-ši, mšina mguwdin l-eṣ-ṣenḍuq dyalha u-ḥăllinah u-ɛămmeṛna želdha b-el-melḥa.*[11] *u-ɛaynnaha*[12] *ḥetta žat. daret iddiha ɛla želdha. ḥit ṣabtu*[13] *ɛameṛ b-el-melḥa matet. hadi hiyya l-kedba l-mluwna.*[14]

Notes

1. The English translation of this word is not quite exact. The people referred to are a negro group living at the southern limit of the Sahara. They are converts to Islam and have had quarrels with the Touaregs. There was for a long time a *soġni* state, see *Encyclopedia of Islam* (first edition), IV, p. 510.
2. 'Sudan', as a general geographic term, not specifically the present Republic of Sudan, formerly the Anglo-Egyptian Sudan. The word is originally an Arabic plural meaning 'blacks, negroes', and the geographical term arose from the Arabic appellation 'country of the blacks'.
3. Synonyms: *ka-iḥkiw ɛlihom, ka-iqulu ɛlihom.*
4. *meḍbuɛ* pl. *mḍabăɛ* 'idiot, fool'; the metaphorical reference is to someone who has unknowingly been given hyena brain to eat, the hyena being considered as a stereotype of stupidity.
5. Refers for example to snakes which take on a new skin and shed the old one in the spring; *slex* means to skin an animal for slaughter.
6. The third person singular masculine suffixed pronoun, usually *-u* after consonants (*šeftu* 'I saw him') and *-h* after vowels (*šefnah* 'we saw him'), takes the form *-eh* after *-w, ixelliweh* 'they leave it, him'.
7. Synonym *skef* 'to suck'.
8. 'Filler of basins', i.e. a teller of tall tales; *keddab* 'habitual liar'; *xeṛṛaf,* someone who tells long, tedious, boring stories; *sariž* pl. *swarež* 'basin', also *săhriž* pl. *sharež*.
9. *xadem* pl. *xdem* 'negro slave woman'. This word formerly designated a male domestic servant, which explains its lack of a feminine ending.

A negro male slave is *ɛăbd* pl. *ɛbid;* from this original meaning has developed the current meaning of *ɛăbd* as simply 'negro, black-skinned'; *šwired* pl. *-at* 'palace slave-child'; *măɛtuq* 'freed slave'. Since the legal abolition of slavery in Morocco these terms, of course, no longer have their traditional implications.

10. *lebset* 'she put on'. The addition of the ending *-u* 'it' entails a change in *lebset* in order to avoid the occurrence of *e* in an open syllable. In much of Morocco the *e* is changed to *a,* thus *lebsatu* 'she put it on'; in Fez the final *t* is doubled, thus *lebsettu* 'she put it on'
11. Demons and all demoniac beings fear salt. In so far as possible one uses rock-salt as a weapon against them: *melḥ ṣḥiḥ* or *melḥa ṣḥiḥa.*
12. *ɛayen* 'to wait'; *ṣbeṛ ɛla* 'to bear patiently, to patiently wait out something'; *tsenna* 'to await, to wait for'.
13. *ṣab* 'he found'; *ṣabet* 'she found'; *ṣabet* + *-u* 'it, him' becomes *ṣabtu* or, in Fez, *ṣabettu,* see note 10 above.
14. *mluwwen* 'vari-colored', here 'enormous, extravagant'.

(15)

Buried Treasures

l-knuz el-medfunin

ḥna l-fasiyin[1] *ɛăndna ṛuḍa*[2] *muṛ bab ftuḥ, fiha medfun sidi yusef*[3] *žeddna l-kbir. u-dak el-muḍăɛ ka-nsemmiwha le-qbeb.*[4] *kollha ɛamṛa b-el-ʔăwliya u-ṣ-ṣaliḥin.*[5] *mnayn nṭelbu ši-ḥaža ɛlihom*[6] *ka-nqulu: "a baṛakt rižal*[7] *el-qbeb." u-qoddam l-qobba d-sidi yusef, qbiba sġiṛa ka-iqulu medfunin fiha sebɛa d-el-ɛulama. ka-isemmiwhom b-sebɛatu rižal.*[8]

waḥăd ṣbaḥ ež-žemɛa ṭḷăɛ le-mqeddem ɛăl l-ɛada iḥell l-biban l-en-nas elli ġadi ižiw itṛaḥmu[9] *ɛla waldihom u-ḥbabhom. huwwa ḥăll l-qobba d-sidi yusef u-men băɛd mša iḥell l-bab d-had eṣ-ṣaliḥin es-sbăɛ, u-huwwa iṣibha mefṛuɛa, u-keṛkaṛ*[10] *d-et-tṛab ṭalăɛ f-el-weṣṭ. zad išuf, ṣab lă-ḥfiṛ f-žder*[11] *l-ḥiṭ u-žuž d-el-lwiz*[12] *mnezzlin ɛla ṭeṛf el-ḥăfṛa. fhem belli kan temma ši-kenz, u-ši-ṭolba swasa*[13] *naḍu bih*[14] *u-xellaw l-imaṛa.*

had eš-ši d-el-knuz mužudin bezzaf f-el-meġṛib. b-el-ḥăqq elli ka-ixerržuhom b-eṣ-ṣeḍq u-l-ufa[15] *ma-bqaw-š. ma-kaynin ġir el-ġeḍḍaṛa lli iḥălbuk aw inetfuk be-ʔsem eṣ-ṣwayṛ.*[16]

Notes

1. With this plural the word means the people of the great family which bears the surname of *l-fasi.* Stemming from the tribe of the Qoraish, this family has produced numerous scholars and holy men; *l-fasiyin* in this sense is to be contrasted with *hel fas* 'the people of Fez'.
2. *ṛuḍa;* in Fez, an enclosed cemetery belonging to a family. Also buried

there, with the permission of the *fasiyin,* are persons outside the family who buy concessions there.

3. A great scholar, who published a very large number of religious works, died in 'the odor of sanctity'.
4. *qobba* pl. *qbeb,* 'cupola'; the plural *qbeb* is also used in the sense of 'cemetery'.
5. *wali* pl. *ʔăwliya* 'holy man', near to God; *ṣaliḥ* pl. *ṣaliḥin,* a synonym of the preceding.
6. Expressions: *neṭḷeb mn-ăḷḷah u-mennek* 'I beg, request of you and of God'; *neṭḷeb Ɛla mulay idris* (or someone else, except *sidi yusef,* who forbade pleas for intercession) 'I pray to Moulay Idris for intercession'; usually the saint is promised something by the one who prays: *wăƐda* 'promise, vow'.
7. The usual plural of *ṛažel* 'man' is *ṛžal;* with reference to saints the plural is *rižal.*
8. The 'seven saints' are also spoken of at Marrakesh, but there their tombs are scattered about the city.
9. To visit the tombs of parents and friends. On this occasion, *ṭolba,* who are present to offer their services for a fee, are hired to recite prayers, and alms are given to the poor, who are always present.
10. The form *keṛkuṛ* is also used, 'pile, heap'; there are also *kṛakeṛ* which are sacred heaps of stone. The anthropologists use the Gaelic term 'cairn' to refer to them.
11. Foot of the wall; literally *žder* 'root'.
12. Invariable word, like such other terms for pieces of money as *ṣoḷḍi* and *fṛenk.*
13. The discoverers of treasures are almost all *ṭolba* from the Sous region.
14. *naḍ b-,* to make off with something despite any and all prohibitions or resistance.
15. *b-eṣ-ṣeḍq u-l-ufa,* 'truly and according to promise'.
16. *be-ʔsem* 'in the name (of)', i.e. under the pretext of defraying the expenses necessary for the discovery of the treasure: The purchase of aromatic plants, magical ingredients, animals for sacrifice, etc.

(16)

Animal Spirits

qalet-li ommwi lalla[1] *kan waḥd el-wold, f-Ɛomṛu ṭnaš-el Ɛam, gales ka-ilƐăb b-waḥd ež-žṛana buriya.*[2] *u-Ɛătteṭ Ɛla xah elli ṣġeṛ mennu u-qal-lu: "aži ndebḥu had ež-žṛana." qal-lu xah elli ttṣab Ɛaqel: "ḥṛam Ɛlik tƐăddeb el-hyuš."*[3] *u-l-axoṛ xella Ɛla klamu*[4] *u-žbed el-mess u-dbăḥ ež-žṛana. ġir huwwa dbăḥha u-r-răƐda*[5] *qebḍettu,*[6] *u-bdat datu kollha ka-teqfez.*[7] *mša xah eṣ-ṣġiṛ l-ḍaṛhom u-Ɛlemhom b-ma uqăƐ. xeržu ka-itsabgu, ṣabuh f-ḥala.*[8] *refduh, dexxluh l-eḍ-ḍaṛ. u-men băƐd ši-saƐa mat.*

u-mešhuṛ Ɛănd en-nas, ž-žṛan u-l-fkaṛen, l-ktir fihom ka-ikunu meskunin,[9] *u-lli adahom ka-yadiweh*[10] *b-el-mtel. ila Ɛăwweṛhom iƐawṛuh, w-ila hărreshom, ihărrsuh, w-ila qtelhom, ḥetta huwwa imut. u-had eš-ši ma-Ɛăndu dwa, la d-eṭ-ṭbib wa-la d-el-fqi,*[11] *ma-Ɛada ila šafah mulana.*

l-qṭuṭ f-el-lil ka-iṛežƐu žnun, biha baš ma-ka-iḍeṛbuhom en-nas f-el-lil.

Notes

1. 'My grandmother'.
2. Collective *žṛan,* noun of unity *žṛana,* 'frog, toad'; a distinction is made between *ž-žṛan d-el-buṛ* or *žṛan buri,* 'dry land batrachian', i.e. 'toad'; as opposed to *ž-žṛan d-el-ma* 'aquatic batrachian', i.e. 'frog'.
3. *hiša* pl. *hyuš,* refers to animals which are neither mammals, birds, nor fishes; *wăḥš* pl. *uḥuš* refers to wild quadrupeds.
4. He paid no attention to his words.
5. *răƐda,* 'trembling of the body'; *ṛăƐda d-el-ma,* with emphatic *ṛ,* 'waterspout'.
6. *qebḍet* 'she, it seized' + *-u* 'him' = *qebḍatu* (Marrakesh, Rabat) or *qebḍettu* (Fez).
7. *bdat datu kollha ka-teqfez,* 'his entire body began to twitch'; i.e., he began having convulsions.
8. *ṣabuh f-ḥala,* 'they found him in a (terrible, awful) state'.
9. 'Inhabited, possessed (by evil spirits)'.
10. *ada* imperfect *yadi,* 'to cause to suffer'.
11. The allusion is to the talismans of magic writing of the scholar-sorcerers.

(17)

The Evil Eye

l-Ɛăyn

kayn waḥd el-matal Ɛaṛabi[1] *ka-iqul: "l-Ɛăyn todxilu ṛ-ṛažula li-l-qăbṛi wa-ž-žamal li-l-qidri."*[2] *u-f-el-ḥadit*[3]*: "tnayn u-sebƐin f-el-mya men ʔommati tamutu b-el-Ɛăyn." ka-nqulu f-fas: "a lli muƐăyyin*[4] *ila šaf*[5] *f-šix el-fellaḥa*[6] *yeṛžăƐ xemmas*[7]*."*

w-ana ka-năƐṛef waḥd el-gezzar măƐyan. kan waḥd el-Ɛšiya gales mƐa ṣḥabu f-el-wesƐa d-wad eš-šoṛfa[8]*, u-d-dula*[9] *kanet ṛayḥa*[10] *f-dik es-saƐa, koll begṛa aw žuž mašyin l-maḥăllhom. waḥăd men dik ež-žmaƐa ḍaṛ f-el-gezzar u-qal-lu: "ḥăbbina netƐăššaw men dik el-begṛa d-flan." f-dik es-saƐa šaf fiha le-mƐăllem u-qal: "aḥ! Ɛla ḍraƐ!"*[11] *ma-ža ikemmelha ḥetta zehqet*[12] *ržel l-begṛa u-ṭaḥet u-therrset. žbed ženwih u-naḍ u-lḥăqha b-ed-dbiḥa.*[13] *u-Ɛad ṣifṭu Ɛla mulaha. mn-ayn ža ṣabha uqăƐ-lha had eš-ši Ɛăbba*[14] *mƐah le-mƐăllem elli dbăḥha huwwa ixdemha.*[15] *u-Ɛṛeḍ Ɛl-en-nas elli ḥaḍṛin, u-ma-ža iṛuḥ el-lil ḥetta tƐăššaw menha.*

Notes

1. 'An Arabic proverb', i.e. one in use among the ancient Arabs.
2. Classical Arabic pronounced in the Moroccan fashion, 'the evil eye sends a man to the tomb and a camel to the cooking pots'.
3. *l-ḥadit,* traditions of the Prophet, concerning his sayings and his acts. Many sententious sayings are falsely attributed to the Prophet.
4. *muɛăyyin,* a person who casts the evil eye; the word is a classical term with Moroccan pronunciation; people with the power of the evil eye are also referred to as *măɛyan.*
5. *šaf eš-šix,* 'he saw the sheikh'; *šaf f-eš-šix,* 'he cast the evil eye on the sheikh'.
6. *šix el-fellaḥa,* 'syndic of agricultural property owners', almost always he is the richest one among them; the syndic of a handicraft guild is called *lamin;* the syndic of butchers is called *ɛrif;* the head of a women's guild is called *amina.*
7. An agricultural worker who contributes nothing but his labor and who receives a fifth of the harvest; the comparable worker in a vegetable garden is called *ṛebbaɛ* and receives a fourth of the produce.
8. The scene is in Fez, *wad eš-šoṛfa* is the name of one of the branches of the river that goes through the city; *f-el-wesɛa,* 'in the open', i.e. ground in or near the city but neither sown nor with buildings on it.
9. *dula,* 'herd of cattle'; in this context, specifically the herd belonging to the local quarter of the city, composed of cows of various ones of the inhabitants; *dula* also means 'dynasty, government'.
10. *ṛaḥ* imperfect *iṛuḥ* 'to return at evening', to an encampment, to a place of residence.
11. 'Ah, what a magnificent teaṭ!' An exclamation of admiration is supposed to bring misfortune to the object admired. In order to avoid it, the expression of praise is preceded by the formula *tbaṛek eḷḷah* 'God be praised!' The butcher deliberately avoided this prophylactic formula.
12. *zheq* 'to slip, to make a false step'; *zleq* 'to slip', as a result of having stepped on some slippery object.
13. *lḥăqha b-ed-dbiḥa* 'he got to her with the slaughter', i.e. he succeeded in cutting the beast's throat before it died; otherwise the flesh would not be acceptable food under Moslem dietary laws.
14. *ɛăbba,* synonym *dda,* 'to take'.
15. *ixdemha,* 'he works it', i.e. cuts up the meat; *slex* 'to skin'; *ṭubeq,* 'to divide into quarters'; *geṛṛeḍ,* 'to cut into pieces'; *semser,* 'to remove the bones from'.

(18)

Children and the Last Judgment

le-mṛa lli mat-lha ṣabi ṣġiṛ aw ṣabiya, žehd ɛamayn aw telt snin, yum el-qiyama[1] *dak eṣ-ṣabi ka-ibăɛtu*[2] *ḷḷah f-sift*[3] *eṭ-ṭiṛ men ṭyuṛ ež-ženna, ka-irekkebha f-ḍăhṛu w-iwoṣṣelha l-ež-ženna bla ḥsab bla ɛqab,*[4] *w-iṛžăɛ l-el-măḥšeṛ*[5] *w-irekkeb bbwah ḥetta huwwa.*

ka-iḥkiw ɛla waḥd el-wali[6] *kan mat-lu ši-ṣabi ṣġiṛ u-ma-ṣbeṛ-ši ɛlih.*[7] *u-f-dik el-lila f-aš mat-lu l-weld, šaf f-le-mnam bin huwwa f-el-măḥšeṛ, u-žah dak el-weld f-sift ṭiṛ u-qal-lu: "a-bbwa, bġit nrekkbek ɛla ḍăhṛi u-ndexxlek l-ež-ženna." bda ka-iɛmel žehdu baš ihezz bbwah fuq ḍăhṛu. iwa ma-qedd-ši, ṣabu tqil ḥit ma-ṣbeṛ-ši ɛăl l-weld elli bġah mulah u-ddah, u-hada huwwa d-denb lli teqqlu. qal l-weld: "kun kan ɛăndi ši-xuya, kun hezzitek ana w-iyyah u-ddinak l-ež-ženna." f-dik es-saɛa l-wali ḍeṛbatu l-fiqa,*[8] *u-tfekkeṛ dik el-mnama u-ṭleb eḷḷah yăɛṭih ši-weld axoṛ w-imut-lu baš itḥamaw ɛlih b-žuž (=itɛawnu ɛlih) w-iweṣṣluh l-ež-ženna. u-ɛṭah eḷḷah dak el-weld et-tani u-mat-lu.*

Notes

1. The Day of Judgment.
2. *bɛăt* 'to raise (from the dead)'.
3. For Classical *ṣifah* 'aspect, form', root *W-Ṣ-F*.
4. *bla ḥsab,* 'without accounting' (for his actions); *bla ɛqab,* 'without punishment'.
5. The place where the resurrected are assembled in awaiting interrogation about their acts during life. See Gaudefroy-Demombynes, p. 55.
6. A Holy Man.
7. He couldn't reconcile himself to the loss of his child.
8. *ḍeṛbatu l-fiqa,* 'he woke up'.

(19)

sidi qaṣem

had es-siyyed huwwa lli medfun ḥda btiža.[1] *kan f-ḥayatu žemmal.*[2] *waḥd el-meṛṛa ɛăbba*[3] *s-smen l-fas. mnin uṣeḷ dxel ɛla bab el-măḥṛuq*[4] *u-huwwed*[5] *ɛl-eṭ-ṭălɛa*[6] *l-kbira. ḥit uṣeḷ l-ṛaṣ et-tiyyalin*[7] *ṣab waḥd eṣ-ṣaliḥ gales f-bab ši-derb ka-iqul: "a men yăɛṭina xobza sxuna iddiha barda?" yăɛni ila ɛṭitih xobza b-eṣ-ṣăḥḥ yăɛṭik ši-kaṛama*[8] *m-el-kaṛamat dyalu, bḥal teṛžăɛ ḥetta-nta ṣaliḥ u-tezhed*[9] *f-ed-denya, kama uqăɛ l-had ež-žemmal, aw teṛžăɛ ġani aw tedṛek ši-mqam ɛali. yeṛžăɛ klamna l-ež-žemmal. berrek žemlu u-šra xobza sxuna u-ḥăll fomm ež-želd lli fih s-smen ɛla ḥaqq kanu zman ta-iɛăbbiw s-smen men blad l-blad f-ež-žlud d-el-begri. mnin ḥăll fomm ež-želd u-ɛmel s-smen f-el-xobza, ġelbu ž-želd,*[10] *bġa yettehṛeq*[11]*; šebbeṛ fih b-el-yedd l-yemniya u-medd l-xobza l-dak eṣ-ṣaliḥ b-el-yeṣṛiya*[12]*; qbeḍha mennu u-qal-lu: "dditiha*[13] *a bu-Ɛăsriya." f-dik es-saƐa smăḥ f-ež-žmel u-ma-žemmel*[14] *u-saḥ.*[15] *u-mnin mat ndfen*[16] *f-eš-šṛaṛda.*[17] *u-l-yum ka-yetsemma b-sidi qaṣem bu-Ɛăsriya.*

Notes

1. *btiža,* the town of Petit-Jean, founded by the French, located on the right bank of the *wad ṛḍem.* The tomb of the saint is on the left bank, in the casbah, among some olive trees. The town is a fairly important center.
2. *žemmal,* 'camel driver', a man who arranges for transport by camel-back; *ḥămmaṛ,* 'muleteer', a man who arranges for transport by mule-back (not donkeys); the former transports only freight, the latter also takes passengers; *ṛeqqaṣ,* 'courier, mail-carrier', goes on foot.
3. *Ɛăbba = dda.*
4. *bab el-măḥṛuq,* 'the gate of the burned'; one of the gates of Fez, so named because of a man who was tortured there by fire; to the west of the old city.
5. *ḥaf* imperfect *iḥuf, hbeṭ,* or *huwwed,* but not *nzel* in this context.
6. *ṭ-ṭălƐa l-kbira,* 'the great slope'; there are two in Fez, one in Salé.
7. *tiyyal,* the craftsman who makes *tila* pl. *tilat,* a fine sieve made with silk or goat hair; *ḥit uṣeḷ l-ṛaṣ et-tiyyalin,* 'when he arrived at the beginning of the tila market'.
8. *kaṛama,* more than a *baṛaka;* 'miracle' is perhaps the closest translation.
9. To renounce the world and consecrate oneself to prayer.
10. *ġelbu ž-želd,* 'the skin conquered him', i.e. he almost lost his grip on it, almost dropped it.
11. *bġa yettehṛeq,* 'it started to spill, it was about to spill'; *ttehṛeq,* 'to spill, to get spilled', with reference to liquid, grain, flour, etc. It is to be assumed that the event happened in the summer and that the butter had melted.
12. *yeṣṛiya,* with both *ṣ* and *ṛ* emphatic; *iṣaṛ = šmal,* 'left'; *Ɛăsriya,* without emphasis, despite the *Ɛ;* it is not proper to hand something to someone with the left hand; *Ɛăsri,* 'left-handed'; the expression *bu-Ɛăsriya* is used only with reference to this saint and his legend.
13. 'you have taken it', i.e. the miraculous reward.
14. A common expression meaning to abandon all that one has in order to withdraw from the world.
15. He began to wander about without a destination, typical of many of the saints of Islam.
16. *ndfen,* Measure VII, medio-passive of Measure I *dfen,* 'to bury'; synonym, Measure Ia *ttedfen,* likewise the medio-passive of Measure I.
17. Tribe of Arab origin. An individual of the tribe is called *šeṛṛadi.*

(20)

l-fqiṛat men el-ḥžiṛat

sidna ℰumaṛ[2] *ben el-xeṭṭab nhana ℰla ℰibadet*[3] *lă-ḥžeṛ ma-ℰada l-ḥažaṛ lă-ℰsad*[4] *f-el-kăℰba l-mušăṛṛafa. qal-lha: "kun ma-šeft ṛaṣul eḷḷah iqebblek*[5]*, ma-qebbeltek." u-waxxa had eš-ši kaynin en-nas lli ka-iḥtaṛmu*[6] *lă-ḥžeṛ w-izuṛuh*[7] *w-ibusuh.*

ḥna ℰăndna f-meṛṛakeš waḥd el-mwiḍℰa ḥda wad isil[8]*, ktira fiha ṛ-ṛemla, u-dak eṛ-ṛmel ktirtha ḥžiṛat mluwnin, fihom el-byeḍ u-lă-ḥmeṛ u-le-ṣfeṛ u-l-mzeṛgeṭ*[9]*. u-dik eṛ-ṛemla d-wad isil ka-teṣlaḥ-lna l-eḍ-ḍeṣṣ*[10] *dyal eṣ-ṣṭuḥa u-d-eḷ-ḷeṛḍ. u-ka-teṣlaḥ tani iℰăṛṛmuha*[11] *fuq el-qbuṛ. u-ḥit ka-ižibuha men dik el-mwiḍℰa dyalha ka-ižebṛu fiha had el-ḥžiṛat elli qolna. w-elli ℰăžbatu ši-ḥžiṛa, ka-ižeṛṛebha*[12]*: ka-ikemmeš ℰliha iddu u-ka-yenfex ℰliha b-ḥălqu, ma-ši b-šwarbu. ḥit iḥell iddu ila ṣabha ℰăṛgana, ka-iqul: "hadi fqiṛa bla šekk!" ℰad ka-yăḥtaṛemha: ka-ilwiha f-waḥd ed-drira nqiyya wolla ši-xniša*[13] *d-el-melf ṣġiwṛa w-idirha f-žibu. u-fin-emma tfekkeṛ*[14] *l-baṛaka dyalha, ka-ixerrežha w-ibusha u-yăℰṭi le-ḥbabu u-l-uladu ibusuha mℰah. w-ila šaf ši-mnama mezyana f-dik el-lila f-aš žbeṛ el-ḥžiṛa, ka-iqul: "bla šekk had el-ḥžiṛa fqiṛa." u-ka-yăℰmel ṣadaqa, ka-iℰămmeṛ ši-geṣℰa d-el-kesksu w-iṣeḍḍeqha ℰăl le-msaken.*

Notes

1. *fqiṛa,* said of a very pious woman, almost a saint.
2. The second of the caliphs of Islam.
3. 'Worship'.
4. The true name of the stone is *le-swed* 'the black', but it is euphemistically referred to as *lă-ℰsad* 'the fortunate, the happy'.
5. *qebbel,* 'to kiss', is the classical term; the colloquial is *bas* imperfect *ibus*.
6. *ḥtaṛem,* 'to honor'; Measure VIII, with the typical colloquial vowel pattern.
7. See the text about *lalla xăḍṛa,* nos. 31-33.
8. The river that flows along the city wall on the north.
9. *mzeṛgeṭ,* 'vari-colored'.
10. Waterproof plaster, made of sand and lime and tamped down.
11. *ℰăṛṛem,* 'to pile up'.
12. 'He tests it', to see whether it is holy, whether it has *baṛaka,* 'blessing, good luck'.
13. 'Sachet, small bag'.
14. *tfekkeṛ,* 'to remember, to think of'.

(21)

I Become the Chief of a Religious Brotherhood

"lli ma-ɛăndu šix[1]*, š-šiṭan huwwa šixu." had el-metla ka-iquluha l-en-nas elli ma-gabḍin ḥetta werd*[2]*, bḥal z-zufriya u-duk elli ka-iɛămmṛu l-qhawi. u-f-el-ɛṛubiya*[3] *qlil elli gabeḍ ši-werd.*

bbwa woṣṣani netbăɛ eṭ-ṭaṛiqa[4] *lli tabăɛha huwwa, dyal sid el-moxtar*[5] *el-konti f-es-sudan; had es-siyyed men el-quṭaba*[6] *l-kbaṛ bḥal mulay ɛăbd el-qadeṛ ež-žilali*[7] *u-sidi bu-medyan l-ġăwt*[8] *u-sidi ben sliman el-žazuli*[9] *u-ġirhom. w-ana kont nawi ma-netbăɛ ma-ɛada l-werd elli šeft mulah f-el-mnan wella f-l-iqda*[10]*. u-uqef ɛliya f-el-mnam š-šix et-tižani*[11]*, u-kont ġadi ntebɛu, saɛa ma-ktab-ši*[12]*.*

waḥd en-nhaṛ kont gales mɛa mwalin ed-dalil[13] *u-ma-ttṣab ɛăndhom mqeddem. ḍaṛ fiya waḥd el-fqi ɛăllama*[14] *u-qal-li: "waš tebġi tkun mqeddem ɛla had eṭ-ṭaṛiqa?" qolt-lu: "ila qebluni ma-fiha bas." f-dik es-saɛa refdu fatḥa*[15] *u-daruni mqeddem ɛlihom. hada huwwa s-sabab b-aš tbăɛt eṭ-ṭaṛiqa l-žazuliya*[16]*.*

Notes

1. *šix,* chief of a religious brotherhood, important personnage; *mqeddem,* chief administrator of a local group of religious brothers of a *ṭaṛiqa;* he is more or less its factotum.
2. *n-nas elli ma-gabḍin ḥetta werd,* 'the people who are not affiliated with any religious fraternity'; the *werd* is the rule of the order containing the text of essential prayers; the prayers vary from brotherhood to brotherhood and are supplementary to the mandatory prayers of Islam in general.
3. *ɛṛubiya,* 'country people, bedouins', sg. *ɛṛubi.*
4. *ṭaṛiqa,* 'way', i.e. mystic way which leads to God, whence the later meaning of 'religious brotherhood'; it is applied to the more respected brotherhoods; the popular brotherhoods with vulgar rituals are called *ṭayfa* pl. *ṭwayf.*
5. The title *sidi* 'my lord' becomes *sid* when the following word begins with the definite article.
6. In the mystic hierarchy, *qoṭb* 'pole' designates the most eminent of the pious men of an epoch.
7. One of the greatest saints of Islam, of Persian origin, buried in Baghdad, has innumerable cenotaphs in all Moslem countries.
8. *ġawt,* 'help', title given to a saint who has arrived at the peak of the mystic hierarchy; he is the *qoṭb* when one pleads for his help; *sidi bu-medyan* is buried in Tlemcen.
9. From the Moroccan tribe of the *gzoula;* the *ṭolba* pronounce the *g* of the colloquial as *ž;* he is the author of the famous *dalil el-xiṛat* 'guide to good works'.

10. *iqḍa,* state of being awake, as opposed to *mnam;* the opposition is the same as that of the more every day terms *fayeq* 'awake' and *naᶜăs* 'asleep'.

11. Buried at Ain-Madhi in southern Algeria.

12. 'It wasn't written', i.e. not destined to be; *ma-ketteb-ši ḷḷah* 'God did not have it written' (by the angels); *ma-ktab-ši,* a Measure IX verb, is exceptional.

13. The members of the brotherhood of which *sidi ben sliman l-žazuli* is the founder are not called *žazuliyin* as one would expect (cf. *tižaniyin, kettaniyin, qaḍiṛiyin,* etc.), but *mwalin eḍ-dalil* 'the devotees of the *dalil*', see note 9; they learn this book by heart and recite it together at the time of their meetings; those who haven't memorized it follow the printed book and recite along with the others.

14. 'Very learned'; the *fqi* was a guest.

15. *refdu fatḥa,* 'they raised a *fatḥa*', i.e. said a prayer to ask the blessings of God; this particular prayer is said with hands touching, held at about the height of the neck, open palms turned toward heaven; it is not necessarily the *fatiḥa,* the first sura of the Koran, which is recited on such occasions.

16. With religious terms, the definite article is not assimilated to a following *ž*.

(22)

lă-ᶜḍam d-el-ᶜid el-kbir

f-eṛ-ṛbaṭ, ṛ-ṛuṣ d-el-ḥăwli ka-ibexxṛu[1] *ᶜlihom kesksu*[2] *u-ka-itᶜăššaw*[3] *bihom nhaṛ el-ᶜid f-el-lil. u-ġir ifeḍḍiw*[4] *b-el-makla, ixerržu lă-ᶜḍam mn-eḍ-ḍaṛ w-isiybuhom.*[5] *f-fas, ka-ibatu ṛ-ṛuṣ f-el-keskas itbexxṛu*[6]*, u-ṣ-ṣbaḥ d-tani ᶜid, ka-ifeṭṛu bihom; ᶜad ka-ixerržu lă-ᶜḍam ḥetta huma. u-had eš-ši f-ktub lă-ᶜyalat*[7]*: ila klaw ṛ-ṛuṣ u-xellaw lă-ᶜḍam f-qelb eḍ-ḍaṛ, ka-idxel-lhom bu-herrus*[8]*; u-ka-ikun l-ᶜam kollu t-tăhras f-el-mwaᶜen d-eḍ-ḍuṛan.*[9]

u-l-luḥa d-el-ktef[10] *l-yemniya, ila kan mulaha fqi u-ka-yăᶜṛef išuf*[11]*, ka-ibda iqul-lhom aš kan w-aš ġadi yuqăᶜ. wolla*[12] *ka-isiybuha mᶜa lă-ᶜḍam f-ez-zbel.*

u-l-kᶜab[13] *d-el-ḥăwli d-el-ᶜid, b-el-xuṣuṣ huma,*[14] *ka-yaxduhom l-ulad w-ixeržu l-ez-zenqa*[15] *ka-ilăᶜbu bihom mᶜa ulad ež-žiran. u-l-bnat ma-ka-ilăᶜbu-š b-el-kᶜab b-el-koll; ka-iᶜămlu ᶜšiša qdira.*[16] *had el-lăᶜb d-el-kᶜab ma-ka-idum-ši bezzaf ᶜla ḥăqq ᶜašuṛa tafrah*[17]*, u-l-lăᶜb ka-itbeddel.*

Notes

1. *bexxeṛ,* 'to cook by steaming'; the couscous is steam-cooked with the water in which the sheep's head is boiled.

2. The form at Fez is *seksu,* doesn't take the definite article.

3. *fṭeṛ,* to take the first meal of the day, noun *fṭuṛ,* 'breakfast'; *tġedda,* to eat the midday meal; *tƐăšša,* to eat the evening meal.

4. *feḍḍa,* 'to finish', is transitive; synonym *sala,* 'to finish', is intransitive, and a following noun complement is introduced by *men* 'from, of'; *qaḍa* imperfect *iqaḍi,* 'to finish', transitive.

5. Synonyms: *ṛma* imperfect *iṛmi, laḥ* imperfect *iluḥ.*

6. *tbexxeṛ,* 'to be steamed', the medio-passive of *bexxeṛ;* see note 1.

7. A mockery aimed at women, who are uneducated; 'their books' (which are compared here to the serious books of the men) are their heterodox beliefs and superstitions.

8. Mythical being who personifies breakage; *herrus,* from *hres* 'to break'; the word has an intensive pattern; a doubled second consonant followed by a long vowel.

9. *ḍuṛan,* verbal noun of *ḍaṛ* imperfect *iḍuṛ* 'to turn', 'everyday dishes'; contrasts with *l-mwaƐen d-el-feṛḥa* 'ceremonial dishes'.

10. 'Shoulder-blade, scapula'.

11. *ka-yăƐṛef išuf* 'he knows how to see (the future)'; i.e., if he is a *šuwwaf* or a *gezzan,* 'clairvoyant'.

12. *wolla,* 'otherwise, if not'; from *wa-in-la* 'and if not'; synonym, *aw la.*

13. 'Knucklebones, anklebones'.

14. 'Especially them'.

15. *zenqa* pl. *znaqi,* 'street'; *derb* pl. *druba,* small dead-end street; *ṭṛiq* pl. *ṭṛuq,* 'road, highway'.

16. *Ɛšiša,* diminutive of *Ɛša,* 'dinner, supper', i.e. a child's play dinner-party; *qdira,* diminutive of *qeḍṛa* 'pot'; *Ɛšiša qdira* is a set phrase.

17. *tfer,* 'to follow closely, soon after'; active participle *tafer,* fem. *tafra,* with affix *-h* 'him, it', *tafrah.*

(23)

Ɛṛifat[1]

kaynin lă-Ɛṛeb d-el-qbayl lli huma saknin f-fas, f-bab ftuḥ u-l-fexxaṛin[2] *u-sidi Ɛli bu-ġaleb u-xrišfa*[3]*, ṛ-ṛžal dyalhom ka-ixedmu f-el-muqef*[4]*, u-l-băƐḍ fe-Ɛyalathom ka-iḍuṛu f-le-mdina ka-ibiƐu tadeqqa d-el-bni l-en-nwafex*[5] *u-tadeqqa d-el-lwani.*[6]

mnayn ka-idxol eš-šheṛ d-el-Ɛid el-kbir, lli Ɛăndha ši-bnita ka-tlebbes-lha bḥal l-mra l-kbira u-ka-tƐăkkeṛ-lha[7] *u-tsuwwek-lha*[8]*, u-tḥăṛqeṣ-lha*[9] *u-tăƐmel eṛ-ṛumiya*[10] *f-ṛaṣha u-l-ḥărraz*[11] *mzuwweq b-el-lwan. f-dak es-saƐa ka-tetsemma Ɛṛifa.*

u-immaha ḥetta hiyya telbes nqiya. u-ka-temši hiyya u-bentha ka-iḍuṛu f-el-ḥwem.[12] *u-bab-eḍ-ḍaṛ lli weṣlu-lha ka-ibdaw iqulu:*

ɛaṛfa[13]*, mbeṛka, mimuna* (repeat)
wa-ya-ḥămmu[14] (repeat)
tăɛṭini ši
wella nemši
năɛṭik ulid
mḥănni-lu b-el-kommiya u-š-šašiya
u-rkab ždid nhaṛ el-ɛid.[15]

u-ka-itnawbu ɛliha[16] *ḥetta iqulu-lhom mwalin eḍ-ḍaṛ "dexlu!" aw "ḷḷah iftăḥ!" ila kanu msellyin*[17] *u-xeṣṣhom ɛl-aš iḍăḥku, ka-idexxluhom w-ifeṛḥu bihom u-yăɛṭihom yaklu w-išeṛbu. u-mnayn ka-ižiw ixeržu ka-yăɛṭihom ši-flisat aw ḥlawi*[18] *aw sokkar.*

u-had eš-ši ka-idum tsăɛ iyyam men uwwel eš-šheṛ ḥetta lilt el-ɛid. u-l-flus elli ka-ižemɛu, bihom ka-iɛaydu.[19]

Notes

1. Doesn't take the definite article; the word derives from *žbel ɛaṛafa* in Mecca; note the emphatic *ṛ*; the word *ɛrifa,* with a non-emphatic *r,* means 'policewoman, woman jailer'.
2. The potters' quarter; all these quarters are on the periphery of the city; *sidi ɛli bu-ġaleb* is the patron saint of the barbers of Fez.
3. 'Little artichoke'.
4. Square where unskilled laborers gather in search of work; it is there that potential employers go to look for them.
5. *tadeqqa,* the kind of potter's clay from which people make, at home, the portable stoves called *nafex* pl. *nwafex.*
6. 'Kitchen utensils', used only in the plural.
7. She puts the vermillion rouge called *ɛăkkaṛ* on her cheeks.
8. She rubs walnut bark, *swak,* over her lips, so that they will look red.
9. She puts the black make-up *ḥăṛquṣ* under her eyebrows.
10. *sebniya ṛumiya,* head-scarf imported from Lyons.
11. A band of pretty cloth which is used to bind the scarf on the head and the ends of which hang down on the back.
12. *ḥuma* pl. *ḥwem,* 'quarter (of a town)'.
13. For *ɛaṛafa,* 'may the day of *ɛaṛafa* be blessed, happy...'
14. Name of a mythical devil-like being; there are those of the land, *berri,* and those of the sea, *băḥri.*
15. 'Made-up with henna, armed with a dagger, and with a cap and new spurs, the day of the feast'.
16. The mother and the daughter repeat this song alternately.
17. *mselli* pl. *msellyin,* 'carefree, happy'.
18. *ḥălwa* pl. *ḥlawi,* piece of pastry with sugar or honey on it.
19. *ɛăyyed,* 'to celebrate a feast', *ɛid; ɛăyyed + -u = ɛaydu* 'they celebrated'.

(24)

Divorce on Account of the Sheep of *l-Ɛid l-kbir*

muḥămmed: a-s-si[1] *Ɛăbd eḷḷah, smăƐt bin xak ṭeḷḷeq le-mṛa. Ɛlaš ttefṛeq mƐaha?*

Ɛăbd eḷḷah: dexlet binathom dik eš-šiṭana d-lă-Ɛguza[2] *nsibtu*[3] *b-xiṭ kḥăl.*[4]

muḥămmed: ḥki-li băƐda kif dayr had eš-ši.

Ɛăbd eḷḷah: le-mƐăllem el-Ɛăṛbi, ṛažel bentha[5]*, šra ḥăwli l-eḍ-ḍḥiya*[6] *b-xemsṭaš-eṛ mya d-er-ryal, u-dexxlu l-eḍ-ḍaṛ. ḥit šaftu le-mṛa Ɛăl luwwel, Ɛžebha. men băƐd šaftu dik eš-šiṭana d-immaha b-Ɛăyn qbiḥa*[7] *u-Ɛawžetha*[8] *u-qalet-lha: "la-tqebli mennu had el-ḥăwli lli qṛinatu ṣġiwṛin*[9]*; šufi bent lalla hăššum! qṛun ḥăwliha fihom neṣṣ mitru f-el-waḥăd, tbaṛek eḷḷah*[10]*!" ġir el bent semƐăt had el-klam men immaha, u-hiyya tḍuṛ Ɛl-eṛ-ṛažel*[11]*. mnin dxel l-ed-ḍaṛ, qalet-lu mṛatu: "had el-kbiyyeš elli qṛinatu gdid hakika*[12]*, ma-nqeblu-ši." qal-lha ṛ-ṛažel: "ṛah măƐluf*[13] *u-smin u-ṣġiṛ u-fti*[14]*, ḥsen men dak mul el-qṛun l-kbaṛ." qalet-lu: "Ɛliya b-es-sna*[15] *la bqa! ġir xerržu Ɛliya!" qal-lha: "ila ġadi ixṛož*[16]*, txorži nti u-yyah." qalet-lu: "be-sm-ellah*[17]*!" u-ṭeḷḷeqha, u-baƐ l-ḥăwli b-el-xṭiya*[18] *u-xella fih xems myat ryal.*

Notes

1. In the vocative the noun takes the definite article, unless it is otherwise definite; *si* 'sir, mister', is a reduced form of *siyyed.*
2. Compare the English construction, 'that devil of an old woman'.
3. *nsiba,* female relation by marriage; in this context, 'mother-in-law'; also 'sister-in-law', 'daughter-in-law'; if one says simply *Ɛguza,* the reference is to the mother of the husband; *nsiba* is added for specification.
4. It is with *xiṭ byeḍ,* 'white thread', that one reunites two adversaries; *xiṭ kḥăl,* 'black thread', is used to bring discord among relaties, married couples, etc.
5. The brother of the speaker is being referred to.
6. The sacrificial animal for *l-Ɛid l-kbir,* and even for a name giving ceremony, is called *ḍḥiya,* a word which is also used for the sacrifice itself.
7. *b-Ɛăyn qbiḥa,* 'with a malevolent eye', i.e. 'she looked askance at it'.
8. *Ɛăwwež,* 'to twist, to make crooked'; here, 'changed her mind, turned her head'.
9. Two diminutives, 'little bitty hornlets'.
10. In order to keep a compliment from becoming an envious malediction of the object admired, one must utter the formula *tbaṛek eḷḷah,* 'God be praised!', which averts evil influences.

Notes

11. She changes her mind and turns against her husband.
12. A torrent of diminutives, from *kebš, qṛun, qedd,* and *hakkak.*
13. 'Fattened'.
14. 'Tender'.
15. *sna,* 'year'; occurs only in this oath used by women, 'may I fast a year if it (the sheep) stays here'; in this context *la* is equivalent to *ila* 'if'; for mockery, the person who hears this oath adds *u-l-kelba le-mḥăssna* 'and the shaved bitch'.
16. Note the *o* of the imperfect and imperative of this verb, *xrež* 'he went out', *xrož!* 'go out!'
17. I.e., 'all right!' A man who is told by his wife that he can divorce her cannot refuse.
18. *b-el-xṭiya,* 'at a loss'.

(25)

Distribution of the Blessed Objects of Pilgrims

tfṛaq el-baṛaka d-el-ḥožžaž

mnin ka-iṛžăƐ l-ġani[1] *m-el-ḥăžž ka-ižib mƐah Ɛadad d-el-ḥwayž baš ifeṛṛeqhom Ɛla ḥbabu*[2] *u-ṣḥabu b-niyt*[3] *el-baṛaka d-mekka u-l-madina. u-had lă-ḥwayž, l-luwwel fihom ma zemzem*[4] *mƐămmeṛ*[5] *f-zemzmiyat*[6] *d-el-qezdir. l-kbira fihom ka-terfed žuž litru, w-elli ṣġeṛ*[7] *men had eš-ši rafdin žehd kas kbir. ka-ifeṛṛquhom Ɛl-en-nas. ka-ixebbiwhom*[8] *ḥetta imutu. men băƐd ikunu mkeffnin naḍyin*[9]*, Ɛad ka-ittžebdu z-zemzmiyat w-itkebbu Ɛăl l-miyyet.*

lli Ɛăndu n-niya[10]*, ka-išṛeb l-ma d-zemzem w-inwi ma-ḥăbb; w-ila bġa ṛebbi, ka-ikemmel-lu niytu. matalan, ila kan ši-waḥăd mṛiḍ, išeṛbu w-idhen*[11] *bih, w-ila tkun niytu mezyana, ka-iƐafih eḷḷah w-išafih*[12]*.*

u-men žmelt ma-ižibu l-ḥožžaž, l-ḥănna. had el-ḥănna meškuṛa Ɛănd lă-Ɛyalat Ɛla ḥăqq žat m-eḷ-ḷeṛḍ l-mubaṛaka (mebṛuka). mṛat el-ḥažž ka-tăƐmel menha ṭubṣil aw qeṣṛiya, w-elli dexlet ka-tbaṛek-lha[13]*, ka-tăƐmel-lha l-baṛaka*[14] *f-keff iddha. w-elli šaṭ ka-itfeṛṛeq Ɛl-en-nas lli ma-žaw-ši.*

ka-ižibu Ɛawd tani t-tmeṛ d-el-madina; ḥetta huwwa ka-itfeṛṛeq Ɛl-en-nas, waxxa temṛa wolla žuž.

w-amma š-šilan[15] *u-ṭ-ṭyeṣ*[16] *u-l-Ɛud el-qmari*[17] *u-Ɛud el-ʔaṛak, ġir l-en-nas el-mwokkdin*[19]*.*

Notes

1. Synonyms: *xwaža* pl. *xwayž, tažer* pl. *tožžaṛ.*
2. 'In-laws'.
3. *niya,* 'intention, thought'; synonym, *qeṣḍ.*
4. From the well of *zemzem;* see Gaudefroy-Demombynes, p. 85.
5. Note the syntax; *mƐămmeṛ* 'filled, full' refers to the water, not the containers; i.e., the water is 'filled into' the containers.
6. Cylindrical containers of sheet metal, decorated to varying degrees.
7. The comparatives are invariable.
8. The subject is not expressed; i.e., those to whom the water is given.
9. *naḍi,* 'all ready, completely ready'; here, ready to be carried to the cemetary.
10. *niya,* in this context 'belief, faith'; further, 'desire, thought, intention', synonym *meqṣuḍ;* the word has many shades of meaning.
11. 'He annoints (himself) with it'; *dhen,* 'to annoint, to grease', is used here as if an oily substance were being spoken of.
12. Both verbs take the sense of 'cure, to give ease after suffering'; synonym; *yăƐṭih ṛ-ṛaḥa,* 'he gives him rest'.
13. *tqul-lha mbaṛek mesƐud l-ḥažž,* 'she says to her "blessed and happy be the pilgrim" '.
14. 'A little'.
15. *šal* or *šan,* piece of light material which one wraps around the head; people bring back 'shawls' from the Arab East and also make turbans out of them.
16. Plural of *ṭaṣ,* 'copper wash-basin'; the pl. *ṭiṣan* is also used.
17. Pseudo aloe-wood; literally 'Khmer wood', from Cambodia; used in fumigation.
18. *ʔaṛak,* tree of Arabia the bark of which is used for cleaning the teeth; in North Africa, the bark of the walnut tree, *swak,* is used for this purpose.
19. Important people whom one may not forget in the distribution of souvenirs from the Arab East.

(26)

The State of Slaves[1]

ḥal lă-Ɛbid[2]

kana lă-Ɛbid u-l-xdem[3] *ka-ittbaƐu f-el-berka. u-l-berka fnidqa ṣġiṛa. kan elli bġa išri xadem wolla Ɛăbd ka-imši l-el-berka u-ka-idwi mƐa d-dellal, ka-iqul-lu: "xeṣṣna Ɛăbd wolla xadem." ka-idexxlu l-el-muḍaƐ elli huma fih u-ka-ibda ixiyṛu*[4]*. u-š-šari ka-ixtaṛ xadem u-ka-iddiha l-ḍaṛu baš iqellbuha*[5] *w-išufu xdemtha. ka-ixelliha Ɛăndu yumayn wella telt iyyam, ka-išriha wella iṛeḍḍha l-el-berka. u-ma-ka-idzaydu-ši*[6] *f-lă-Ɛbid u-huma ḥaḍṛin. u-f-koll* *mdina, kanet lamina d-el-xdem tăḥt naḍaṛ l-qaḍi, u-huwwa ka-iɛăyyenha*[7]. *u-had lamina, sġolha, lli ibġi ibiɛ ši-xadem ka-iddiha l-ɛăndha l-eḍ-ḍaṛ, ka-tebqa ɛăndha ḥetta ka-tettbaɛ, u-ma-ka-texrož-ši ġir baš temši l-el-berka f-el-ɛaṣeṛ wolla ila bġa ši-waḥăd iqellebha*[8]. *u-mnayn ka-tettbaɛ ka-yăɛṭi sidha lli baɛha l-lamina l-muna*[9] *mtaɛ l-xadem f-el-modda lli kanet galsa ɛăndha.*

l-ɛăbd, syadu ka-iwokkluh w-išeṛṛbuh w-iksiweh, u-ma-ka-yăɛṭiweh l-flus. u-huwwa măɛguṛ[10] *ɛănd syadu, ḥetta ila txaṣem mɛa ši-ḥădd, ka-iqul-lu: "ya qimt el-melḥ!*[11]*, ma-ɛăndek užăh! saɛa ḥna qedd qedd*[12]*?" u-sidu, ila ma-kan-ši ɛla xaṭṛu wolla dar el-ɛăbd ši-ḥaža xayba, ka-ibrek*[13] *ɛlih b-eḍ-ḍeṛb.*

Notes

1. Excerpt from Louis Brunot, *Textes arabes de Rabat*, I, p. 85. For slavery, see the article *"ᶜabd"*, by Brunschvig in the *Encyclopedia of Islam*, second edition.
2. *ɛăbd,* in the sense of 'slave' the pl. is *ɛbid,* in the sense of 'worshipper of God' the pl. is *ɛibad.* The town crier begins his proclamations with the vocative *a ɛibad eḷḷah!* Even when freed, a negro is still called *ɛăbd.*
3. *xadem* pl. *xdem,* 'female slave'; this word, masculine in form and feminine in meaning, originally meant 'male servant'.
4. *xiyyeṛ,* 'to make choose'; *xiyyeṛ* plus *-u* becomes *xiyṛu.*
5. The subject is not expressed, 'the folks at home, the household'.
6. 'To bid', at an auction.
7. *ɛăyyen,* 'to appoint', someone to a task, position; the word also means to cast the spell of the evil eye upon someone.
8. 'He tries her out'.
9. 'Expenses of upkeep'.
10. 'Scorned'.
11. 'Value of salt', someone who is worth no more than salt; Moroccan slave-traders in the Sudan secured slaves by offering salt to the negroes who held them prisoners; salt was very rare and much valued in the country.
12. 'Are we equals?'
13. *brek ɛla,* 'to dog, to be always after'.

(27)

Visiting the Sick

ila smăɛna b-ši-waḥăd men ṣḥabna mṛiḍ ka-nemšiw nṭeḷḷu ɛlih[1]. *b-el-ḥăqq had eš-ši f-eṣ-ṣbaḥ wella f-weṣṭ en-nhaṛ. w-ila mša ḥetta*[2] *tkellem*[3] *l-ɛaṣeṛ ma-ka-ndexlu-ši ɛăl l-mṛiḍ baš ma-itzad ɛlih l-ḥal*[4]. *lă-ɛyalat rafdin fiha ṭ-ṭiṛa*[5]. *ka-inwiw ma-išuf l-mṛiḍ f-lă-ɛšiya ġir ila kan măɛdum*[6].

ḥit ka-idexlu Ɛăndu n-nas, ila kanu ṭolba, ka-iqulu-lu: "ṭahuṛ"[7] *Ɛad ka-izidu: "la-bas Ɛlik in-šaʔ-ḷḷah", u "ma-ikun Ɛăndek bas, ḷḷah igăƐƐăd usadek*[8] *w-inḍeṛ men ḥalek*[9]*, u-lăhla ixeṭṭik Ɛla ulidatek*[10] *". u-huwwa ižawbhom w-iqul: "lăhla iwerrikom bas*[11] *w-išufkom l-xir. mn-el-lil ka-tžini s-sxana u-Ɛḍami ka-itburšu*[12] *Ɛliya, u-ma-ka-năƐṛeg-ši*[13] *", u-sir men had eš-ši*[14]*. koll waḥăd ka-iqul-lu klam f-škel. ši ka-iqul-lu: "ixeṣṣek t-tăƐṛiqa baš iṭelqek l-ḥal"*[15]*. u-ši ka-iqul-lu izuṛ ši-siyyed aw lalla xeḍṛa f-meṛṛakeš*[16]*, Ɛla ḥăqq ka-iqul: "uqăƐ biya bḥal hakka, ma-nfăƐni ma-Ɛada had eš-ši lli qolt-lek." ka-iqulu n-nas: "sal le-mžeṛṛeb*[17] *la-tsal ṭ-ṭbib." ka-iži waḥăd axoṛ ka-iqul-lu: "ma-inefƐăk ma-Ɛada ṭ-ṭbib*[18]*, amma iži l-Ɛăndek huwwa wella neddiwek l-eṣ-ṣbiṭaṛ."*

lli huwwa b-Ɛăqlu ka-imši yetdawa f-eṣ-ṣbiṭaṛ w-ithenna men eṣ-ṣḍăƐ[19] *dyal eḍ-ḍaṛ. b-el-ḥăqq duk lă-Ɛyalat el-qdam ma-ka-itiqu ġir b-es-sbub*[20] *dyal eṭ-ṭolba.*

Notes

1. *ṭeḷḷ* and *ṭeḷḷel,* to pay a visit to a sick person; also, to look down from above on something which is passing below.
2. 'If it so happens that'.
3. 'To resound', subject not expressed, i.e. the cry of the muezzin.
4. 'So that his condition won't get worse'.
5. They take it as a bad omen; *ṭiṛa,* 'bad omen'; a good omen is *fal.*
6. *măƐdum,* 'lost' in speaking of a sick person.
7. A classical word meaning 'purification'. The sickness 'purifies' the sick person of his sins; people also say, *men ġeffaṛet d-dnub,* 'for the remission of sins'.
8. *usada* pl. *usayd,* 'pillow'; 'may God straighten up your pillow', i.e. the sick person is wished a quick recovery.
9. 'May he view your condition' (and take it into consideration).
10. 'God forbid that you should be lost to your little children'.
11. *werra,* 'to show'; has two direct objects, one a pronoun, the other a noun.
12. *tbureš,* 'to shiver'; *tburiša,* 'shivering, a shiver'.
13. It is believed that the evil comes out of the body with perspiration.
14. *u-sir men had eš-ši,* 'and go from this', i.e. 'and so forth, etcetera'.
15. 'You must have an (induced) sweating so that the evil (the condition) will leave you'.
16. See the text *lalla xeḍṛa,* nos. 31-33.
17. Someone who has stood the test, been tried, had experience.
18. *ṭbib* pl. *ṭebba,* 'physician'; *ṭbiba,* woman physician or nurse who administers medicines; *fremli* pl. *fremliya,* 'male nurse'.
19. 'Noise, tumult, bother'.

20. *sbub,* pl. with no singular; magic remedy intended to do good; *sḥur,* magic intended to do harm; *ṭaleb musebbib,* a cleric who writes amulets; *ṭ-ṭaleb ka-isebbeb l-en-nas lli mṛaḍ,* 'the *ṭaleb* gives magic remedies to those who are sick'; *ḷḷah išafik w-ed-dwa huwwa s-sabab,* 'God cures you and the medicine is the means'.

(28)

Education in the Family

t-terbiya[1] f-el-familya[2]

l-waldin ka-iweṣṣiw[3] uladhom ma-iṣeffṛu-ši, Ɛla qibal ka-iqulu: "t-teṣfaṛ ka-iḥăḍḍeṛ[4] š-šiṭan[5] u-ka-ihăṛṛeb l-malayka[6]." u-iƐăllmu[7] d-derri[8], ḥit yetfuwweh[9] idir iddu Ɛla fommu u-iqul: "ʔaƐudu bi-llahi min eš-šiṭan ṛ-ṛažim[10]!" w-ibzeq[11] tlata d-el-meṛṛat f-eḷ-ḷeṛḍ. u-kun ma-dar iddu Ɛla fommu, kun idxol fih š-šiṭan.

u-hadi Ɛada[12] oxra: ila l-weld, aw l-bent, nezzel[13] iddu Ɛla xeddu, ka-iwebbxuh[14] waldih u-ka-iqulu-lu: "dak tenzil el-yedd ġadya[15] tṛeḍḍek ġir itim." u-hakda tani ila gles f-el-Ɛătba[16] d-bab eḍ-ḍaṛ.

u-l-waldin ma-ka-iƐžebhom-ši uladhom yaklu f-ez-zenqa. ka-iqulu: "ila kla ši-ḥădd u-huwwa maši f-ez-zenqa, š-šhada[17] dyalu ma-dayza-ši[18] qoddam el-qaḍi; Ɛla ḥăqq ka-isemmiweh ṛažel qlil lă-Ɛqel[19]." u-zyada Ɛla had eš-ši, yemken išufu ši-ḥădd žiƐan u-huwwa ka-yakol; u-dak eš-ši ḥṛam[20] f-ed-din, layn[21] qal waḥd el-ḥadit[22]: "Ɛăynin waklin u-Ɛăynin šayfin kollhom mohhbin l-ež-žăhnam[23]."

Notes

1. Also *trabi,* morphologically plural, syntactically feminine singular: *irebbi uladu trabi mezyana,* 'he is raising his children well'; synonym, *ʔeddeb,* 'to educate, to rear', has no verbal noun.
2. *familya,* 'family', borrowed from Spanish; *Ɛaʔila,* 'family', in polished speech; *Ɛaʔila saqṭa,* 'vulgar family', with no background; *Ɛaʔila šrifa,* 'famous family, of good repute'; *Ɛyal,* 'household'.
3. *weṣṣa:* (1) 'to prescribe, to order'; (2) 'to recommend', a dish, a remedy; (3) 'to recommend, to commend', *weṣṣi woldi Ɛla flan,* '(re)commend my son to so-and-so'; (4) 'to order', shoes, clothing, etc., from a craftsman; *nsăḥ,* to give good advice for conduct; *waƐăḍ,* to exhort to the good, from the pulpit on Friday.
4. *ḥăḍḍeṛ,* to cause to be present, 'to attract'; *kellem,* 'to summon'; *Ɛăyyeṭ (Ɛla, l-),* 'to call'.
5. Satan, the rebel angel who refused to prostrate himself before man, whom God had just created. People who have evil malicious, minds are called *šiṭan* pl. *šyaten;* synonym, *iblis;* collective *ženn,* sg. *ženni,* pl. *žnun,* 'demon', created from fire; the popular notion is that the

žnun are the children of Satan, although the latter, a fallen angel, was presumably created from light like the other angels. See Gaudefroy-Demombynes, p. 51 ff.

6. The singular *malak* 'angel' is rarely used. Names of certain angels: *sidna žbril* or *žbṛayn*, 'Gabriel', messenger of God; *sidna mikaʔil*, watches over the order of nature; *sidna israfil*, announces the Day of Judgment by blowing on a trumpet; *sidna ʕăẓṛin* or *ʕăẓṛaʔin* or *ʕizraʔil*, the angel of death, *qebbaḍ eṛ-ṛwaḥ*, 'collector of souls'; *sidna ṛeḍwan*, the guardian of paradise; *nakir u-menkuṛ*, they interrogate the dead person in his tomb.

7. *ʕăllem*, 'to teach', takes two direct objects, *ʕăllemni l-ʕăṛbiya*, 'he taught me Arabic'; with *l-* 'to' introducing the person taught, the implication is pejorative, *škun ʕăllem-lek had eṣ-ṣenʕa*, 'who taught you to act in such a way?'

8. *derri* pl. *drari*, 'boy, child, young man, servant'; *weld* pl. *ulad*, 'boy, young man, son'; *ṭfel* pl. *ṭfal* (bedouin speech), boy of more than ten years of age, the feminine is pejorative; *ṣabi* pl. *ṣebyan*, child of from six to ten years of age; *tribya*, 'suckling', i.e. a child not yet weaned.

9. 'to yawn'; *tfuwweh mʕa ṛaṣu*, 'to take a breather, to go out for a breath of air'; *mfuwweh*, 'airy', of a room, house, etc.

10. 'I seek refuge in God against accursed (literally, 'deserving to be stoned') Satan', the phrase is Classical Arabic, pronounced in the Moroccan fashion; *lă-ʕyadu be-llah mennu, ṛažel*, 'the refuge is with God (i.e., God save us from) against him, that man'.

11. *bzeq*, 'to spit'; with reference to birds, 'to excrete'; rural people say *dfel*; *bezqa*, 'spittle, a spitting', or 'bird dropping'; *defla*, pl. *dfali*, oleander, rose-laurel' throughout Morocco in this meaning, *defla* also means 'spittle, a spitting' among rural people.

12. *ʕada* pl. *ʕwayd*, 'custom'; *qaʕida* pl. *qawaʕid*, 'tradition'; *lă-ʕwayd w-el-qawaʕid*, 'customs and traditions'.

13. *nezzel*, 'to set down, to lay down, to put down'; *ḥăṭṭ*, 'to alight', of a bird, of a family installing itself in its tent.

14. *wobbex*, 'to rebuke, to chide'; *lam* imperfect *ilum*, 'to blame'; *xaṣem*, 'to reproach'; *ġuwwet ʕla*, 'to carp at, to scold'; *ʕayer*, 'to insult, to reproach insultingly'.

15. The agreement is with the gender of the second word of the complex; here it is *yedd* which is feminine.

16. Proverb: *l-itim, ila mat bbwah ka-iwossed ʕl-er-rekba, w-ila matet-lu immah, ka-iwossed ʕăl l-ʕătba*, 'the orphan whose father dies has his mother's knees for a pillow, the orphan whose mother dies has the door-step of the house as a pillow'.

17. 'Testimony', at law; 'profession of faith'; 'certificate, diploma'.

18. *dayz*, 'admissible, admitted'; see note 20.

19. 'Man of little reason', i.e. 'crazy, hare-brained'; *qlil ed-din*, 'having little religion, irreligious'; *qlil l-iman*, 'of little faith, unbeliever'.

20. *ḥlal*, '(religiously) lawful, licit'; *ḥṛam*, '(religiously) unlawful, illicit'; *dayz*, 'acceptable'; *mekṛuh*, 'detested, scorned'; *ḍifanḍi*, 'forbidden' (by the police).

21. For Classical *liʔanna,* 'for, because'.
22. In this form at least it is a false hadith, since the verb *šaf* imperfect *išuf* 'to see' was never used at the time of the Prophet.
23. 'Hell', cf. English 'gehenna', from the Hebrew *gai-hinnom,* name of a valley where the idolatrous Jews made their children pass through fire in honor of Moloch.

(29)

Magnanimity and Generosity

l-žud[1]w-el-kaṛam

kan waḥd eṛ-ṛažel ɛăndu bent ḥadqa[2] u-ɛayqa u-fayqa[3]. ila ẓeḍmet ɛl-ez-zbiba ka-teṭlăɛ mɛaha ḥlawtha[4]. waḥd en-nhaṛ qalet-lu: "ḥăbbit nseqṣik[5] ɛla waḥd el-kelma, ka-iquluha n-nas, waš ka-ifehmuha ɛla ḥqiqetha[6] aw la. — qal-lha: "šni hiyya?" —qalet-lu: "ka-iqulu: 'l-žud w-el-kaṛam', mnayn huma mažyin[7]?" —qal-lha: "m-el-mužud." —qalet-lu: "lla!" —qal-lha: "u-mn-aš?" — qalet-lu: "men ṛeqq ež-žlud[8]." — qal-lha: "u-šnu huwwa ṛeqq ež-žlud?" — qalet-lu: "ḥit ikun eṛ-ṛažel nafeḍ alla yažid[9], w-ižiweh[10] ḍ-ḍyaf ɛla beġta[11], w-inuḍ yexrož iḥăššem wežhu[12], imma isellef aw yeṛhen ḥwayžu w-išri ma ka-ixeṣṣu u-yăɛmel l-wažeb ɛlih, ḥetta imši ḍ-ḍif našeṭ[13]; hadak huwwa l-žud. w-amma ila kan l-mužud, ṭɛam žuž yakluh tlata; w-ila kan waṛṭu men ždudu, ma-tɛăb fih ma-šqa[14], ma-yetsemma žud.

Notes

1. *l-* instead of *ž-* for the definite article here in imitation of Classical Arabic; the two words *žud* and *kaṛam* are more or less synonyms and reinforce each other by their use together.
2. *ḥadqa,* 'bright, intelligent, quick-witted'; *ḥadqa,* 'diligent', in speaking of a maid servant.
3. *ɛayqa u-fayqa,* the two words always go together, sort of a compound adjective, 'bright and perceptive'.
4. *ẓḍem (=zṭem) ɛla,* 'to crush with the foot'; *ḥălwa,* a sugared confection, becomes *ḥlăwtha* with the affix; she didn't need to chew a raisin to recognize its flavor, all she had to do was step on it, because her senses and intelligence were so finely developed.
5. *seqṣa,* 'to ask' (a question); the remnant of a Classical Measure X; the forms *seqsa* and *ṣeqṣa* are also heard.
6. *ḥqiqa,* 'truth'; i.e., do people understand the true sense of these words?
7. Active participle of *ža* imperfect *iži,* 'to come'; formed by analogy with *maši,* active participle of *mša* imperfect *imši,* 'to go'.
8. 'fineness of the skin', i.e. the faculty of blushing under the influence of an emotion; by extension, to have a keen and sensitive sense of honor.

9. *nafeḍ,* 'deprived of everything'; *alla yažid* reinforces the sense of *nafeḍ;* quote from the Koran, sura IX, verse 93, 'not having found'.
10. *iži,* 'he comes'; *ižiw,* 'they come'; *ižiweh,* 'they come to him', with *-eh* instead of *-u* 'him' after a preceding *w*.
11. Synonym, *ɛla ġefla,* 'unexpectedly'.
12. 'He puts himself to shame', i.e. he obligates himself.
13. Synonyms: *ɛla xaṭṛu, ɛla gantu, mesṛuṛ, feṛḥan.*
14. 'Neither trouble nor fatigue'.

(30)

Jha and the Fast of Ramadan

žḥa, f-weṣṭ ṛemḍan dar ḥila baš yakol ṛemḍan[1] *qoddam en-nas dyal fas kollhom. u-ḥit bġa idir dak eš-ši ɛṛeḍ*[2] *ɛăl l-qaḍi u-žuž d-lă-ɛdul f-el-lil u-ddahom l-ḍaṛu. dexxelhom l-waḥd ed-dăhlis*[3] *mfeṛṛeš tefriša mezyana u-gelleshom u-nezzel-lhom waḥd el-makla ldida u-men băɛd qam-lhom atay*[4] *u-dar lă-ḥšiša*[5] *f-el-berrad bla xbaṛhom. ma-bṭat-ši lă-ḥšiša f-dmaġhom ḥetta tduwxu*[7]. *xellahom žḥa hakdak ġaybin ɛl-ed-denya ḥetta lla-ġedda f-el-luwli; ɛad fiyyeqhom u-qal-lhom: "daba ɛad neṣṣ el-lil." u-nezzel-lhom ṣ-ṣḥuṛ*[8] *fuq el-mida u-xrež. mnin uṣel l-el-bab el-kbira d-el-qăṛwiyin*[9] *gles u-bda ka-yakol. n-nas kollhom bdaw ka-iɛaybu*[10] *ɛlih ɛla makelt ṛemḍan u-huwwa ižawbhom u-qal-lhom: "had en-nuba ṛemḍan ma-fih ġir xemsṭaš-eṛ yum, u-ṛa l-qaḍi mɛa lă-ɛdul ɛăndi f-eḍ-ḍaṛ ka-yaklu u-huma lli ṣifṭuni năɛlemkom b-el-ɛăyd ṛa ža." u-dda n-nas mɛah baš iwerri-lhom el-qaḍi u-lă-ɛdul ka-yaklu. ġir huwwa ḥăll bab ed-dăhlis u-l-qaḍi u-lă-ɛdul šafu n-nhaṛ ḍawi u-huma ma-zalin ka-yaklu. n-nas ɛăṛfuha ḥila men ḥilat žḥa u-qalu: "wa-laynni had žḥa miṣṣeḷ*[11] *mn-eš-šiṭan ḥit zɛăm*[12] *yelɛăb ḥetta b-el-qaḍi dyalna.*

Notes

1. Notice this telescoped expression, *yakol ṛemḍan,* literally 'he eats Ramadan', i.e. he breaks the fast by eating during daytime during the month of Ramadan.
2. *ɛṛeḍ l-luḥa,* to recite the lesson written on the Koranic wooden slate; *ɛṛeḍ ɛla,* 'to invite'.
3. More common than *dăhlis* is *lakaf* or *lakab.*
4. *qam* imperfect *iqim,* 'to prepare', e.g. *iqim atay, iqim ṭenžiya; iqim eṣ-ṣla,* 'he prepares the (communal) prayer', i.e. he calls the faithful to prayer; *iqama,* 'preparation', by extension 'condiments, spices' in cooking, and with specific reference to tea, 'mint'.
5. Marihuana, hashish; the seed of the hemp plant, produces intoxication.
6. Did not delay, i.e. in making its effects felt.
7. They fell under the influence of the intoxicant.
8. The last meal of the night during Ramadan.

9. Famous mosque-university, built in the quarter of the Kairouanais.

10. *Ɛăyyeb* plus *-u* becomes *Ɛaybu,* 'to reproach', to say *Ɛib Ɛlik* 'this is bad of you' to someone.

11. From *ʔaṣeḷ,* 'origin'.

12. 'To dare'.

(31)

lalla xeḍṛa

kanu ši-Ɛyalat ḥramiyin qal-lhom eš-šiṭan idiru ši-sebba[1] *baš irebḥu*[2] *l-flus bezzaf. u-kanu ka-iƐăṛfu waḥd el-ḥăžṛa kbira u-mkerkba*[3] *f-ši mwiḍăƐ Ɛla beṛṛa m(en) el-blad. u-ttafqu, u-tfeṛṛqu Ɛăl lă-ḥmaḥem*[4] *dyal meṛṛakeš, u-qalu ḥălmu ši-mnama*[5] *bin lqaw waḥd el-ḥăžṛa xeḍṛa mažya ka-tkerkeb b-uḥedha men mulay ibṛahim*[6]*, ṭiṛ ež-žbel*[7]*, ḥetta qeṛṛbet tedxel l-meṛṛakeš, u-ṛaḥ Ɛliha l-lil*[8]*, u-neṭqet b-el-lsan el-faṣiḥ*[9]*: "ila dxelt l-meṛṛakeš ġadi ndawihom mn-es-sxana." u-ḥit ttšenƐăt*[10] *had el-xbaṛ f-el-blad, nhaṛ axoṛ Ɛawdu tani*[11] *duk lă-Ɛyalat Ɛălmu l-ḥṛamiyat lli bḥalhom, u-xeržu men meṛṛakeš huma w-iyyahom u-mšaw tḥamaw*[12] *Ɛla dik el-ḥăžṛa u-bdaw ka-ikerkbuha ḥetta qeṛṛbuha l-bab eṛ-ṛebb*[13]*. u-sebġuha b-es-sbaġa xeḍṛa, u-dexlu l-le-mdina u-xellaw temma.*

Notes

1. 'Device, strategem'.
2. *rbăḥ,* to earn money in a commercial transaction or something similar; *ṣuwweṛ l-flus,* to earn money by work, labor.
3. *mkerkeb,* 'spherical, round'; *tkerkeb,* 'to tumble, to roll down'; *šƐăṛ mkerkeb,* hair with a permanent (recent usage).
4. *ḥămmam,* 'moorish bath', has the pl. *ḥmaḥem* at Marrakesh, *ḥămmamat* elsewhere.
5. *ḥlem,* 'to dream'; *mnama,* 'dream, vision'.
6. A Saint buried near Marrakesh, to the south, on top of a hill.
7. The epithet with which the name of this Saint is traditionally followed.
8. 'Night came upon her'.
9. 'She said very clearly'.
10. Synonym: *tšăhret,* 'to spread', a rumour, a piece of news.
11. *Ɛawd tani,* indicates a reptition of the action, here *Ɛălmu,* 'they informed'.
12. Synonym: *tƐawnu,* 'they helped each other'.
13. One of the numerous gates of Marrakesh on the south; it is from there that the route toward the Atlas begins.

(32)

lalla xeḍṛa (continuation)

u-Ɛawdu šenƐu f-le-mdina bin Ɛawdu ḥălmu f-le-mnam dik el-ḥăžṛa qalet-lhom: "ha-(a)na bayta f-fomm el-bab, xoržu ya hel meṛṛakeš, dexxluni u-thăḷḷaw fiya nethăḷḷa fikom." u-lla-ġedda xeržu hel meṛṛakeš itebbtu had eš-ši. ṣabu dik el-ḥăžṛa xeḍṛa u-dexxluha, ka-ikerkbu fiha[1] *b-ez-zġarit, ḥetta l-waḥd eḍ-ḍaṛ kanet mxerrba*[2]*; bnawha u-ḥăbbsuha Ɛla dik lalla xeḍṛa. u-bdaw duk el-mqeddmat elli ṣenƐu*[3] *had el-ḥila ka-iqulu l-eẓ-ẓuwwaṛ: "lli kan Ɛăndu ši-ḥădd mṛiḍ b-es-sxana, ižibu-lna ndawiweh-lu*[4]*."*

u-ḥit ka-ižibu-lhom ši-waḥăd, ka-iqulu-lhom: "siru žibu telt eṛṭal d-et-tmeṛ." ḥit ka-iži t-tmeṛ, ka-išebbṛu le-mṛiḍ w-iziyduh l-Ɛănd lalla l-ḥăžṛa[5] *w-igellsuh w-ikebbu Ɛlih dik el-qeffa d-et-tmeṛ Ɛla ṛaṣu, w-ižemƐu dak et-tmeṛ w-idefƐuh*[6] *l-el-mqeddma; u-men băƐd ka-inuwḍu le-mṛiḍ w-iqulu-lu b-el-ġwat: "bus lalla xeḍṛa baš tebṛa!", baš tṭiṛ mennu d-dăhša*[7] *d-es-sxana. w-iziydu tani ḥda l-bir w-iḥiydu-lu ḥwayžu w-iƐămmṛu tlata d-ed-delwan*[8] *men el-bir w-ikebbuhom Ɛlih baš texrež dik el-baqiya*[9] *d-es-sxana.*

Notes

1. They rolled it in front of themselves.
2. In ruins.
3. Who had engineered this trick.
4. *ndawi* pl. *ndawiw,* takes *-eh, ndawiweh,* instead of *-u* 'him' because of the preceding *w.*
5. Mocking expression, 'Madame the Stone' instead of 'Madame the Green'.
6. Here, 'to hand over to, to give'.
7. The frightened torpor which fever brings about. The popular belief has it that it is this torpor which keeps the fever in the body of the sick person.
8. *dlu* pl. *delwan,* leather well-bucket.
9. The remainder of the fever.

(33)

lalla xeḍṛa (end)

ana b-ṛaṣi ka-năƐqel ḥit kont ṣġiṛ žatni s-sxana u-daru-li had ed-dwa. u-šafani rebbi bla xeḍṛa bla ḥežṛa.[1] *u-bqat dik el-xedma modda u-l-mqeddmat qḍaw ḥaža*[2] *u-šebƐu flus mƐa ṛuṣhom. ḥetta žab eḷḷah waḥd el-qaḍi ždid u-smăƐ had el-xbaṛ elli mxalfa š-šṛăƐ u-qal-lhom: "men ġir l-ḥažaṛ es-swed*[3] *ma-wažeb Ɛlina nqebblu*[4] *ḥetta ḥăžṛa. u-daba tăḥtažu txerržu dik el-ḥăžṛa men dak el-maḥăll u-tkerkbuha ḥetta tweṣṣluha l-el-mwasim*[5]*, u-tdăƐƐmu*[6] *biha d-deffa dyal l-fḥel*[7] *elli ḥda seqqayt es-sebbaġin, Ɛad nšufu ḥetta ḥna l-baṛaka dyal had lallakom xeḍṛa; baš ila hiyya ṣebḥet f-el-maḥăll mn-aš* *žebtuha nƐăŗfuha bin ṣaliḥa u-năƐṭiw ḥetta ḥna ḥăqqna*[8] *b-had eš-ši, w-ila ṣebḥet mdăƐƐma d-deffa nƐăŗfuha bin ġir ḥăžŗa u-ma-Ɛăndha qaḍaŗ, la baš tdawi wa-la baš tʔadi*[9]*."*

Ɛămlu dak eš-ši u-bqat mdăƐƐma dik ed-deffa ḥetta l-daba, u-l-yum u-l-ġedda ila iṣbăḥ[10]. *w-amma ḍ-ḍaŗ elli kanet mḥăbbsa Ɛla dik el-ḥăžŗa, dexlet f-lă-ḥbas mtaƐ ež-žamăƐ.*

Notes

1. A mocking expression.
2. They made a lot of money.
3. The reference is to the black stone enshrined in a wall of the Kaaba in Mecca, which the pilgrims kiss. See Gaudefroy-Demombynes, *Institutions*.
4. *qebbel,* 'to kiss'.
5. The name of a quarter in the center of Marrakesh.
6. *dăƐƐăm,* 'to prop, to stay'; here the reference is to keeping a wing of an open gate pressed against the wall.
7. *fḥel,* the name of the large gates which give access from one quarter to another.
8. *ḥăqqna,* here 'what we owe'.
9. *ʔada* imperfect *iʔadi,* 'to do harm to, to give a sickness to'.
10. 'Today and tomorrow, if there is a tomorrow'.

(34)

ḥkayt[1] *sid et-torki*[2]

l-qobba dyal sid et-torki qŗiba l-el-qobba dyal sid el-ḥažž Ɛăbd eḷḷah el-yaburi[3] *Ɛla šeṭṭ le-bḥăŗ f-eŗ-ŗbaṭ. ka-iƐawdu*[4] *Ɛlih kan f-luwwel siyyaġ*[5] *u-ka-ixdem f-eš-šeŗq. waḥd en-nhaŗ kan huwwa xeddam ka-iḥăyyed waḥd ež-žuhŗa men ši-ḥaža men ḥwayž ed-degg*[6]*, u-men žmelt ež-žhed dyalu ṭaŗet-lu f-qennuṭu*[7] *u-ŗṣat-lu f-xwašmu*[8]. *u-b-dak eš-ši ḍeŗŗu l-ḥal bezzaf. mša išaweŗ Ɛadad men eṭ-ṭebba*[9]. *ši menhom bġa yeftăḥ-lu l-menxaŗ w-iḥiyyed-lu dik ež-žuhŗa, u-ši qal idawih b-ed-dhin*[10] *u-ši ma-qḍa bih*[11]. *waḥd en-nhaŗ tlaqa b-ši mġeŗbi woṣṣah yemši izuŗ sidi ben Ɛašer f-sla. dak eṣ-ṣiyyaġ faḍet niytu*[12] *f-eṣ-ṣaliḥ, u-serrež el-beġla dyalu u-ṣafeŗ*[13]. *u-kan el-qbeŗ d-es-siyyed, f-dak et-tarix, ḍayŗ bih ġir ši ḥwiyyeṭ qṣiweŗ u-mŗebbăƐ. ḥit qeŗŗeb-lu u-šafu hakkak măhmul*[14] *tƐăžžeb u-qalet niytu u-qal: "hada huwwa ṣ-ṣaliḥ elli žit Ɛlih men blad bƐida?" ma-kemmel klamu mƐa ŗaṣu ḥetta tgerdƐăt*[15] *bih l-beġla, u-ḍŗeb eḷ-ḷeŗḍ b-ŗaṣu, u-ṭaḥet ež-žuhŗa men menxaŗu, u-bŗa.*

Notes

1. *ḥkaya,* a true story or one considered as true; *qeṣṣa,* a true story or else plausible with a semblance of truth; *xṛafa,* 'fantastic tale', usually told at night, cf. the proverb *lli ḥka xṛafa f-en-nhaṛ ixeržu uladu quṛăɛ,* 'whoever tells a *xṛafa* during the day, his children will turn out bald (with scalp disease)'.
2. *sidi* becomes *sid* before the definite article, cf. *sidi ɛali* and *sid el-beṛnuṣi.*
3. Patron Saint of sailors of Rabat and Salé.
4. Synonyms: *ka-iqulu ɛlih, ka-iḥkiw ɛlih.*
5. Synonyms: *deggag, nqayṛi.*
6. The word 'jewel' has no equivalent in Arabic; the nearest equivalent is *ḥaža d-ed-degg,* the word *degg* meaning 'silver jewelry' and by extension jewelry in general.
7. *qennuṭ* pl. *qnaneṭ* (synonym: *žăɛba* pl. *žɛab*), 'nostril'.
8. *xwašem,* i.e. the nasal cavity.
9. Pl. of *ṭbib,* 'doctor, physician'.
10. *dhin,* 'action of oiling, annointing', also 'ointment'.
11. Nothing helped, he accomplished nothing with it.
12. 'His confidence in the Saint was overflowing', i.e. he was convinced that the Saint would cure him.
13. *mša f-ḥalu,* 'he went away'; *ṣafeṛ,* 'he set off on a (long) journey'; *ṣaḥ* imperfect *iṣiḥ,* 'to wander, travel about'; *žal* imperfect *ižul,* 'to make a tour'.
14. 'Humble, modest', unprepossessing and not attracting attention.
15. *tgerdăɛ,* 'to take a violent tumble, fall'; *flan gerdăɛ ṣaḥbu,* 'so-and-so hurled his comrade violently to the earth'; synonyms: *ṭaḥet bih, žat ṭayḥa bih.*

(35)

ḥaguza

ḥit kont ṣġiṛ žehd xems snin kanu waldiya ka-ixuwfuni b-ḥaguza. ka-iqulu-li: "ila ma-ɛămmeṛti-ši keršek bezzaf ġadi tžik ḥaguza f-neṣṣ el-lil u-tqelleb-lek keršek w-ila ṣabetha xawya ka-tɛămmeṛha-lek b-et-tben u-lă-ḥžeṛ. u-had eš-ši ka-ikun nhaṛ lilt en-nayr l-filaḥi. w-ed-drari kollhom ka-ixuwfuhom waldihom b-had eš-ši. iwa dik el-lila klit bezzaf men šeṛsma u-ġirha bḥal le-mxemmer w-er-rfisa u-beġrir medhun b-el-ɛsel w-es-smen. u-mšit nɛăst. saɛa men quwwet el-makla lli klit bla qyas žani bu-ġeṭṭaṭ f-neṣṣ el-lil u-xlăɛni u-bdit ka-nġuwwet u-nɛăyyeṭ ɛla imma. ḥit semɛu l-ġwat, naḍu waldiya men en-nɛas u-seqṣawni: "ma-lek? w-aš ṭṛa-lek? yak ma-šefti-ši ši-ḥaža lli txelɛek?" qolt-lhom: "ḥăssit b-ḥaguza žatni ta-teḍḥek b-ši-snader kbaṛ u-bġat teftăḥ-li kerši b-waḥd ež-ženwi fih dṛaɛ u-šbeṛ. u-ḥit ġuwwett xafet menkom u-mšat heṛbana u-ṭayṛa f-es-sma bḥal ši-soġniya. u-bdaw waldiya ka-iseddu l-biban, u-qolt-lhom iseddu l-bir u-s-sṛažem u-bab eṣ-ṣṭaḥ. u-ġellqu l-qwades u-ziyru le-bzabez baš ma-tedxel Ɛliya ḥaguza menhom.

(36)

ḥaguza dyal fas

ta-tkun en-nhaṛ l-luwwel f-yennayr l-filaḥi. u-ta-ibdaw b-eṛ-ṛġayef mextemṛin. w-en-nhaṛ et-tani beġṛiṛ, w-en-nhaṛ et-talet sfenž, w-en-nhaṛ eṛ-ṛabeƐ herbel b-el-ḥlib, u-nhaṛ el-xames el-bişaṛa, we-nhaṛ es-sades (=s-satet) seksu be-sbăƐ xḍaṛi, w-en-nhaṛ es-sabăƐ l-fwaki. u-nhaṛ herbel ta-iƐămmṛu ġṭaṛ w-ixelliweh ḥetta ibred w-iteqbuh ṛebƐa d-et-teqbat w-ixebbƐu, w-ila ṣebḥu Ɛamṛin b-el-ma, ta-iƐăṛfu l-Ɛam šati w-eš-šaba mezyana. ta-iqulu l-ed-drari: "kulu bezzaf u-Ɛămmṛu kruškom, ṛaha ila žat immakom ḥaguza u-ṣabet kruškom xawya, ṛaha tetqebha u-tƐămmeṛha-lkom b-et-tben. u-f-el-lil ta-ižibu l-fakya, u-ta-isemmiwha "l-fakya l-messusa". u-had l-fakya hiyya: l-guz, w-en-nwa, w-et-tmeṛ, u-z-zbib, kawkaw, l-keṛmuṣ, u-l-ḥămmuṣ meqli.

u-Ɛlaš ta-ibdaw b-el-xmiṛa n-nhaṛ l-luwwel, ta-issfalu b-el-xir, baš ta-ixṛež l-Ɛam kollu mezyan u-Ɛămmeṛhom ma-ta-ižuƐu fih. u-dima lă-Ɛžin u-dima l-makla mužuda.

(37)

kan zman (qbel had es-saƐa) l-metḥăsseb ka-iḍuṛ f-le-swaq d-el-mdina baš igadd le-ṣƐaṛ. ka-ixṛež rakeb Ɛla beġla b-es-sriža u-tabƐinu ṣḥabu, žuž wella tlata w-el-fqi. ka-ixleṭ Ɛăl l-beqqal w-iqul-lu: "aṛa duk eṣ-ṣṛuf baš ta-tăƐbeṛ l-en-nas", w-igaddhom mƐa ṣ-ṣruf lli Ɛăndu. ila lqahom naqṣin, ka-isžen dak el-beqqal w-isedd-lu l-ḥanut w-idăƐƐṛu. waḥd en-nhaṛ l-metḥăsseb žbeṛ waḥd el-beqqal mxeḷḷeṭ s-smen b-eš-šăḥma. xerržuh ṣḥabu m-el-ḥanut u-rekkbu-lu l-falaqa f-režlu u-bdaw ta-iḍeṛbu b-el-mṣuṭa Ɛla qaƐ režlu u-Ɛṭah ḍƐiṛa u-ṭiyyeḥ-lu men dak es-smen en-neṣṣ f-tamanu. w-elli Ɛmel tlata d-el-falṭat, ka-iṭuwfu nhaṛ l-xmis Ɛla ḥăqq ta-ikunu l-ulad mḥăṛṛeṛin m-el-qṛaya. ka-irekkbu dak el-mṭuwwef Ɛla ḥmaṛ Ɛṛež baš ḥit ibda ittemxeḍ, ta-ibdaw n-nas iḍăḥku Ɛlih. u-mrekkbinu užhu žiht qezzibt lă-ḥmaṛ u-ḍăhṛu men žiht eṛ-ṛaṣ. ḥit išufuh en-nas ġadi b-el-luṛi u-l-ḥmaṛ ta-iƐṛež bih u-huwwa bḥal lli ka-ižded, bezz menhom ka-iḍăḥku Ɛlih.

(38)

Ɛašuṛa Ɛăndna f-fas Ɛid lă-Ɛyalat u-d-drari, u-le-mwokked f-had eš-ši huwwa dxul d-drari l-le-msid, u-l-ḥwayž d-el-lăƐb.

mnin ka-tebqa ši-sebƐ iyyam l-Ɛašuṛa, ta-iƐăwšru. u-ta-ižib le-fqi xabya aw žuž w-inezzelhom f-le-msid. u-l-mḥaḍṛa lli Ɛăndu ka-ibdaw ižibu z-zit w-ikebbuha f-el-xwabi. mnin ka-tebqa yumayn ka-ikteb l-fqi bṭaqa l-en-naḍiṛ d-el-qăṛwiyin baš yăƐṭih le-mṣabăḥ w-et-triyat. ka-imšiwi ši-mḥaḍṛa kbaṛ be-Ɛqelhom ka-ižibu had eš-ši. w-išriw Ɛawd tani ḥămza d-eṣ-ṣmeṛ w-el-qṭen w-el-qezdir baš iṣuwbu le-ftayl lli ka-išăƐlu f-el-mṣabăḥ, u-lilt Ɛašuṛa ta-iƐăllqu le-mṣabăḥ Ɛl-eṣ-ṣṛužeb u-l-bab. u-f-el-weṣṭ et-triyat ḍayṛin bihom le-mṣabăḥ bḥal l-xwami, b-et-tqaweṣ u-l-lwan. nhaṛ el-lila ka-itteġsel le-msid w-ižibu l-ḥyaṭi w-el-fṛaš u-ẓ-ẓṛabi. f-lă-Ɛša ta-ibdaw ižibu ulad et-tožžaṛ w-elli ḥăbb lă-Ɛšawat f-el-mžadi. ka-yăƐṛeḍ le-fqi Ɛl-eṭ-ṭelba ṣḥabu. ta-ižiw ta-iṣibu l-msid bḥal ḍaṛ el-Ɛers. imma l-ʔaliyin, aw l-musemmiƐin, aw mwalin ed-dalil. ka-itƐăššaw l-măƐṛuḍin w-irefdu fatḥa w-ixeržu w-iḍuṛu Ɛl-elli Ɛaṛḍin Ɛlihom. u-men băƐd ka-itƐăššaw le-mḥaḍṛa l-kbaṛ lli baytin.

u-f-le-fžer, ka-itxemmel le-msid. u-mnin iṣebbăḥ l-mwodden ta-ibdaw ižiw le-mḥaḍṛa ṣ-ṣġaṛ w-elli Ɛad ġadi ižiw idexlu le-msid. u-ta-ižibu f-iddihom š-šmăƐ l-xemm u-l-flus. u-l-Ɛada lli bġa idexxel woldu l-le-msid, ka-idexxlu ṣbaḥ Ɛašuṛa b-šeṛṭ.

(39)

ṣ-ṣyam el-luwwel dyal l-bnitat

nhaṛ setta u-Ɛăšrin d-ṛemḍan, ta-tqiyyel l-bnita ṣayma. ila kanu waldiha tožžaṛ u-ḥăbbu ifeṛḥu b-benthom, ta-iƐămlu-lha l-ḥănna b-ez-zwaq f-iddiha u-režliha, u-ka-iƐăṛḍu Ɛla ḥbabhom u-nsabhom, ġir lă-Ɛyalat. u-ka-iwožždu l-mwakel Ɛl-eš-škal, u-l-ḥlawi d-lă-Ɛsel u-l-ḥlib u-t-tmeṛ.

u-men băƐd el-Ɛaṣeṛ ka-ilebbsu-lha w-iƐăllqu-lha ḥetta ka-teṛžăƐ bḥal lă-Ɛṛuṣa. u-duk lă-Ɛyalat el-măƐṛuḍat ta-iṭellƐuha l-eṣ-ṣṭaḥ w-iṭellƐu šelya u-l-mwaƐen d-et-teṭbil. w-igellsuha Ɛl-eš-šelya w-iḍuṛu biha w-ibdaw iṭebblu w-iġenniw. ž-žwaren ta-iṭelƐu ḥetta huma l-ṣṭaḥathom, Ɛăndhom aw ma-Ɛăndhom ši-ṣyam, w-itfeṛṛžu w-ibarku-lhom ila kanu ka-iƐăṛfuhom.

u-qṛubat el-moġṛeb ta-ihebṭu, ta-iṣibu ḍ-ḍaṛ koll-ši mwožžed: ṭ-ṭbali mnezzlin u-z-zlayf msettfin u-l-ḥlawi u-koll-ši myisser. u-ḥit ka-tetkellem l-moġṛeb ta-yăƐṭiw l-le-bnita ṣ-ṣayma tefṛeq eṣ-ṣum b-el-ḥlib u-t-tmeṛ Ɛad ibdaw išeṛbu lă-ḥrira u-yaklu l-ḥălwa u-t-tmeṛ.

w-amma r-ržal ka-ikunu b-waḥdhom f-ši-bit. u-men băƐd lă-Ɛša duk lă-Ɛyalat lli ġadya tbat ha-hiyya bayta, u-lli ġadya temši, tṣifeṭ mƐahom u-telbes ḥaykha u-temši f-ḥalha.

(40)

l-ḥămmala w-eḍ-ḍḥiya d-l-imam f-el-Ɛid el-kbir

mnin ta-tebqa ši-telt iyyam l-el-Ɛid, ta-iṣifṭ en-naḍiṛ Ɛla lamin d-el-ḥămmala men fendeq eš-šemmaƐin, ta-ifeḍḍi mƐah l-klam Ɛl-en-nas lli ġadyen ihebbṭu ḍ-ḍḥiya men l-mṣeḷḷa d-fas ždid u-l-mṣeḷḷa d-bab ftuḥ ḥetta l-ḍaṛ l-xṭib. u-l-xṭib huwwa l-imam, men băƐd eṣ-ṣla ta-ixṭeb, Ɛad ta-idbăḥ. u-had lamin huwwa ta-iƐzel n-nas lli iṣlaḥu u-Ɛăndhom bhaym ṣḥaḥ. ta-iqṣemhom Ɛla žuž d-el-qesmat, u-koll qesma b-ṛaiṣha.

u-men băɛd ta-imšiw w-ibdaw iṛiyḍu bhaymhom men l-mṣella ḥetta ḍaṛ l-xṭib, žuž aw tlata d-el-meṛṛat f-en-nhaṛ. ɛla dak eš-ši ta-yettsemmaw ḥămmaṛa, ġir dak en-nhaṛ d-el-ɛid.

u-ṣbaḥ el-ɛid ta-iṭelɛu labsin mezyan, u-ḥetta bhaymhom mɛawminhom. ta-igelsu muṛ ḍheṛ el-meḥrab. u-n-naḍiṛ ta-iṭlăɛ w-iṭellăɛ mɛah l-ḥăwli w-izaṛ ždid d-el-meṛzaya. mnin ta-ifeḍḍi l-xṭib men l-xeṭba w-iḥuf men el-menbaṛ, ta-iṣib l-ḥăwli mwožžed, w-ež-ženwi mužuda, w-el-ḥămmaṛa waqfin ɛla bhaymhom, u-l-mɛăllem fihom huwwa l-luwwel. ġir ta-iduwwez l-iman ɛla ɛonq el-ḥăwli, ta-iluwwiweh b-dak l-izaṛ baš ibqa d-demm măḥṣuṛ u-yuṣel ɛăyyeš' l-ḍaṛ l-imam. f-dak es-saɛa ta-ihezzuh l-ḥžer dak el-mɛăllem, u-huwwa ta-iṭiṛ b-es-sbeg u-l-oxṛin tabɛineh ta-iɛăššqu f-en-nbi: a l-ɛašqin f-en-nbi, ṣeḷḷiw ɛlih, a ḷḷahu mṣeḷḷi ɛlik ya ṛaṣul ḷḷah.

ta-inwiw dak eḍ-ḍḥiya ila weṣlet ɛayša l-eḍ-ḍaṛ, l-ɛam mezyan u-ṣ-ṣelṭan ɛla xaṭṛu; w-ila weṣlet miyta, l-ɛam ikun mfelles u-ṣ-ṣelṭan ši-ḥaža mašya tuqăɛ-lu.

(41)

š-šhada

ɛănd le-mselmin f-eš-šṛăɛ u-f-el-mexzen koll-ši b-eš-šhud. lli šehdu fih en-nas ḍalem ka-yăɛṭi l-ḥăqq, u-lli šehdu fih meḍlum ka-iqbeṭ el-ḥăqq.

kanet ɛăndi waḥd eḍ-ḍaṛ dyalti u-ḍaɛu-li l-kwaġeṭ b-aš šariha. ža waḥăd men l-quṛaba ṭleb menni yeskon mɛaya, u-ɛṭitu maḥăll bla kra. nhaṛ bġit nbiɛ eḍ-ḍaṛ qal-lek ɛăndu l-ḥăqq fiha. mšina ɛănd eš-šṛăɛ u-ɛṭani l-aden baš năɛmel biyna, yăɛni ṭnaš-eṛ šahed. lqit ḥḍaš f-el-ḥuma, u-ṛeḍḍit le-xbaṛ ɛăl lă-ɛdul. qalu-li: "žib žuž ɛyalat nkemmlu bihom." lqitḥom huma waxedhom waḥăd men duk lă-ḥḍaš. ɛla ḥăqq šhadet lă-ɛyalat, žuž menhom dayzin f-šhadet ṛažel waḥăd.

ila kan ši-ɛadel ka-yăɛṛef dik el-ḥaža u-šhed biha, dayza šhadtu f-setta d-en-nas. w-ila kanu žuž ɛdul, dayzin f-ṭnaš d-en-nas. w-ila kan l-qaḍi ɛaṛef dik el-ḥaža kayna u-šhed, dayza šhadtu f-ṭnaš d-en-nas.

w-ila kanet dăɛwa mexzaniya, ma-năḥtažu-ši nkemmlu ṭnaš d-en-nas. ila šăhdu ġir tlata wolla ṛebɛa, šhadthom tabta. u-ḥetta šhadet eṣ-ṣebyan, ulad u-bnat, dayza, ila ma-dxel binathom ši-waḥăd kbir.

n-nas el-măɛyubin, bḥal š-šeffaṛ u-l-ġeḍḍaṛ u-l-ḥmeq u-ġirhom, šhadethom meṛžuɛa.

(42)

waḥd en-nhaṛ tneffxet-li l-maɛida. ṣifeṭt ɛl-eṭ-ṭbib ɛla ḥăqq ma-qeddit-ši nnuḍ u-nemši ɛla režliya. mnayn ža u-qelleb, uwwel ma qal-li: "ftiḥ!" qolt-lu: "ma-qṛiti ġir le-ftiḥ? xemmem ila kaynin ši-ibari aw fanid aw ma aw dhen, w-ila ma-qḍaw-šay ɛad nfetḥu!" qal-li: "kaynin ši-ibari dyal le-mṣaṛen, nžeṛṛbuhom Ɛla adnek." qolt-lu: "waxxa." u-ḍṛeb-li waḥda f-fexḍi. bett had el-lila la-bas, u-f-et-tanya ttfeššet el-maƐida. men bắƐd šaf had eš-ši qal-li: "nta huwwa ṭ-ṭbib. u-daba xeṣṣek tqelleb ed-demm, u-tduz f-eṛ-ṛaḍyu baš nƐắṛfu aš kayn." Ɛmel dak eš-ši kollu u-ma-tṣab walu ma-Ɛada ši-usex d-el-makla d-ṛeṣṭuṛat. u-men bắƐd rtaḥit ṭlebt mennu iserreḥ-li l-makla Ɛla ḥắqq kont qaṭắƐha bla klamu. qal-li: "kul koll-ši ma-Ɛada l-biḍ u-š-šeklaṭ u-l-xliƐ u-l-ḥut, ġir merla. ḥetta l-felfel ma-takolha-ši." qolt-lu: "had eš-ši kollu ḷḷah ihennik, u-l-felfel lazem nakolha." qal-li: "u-tƐawd temṛeḍ." qolt-lu: "nƐawed nši Ɛắndek tdawini." qal-li: "yemken tmut." qolt-lu: "l-mut ma-hiyya la b-felfel wa-la b-baṛuḍ. ḥna le-mselmin Ɛắndna l-aƐtiqad ṣḥiḥ, l-mut b-el-ˀažal.